The Slate Diaries

The Slate Diaries

EDITED BY

JODI KANTOR, CYRUS KROHN, AND JUDITH SHULEVITZ

PublicAffairs New York

Book design by Mark McGarry, Texas Type & Book Works
Set in Aldus

Cover design by Kathleen Kincaid.
Cover illustration by Robert Neubecker.

Library of Congress Cataloging-in-Publication Data
The Slate diaries / edited by Jodi Kantor,
Cyrus Krone, and Judith Shulevitz.
p. cm.
Selected articles from the online magazine Slate.
ISBN 1–58648–007–3 (pbk)
1. Biography—20th century.
2. Celebrities—Diaries.
3. Authors, American—20th century—Diaries.
I. Kantor, Jodi, 1975– . II. Krohn, Cyrus, 1970– .
III. Shulevitz, Judith, 1963– . IV. Slate (Redmond, Wash.)
CT120.S55 2000
818′.540308′dc21
00–057582

FIRST EDITION
10 9 8 7 6 5 4 3 2 1

Contents

Introduction

By Michael Kinsley

Like every journalist (or so I assume) I always wanted to start a magazine. Twice before, at *The New Republic* and *Harper's,* I came close. Both publications needed substantial overhauls when I lucked into the editor's job. But at *TNR* there was an owner who also acted as editor-in-chief. (Which he had every right and reason to do. You don't buy an expensive toy just to let other kids play with it.) And at *Harper's* I spent 18 months quarreling with the Board of Trustees before taking the hint that I wasn't wanted.

So in 1995 I was having a good time writing for various publications and playing TV pundit on CNN's *Crossfire,* but I still wanted that magazine. Then I became one of the earlier people — not the first, but far from the last — to have the brilliant insight that has transformed life as we know it. (Or certainly life as I know it.) This insight was that people will let you do almost anything you want if you slap the magic words "dot-com" on it. (Sadly, the magic no longer works. Even the successor term — "B2B" — has lost its magic. Try "human genome.")

When *Newsweek* reported that Microsoft was looking for

someone to spearhead its online journalism efforts, I wrote to Steve Ballmer, then a Microsoft vice president, now president of the company, asking if I qualified. He replied that the *Newsweek* story was untrue (can you imagine?), but he put me in touch with Russ Siegelman, another Microsoft VP (now a venture capitalist at Kleiner Perkins), who was about to launch MSN, the Microsoft Network. Within less than three months I had left one Washington for the other, had started hiring colleagues, and we were planning an online magazine.

Microsoft has been the perfect owner: financially and techno-logically supportive, but completely hands-off editorially. (The moral may be that if you're rich enough, you do buy expensive toys just to let other kids play with them. Or it may be that a for-profit corporation is going to value editorial independence more than either a nonprofit board of trustees or an individual owner with strong views of his own.) And while a corporate campus in suburban Seattle is an odd place from which to publish a news and culture magazine — not just odd but impossible if not for the In-ternet — there are advantages, too. No time wasted wondering where to have lunch, for example. And at the company cafeteria, there's never a problem getting a table.

The name "Slate" came from a Microsoft manager named David Weld. We had been thinking about "Boot" — as in boot up a computer, as in giving someone a boot (i.e., a kick in the rear, not firing them), and as in John Boot, the journalist hero of Evelyn Waugh's great comic novel *Scoop*. But then someone noted that, as a verb, "to boot" also meant "to vomit." This was discouraging. Then David came up with "Slate" and we quickly settled on it, out of imaginative exhaustion more than anything else.

In the first issue, June 26, 1996, I wrote that we picked the bland name "Slate" as "an empty vessel into which meaning can be poured." Unbeknownst to us, Levi Strauss was planning a new line of pants called Slates. When Slates pants were launched, the mar-keting director told the *New York Times* that the name had been chosen as "an empty vessel into which meaning can be poured." But we didn't make a fuss. And the name has worked out better for *Slate.com*, the online magazine, than for Slates, the pants.

Arriving at *The New Republic* 25 years ago, I started a diary column. It was called "Washington Diar*ist*" in a petty attempt to distinguish it from the diary columns in many British publications, from which it was, in fact, indistinguishable (except that fewer Americans have the talent for clever triviality). Two decades later we called a feature in *Slate* the "Diary," to distinguish it from *TNR*'s "Washington Diarist," which had become somewhat an institution.

But *Slate*'s diary column is different from columns with the same or almost the same label in print publications. First, it is a real daily diary—filed and published daily, not composed and published all at once at the end of the week. Second, reflecting the instantaneousness of publishing on the Web, it is supposed to be an actual description of what-I-did-yesterday, rather than a mini-essay or a random collection of *pensées* and *aperçus*. Third, it has —or at least we want it to have—the special voice of e-mail, combining the spontaneity of talking with the reflectiveness of writing (when it works—the other way around when it doesn't).

If anything was the inspiration for the *Slate* Diaries, it was the diaries of Alan Bennett, the British playwright, published in 1995 as *Writing Home*. Bennett's subject matter was almost aggressively mundane—a typical day's entry might describe what he watched on television the night before—but completely and mysteriously fascinating. Unfortunately, even talented professional writers often don't have this particular form of genius. We started out urging our *Slate* Diary contributors to make each item what-I-did-yesterday, described with as little art or shape or thematic unity as possible. Now we usually choose people who have interesting jobs or are going through a noteworthy experience, in order to give these quotidian observations a bit of a head start.

Still, the fact that they're published on the Web within hours or even minutes of the events they describe does affect these diaries in ways we failed to predict. One such way is the fast reader-feedback loop. A diary entry about what you did Tuesday gets posted Wednesday morning, and by lunchtime there are dozens or hundreds of responses and reactions in "The Fray" (*Slate*'s reader discussion forum). These then become part of the Wednesday experience you describe for the world on Thursday. Either that or the ferocious reaction of some Fraygrants (as we call them)—not just to your writing, but to your life, as you have chosen to present it—is so dispiriting that you call your editor at *Slate* and say, "I can't go on." It's happened a lot more than once. But all *Slate* editors are certified trainees in Emergency Psychological Respiration, and I'm pleased to say we haven't lost a Diary writer midweek yet.

The *Slate* Diaries, like many features on *Slate.com* and other Web sites, are a continuing experiment. This is a new medium, and the appropriate styles and conventions of writing for it are still being invented. Watching writers learn to use the new medium—play around with its special advantages, work around its special burdens—is a big part of the fun. The next collection of *The Slate Diaries*, four or five years from now, will include (we hope) just as much fine writing. But a certain sense of discovery and adventure will be missing.

Slate's Judith Shulevitz, Cyrus Krohn, and Jodi Kantor have been in charge of the Diary for different pieces of our brief history. Jodi and Michael Brus did most of the work of putting together this book. But all present and former members of the *Slate* team—writers, editors, businessfolk, heck! even the software developers—deserve a share of the credit. Working with them has been the best thing about *Slate* for me.

The Slate Diaries

Haleh Anvari

Haleh Anvari is a translator and "fixer" for foreign journalists in Tehran, Iran.

POSTED Monday, Feb. 14, 2000, at 10:30 A.M. PT

I missed the Iranian revolution when it happened, 21 years ago this week, because I was at school in the U.K. I was 16 then and, like most Iranians, extremely excited about an event that would prove to be momentous not just in the life of this nation but also in all our personal lives. It took 16 years for me to be able to return to my country. I have been back now for seven. I am now witnessing the maturing process of that revolution firsthand through my work with foreign journalists. So I kind of console myself for having missed the main gig by listening to the stories and hopes of those who were here and on the front line. But more of this later; right now you will want to know what exactly you will be reading in the next few days.

I work with foreign journalists; they call us fixers. An odd name, I always thought: at best reminiscent of glue; at worst implying some kind of wheeling and dealing. In fact, the job is to provide guidance to journalists, who are often unfamiliar with the terrain and the culture, managing their time, arranging their interviews,

and generally getting them over the hurdles of a massive bureaucracy that they must navigate if they are to use their limited time in
this country in an efficient way. I get to meet the personalities who
count here and translate their stories and commentary. It gives me
a privileged, inside look at the politics of the place and a chance to
understand an ancient country's remarkable transition from a politically undeveloped system to one that is finding its feet on its quest
for real democracy. I like to see my job as a bridge between two cultures, two peoples — in the context of Iran, a bridge between two
worlds so set apart in the Western media and the attitudes that have
prevailed in my country since the revolution. I am not just a translator of words; I'm an interpreter of mannerisms and a reader of
fine lines in the seemingly obvious.

The countdown to the parliamentary elections has begun, and
we are receiving a rush of reporters from all over the world. My
first team arrived this morning from Oslo. Our first stop, the
Ministry of Culture and Islamic Guidance for our permits and
press cards. To see anyone in a position of power will require a
letter from the intimidating-sounding but actually rather
friendly ministry. So I sat down with a huge piece of paper and a
new pen, expecting to write an impossibly long list of ayatollahs
and ministers. But Joy, my Norwegian reporter has worked in the
Middle East for many years and doesn't waste his time with requests for interviews he knows he is unlikely to get. We spend
half a day hanging around the ministry's emergency offices
arranged on the top floor of one of the main hotels in Tehran,
previously owned by the Inter-Continental chain. It's now part of
one of the financial foundations that took over foreign hotels, the
Foundation for the Oppressed, I think. There are 500 reporters in
town: Fixers are like gold dust and about as expensive! The reporters will probably be eligible as oppressed themselves by the
end of the week.

POSTED Tuesday, Feb. 15, 2000, at 10:00 A.M. PT

The *Toronto Star* correspondent arrived late last night; the *News-day* correspondent followed late this morning. I'll spare you another account of a day spent getting papers. Now that we have them, I need a mobile filing cabinet for all the permits we have to carry around with us.

These two are an interesting duo to work with. The Canadian is a soft-spoken Montrealer, the kind of guy you would like to have as your child's pediatrician after a household accident. He never raises his voice above a soothing pitch, even when you know he is despairing of getting that one vital interview with some conservative cleric that he needs to make his report work. The *Newsday* correspondent is a young Scotsman, now an honorary New Yorker, who is more likely to pine for a bagel than a plate of haggis. We don't get bagels in downtown Tehran; they probably wouldn't get a visa! But I further digress amid my main digression. His quintessentially British sense of humor makes me homesick for the rainy island. The last time he was here I spent more time catching up on jokes than on fixing.

Our first appointment was with the publisher of a reformist newspaper that has been shut down four times by the authorities for stepping over the so-called red line in journalism. The press court shuts them down, then they publish again with a new name and a new license. I changed their particulars in my phone book so many times I couldn't keep up. So now I just call their paper the "Phoenix" — rising from the ashes. It saves my new book from turning into a mess.

Jalaii-pour, the publisher, epitomizes the changes in Iran. He has an impeccable revolutionary background. Born into an Islamic family opposed to the deposed Shah, he lost three brothers in the war with Iraq. At the beginning of the revolution, he was the governor of Kurdistan when there was an uprising by the Iranian

Kurds who wanted autonomy from the central government. About a year and a half ago, he and three of his journalists were arrested and imprisoned for a month. They were released only because Jalaii-pour's mother wrote an open letter to the supreme leader of the country, Ayatollah Khamenei, asking for the release of her only remaining son. I can't remember the exact words, but they went something like, I have given the nation three martyred sons, and I would like this one safely home. It was weird that at that time we were reading about a new film with Tom Hanks called *Saving Private Ryan*. Here was our very own Ryan, but in a different situation.

Ironically, Jalaii-pour was rejected as a candidate for the parliamentary elections last month; once an insider, he is now deemed too radical as a reformist. And he is not alone: There seem to be legions of revolutionaries turned reformists who have found a voice and a new sense of purpose since President Khatami's election. They are, like Jalaii-pour, still supporters of the Islamic revolution; they simply maintain that the time for revolutionary behavior is over. It is now time to try and reach the ideals for which the revolution happened in the first place, namely a populist democracy with Islamic values. This naturally rubs some people the wrong way. So, he and his colleagues find themselves moving toward the edge of what has always been the ruling circle. Some would say the cutting edge. His paper has one of the largest circulations among the new papers, and the party he is associated with seems to be the one most popular with the younger generation of Iranians, who form 60 percent of the population here.

While waiting in the foyer of the "Phoenix" newspaper, a friendly and pretty young woman was asking one of the female reporters whether she'd got any Valentine's Day presents. My ears perked up. I had not heard the occasion mentioned in the seven years I had been back. To be honest, I was quite happy to be away from the paranoia that goes with the day. The dreadful start to the day, when you get to pretend not to be expecting any mail. The pathetic attempt at playing it cool just like an Oscar nominee when the bunch of flowers delivered to the office finds its way to the desk next to yours. Who needs the emotional trauma? I couldn't help asking the girl what she knew about Valentine's Day and where she had heard about it. It's the second year, she told me, that this new consumer craze has become all the rage among young Iranians. They flood to card shops and gift shops and flower shops and send each other presents. It has to be secret, she said. It came from the Internet. Aaah, the wonders of technology!

You could see the sparkles in her beautiful Persian eyes; it was early afternoon, and she was still hoping and waiting.

I gave her a tip from my previous life: Save yourself the suspense and the loss of face — send yourself a valentine. I think I may have started something here.

POSTED Wednesday, Feb. 16, 2000, at 10:30 A.M. PT

Three days to the elections.

The North American team is on the trail of Ayatollah Khomeini's family for interviews. The Norwegians want to talk to people in the arts. We go to the house of a famous theater director who has recently staged *The Blood Wedding* by the Spanish writer Lorca. It's a tale of love, hope, and betrayal with a lot of old resentments and revenge. It received a great deal of attention from the audiences here. It must have touched a nerve with them. There are many women in the play who perform in Spanish-style clothes cleverly manipulated to observe the Islamic cover. After a few minutes you are no longer aware of the lack of visible manes on the actresses. There were also many scenes that required men and women to dance together or embrace one another. In Iran, unrelated men and women may not touch. If you want to stage a play, you have to get around these problems somehow. The director explained to the reporters how he managed to do this by the use of the Spanish shawls the women wore, which would be used as a connecting device for the actors. The Indian filmmakers for years got around the same cultural restrictions by inventing the indirect kiss: Boy kisses apple, throws it at girl, both dancing very improbably around a tree. The girl catches it and plants her kiss on the apple. The connection is made and the sensibilities of the more conservative viewer remain intact. Nowadays, the Indian TV shows we receive from satellite dishes illegally perched on top of our roofs indicate that indirect is out. Most of the girls are in wet saris, and they receive their kisses full on the lips.

When Iran became an Islamic state, the most visually obvious thing was the change in the code of dress for women. Whenever the reporters want to show they are in Iran they use the covered women, usually the ones in the black chadors; that image shows the chasm between our two cultures with greater force. Unfortunately it also reinforces the clichés.

I give you an example: We went to an art gallery to interview the owner because he was the first to exhibit a foreign artist's work in Iran. The photographer decided that just taking a picture of him next to the paintings would be boring—he needed to show more obviously he had taken this picture in Iran. What will immediately tell the reader where he was? Women in their *hejab*. Unfortunately, by the time he decided to take his pictures it was lunch time and there were no visitors left in the gallery. So we had to "fix" it. I had to go into the street and ask some women to come and help us out. No shy wallflowers, the women I talked to came into the gallery, took a painting each, and posed for him outside, with a view of the Alborz mountains in the background. I guess the mountains could have been anywhere in the world, too, but with our scarves and long coats, we made the image complete: We are the trademark of revolutionary Iran.

Later we went to a newsstand to do some vox pops on the press and its role in the elections. The reporter wanted to interview a man who was buying a paper. I explained who we were and what we wanted. Would he answer some questions? "No," came the reply. Why not? "I don't want any trouble," he said. Before I could fully translate his sentence, a woman at the other end of the stand put up her hand and said in Farsi, "I will. You can interview me." And so we did. We actually got a lot more than we'd bargained for.

She gave us a full frontal assault on the political system in the past 20 years. Would she vote? Of course. A few other people were gathering round. Foreigners are always of interest here. A man said what's the point of voting, it won't change anything. The woman laid into him. That's exactly what the conservatives want. To discourage you from exercising your right for change. We left the circle of debate as it was really heating up. We had to run to another interview on the other side of town. The men were still being lectured by the woman on the power of the plebiscite as we drove away. She didn't seem too oppressed to me even in her *hejab*. She knew exactly what forces were trying to keep her down. Don't they say recognizing the problem is halfway to solving it?

POSTED Thursday, Feb. 17, 2000, at 10:00 A.M. PT

I was brought up in a staunchly nationalist home. My father had spent time in the Shah's prison as a young journalist supporting Mossadeq. The Shah was, as soon as I could understand what I heard around me as a child, not the father of the nation, as my school textbooks told me, but a dictator. When the revolution began, my father and his friends were taken by surprise by the path it actually took. It didn't take him long before he fell afoul of the new system and left the country to live in the U.K. as a political refugee. His property was confiscated. His name went on the list of antirevolutionaries. It probably didn't help that he spent his time in London publishing a newspaper critical of the Islamic Republic. He came back to Iran soon after my return, spent two years to-ing and fro-ing from one revolutionary court to another until he got his home back, only to fulfill a wish to die in it on Iranian soil. He didn't see the election of President Khatami. He would have got a kick out of it. He believed that the Iranian revolution would come to fruition, but with time and from within the system. He would have voted.

It's a strange sensation, the death of a parent; next to the grief sits a sense of growing up. The parent gone, you are your own person to please. When I refrained from voting in the presidential elections three years ago, I was still carrying my childish interpretation of my father's politics from 30 years back. The justification of my position was ostensibly shaped by my claim to a mediocre degree in politics and philosophy. How could anyone with a modicum of intelligence take part in an election that would allow only a handful of pre-selected candidates? Why would anyone want to give legitimacy to a system that by nature shunned the power of the populace? I obstinately refused to vote, but 20 million people went out that day and voted for Khatami. They returned a candidate of choice, albeit a limited choice.

The 15-year-olds who got Khatami elected against all odds are now 18. Their initial euphoria of empowerment may have paled in the face of political realities. Some will be disillusioned, no doubt; others are more pragmatic. Either way they are better-educated than we were at their age, both academically and politically. When I was 15, voting was what people in faraway lands did. These youngsters have lived within a system that has shown them the framework of democracy. They read papers that provide them with a critique of what has happened during the past 20 years. They are practicing the art of participation, however limited it may appear to the Western eye. And they are from all walks of life.

My mistake in abstaining in the presidential elections was exactly that I was looking at that event as a person brought up in the West. I wanted the whole thing. The whole thing was not handed to any country on a plate; they had to work for it and learn its process. People of my generation are taking their cue from these "kids" running between cars in the cold winter night. I asked the next boy with pamphlets if he had a list of recommended candidates. He gave me three and told me how to use the codes next to the names.

Now I've got my election list. I've told my reporters I need time off on Friday to go and vote. I'm voting this time. So what if it'll take a while for things to change. The point is that the process has begun. In the words of one political analyst to an American journalist who saw the pace of change as way too slow, "This is the land of Persian carpets, it takes years for the pattern to be woven, you may have sore fingers weaving it, but when it's done it'll be a work of art and it will last a hell of a long time."

Alison Bechdel

Alison Bechdel writes and draws the comic strip "Dykes to Watch Out For" and has published a series of books of the same name.

POSTED Monday, March 30, 1998, at 4:30 P.M. PT

The road up our hill is a mess. The first couple of years I lived in Vermont, I thought "mud season" was just a figure of speech, a concept people clung to out of regional pride or pre-Interstate nostalgia. But now I live on a dirt road. The thaw has transformed it into a living thing, a quivering, tire-sucking semisolid interspersed with bone-jarring ruts and ridges. Driving on it is like wrestling a huge serpent. It makes me feel heroic, like a latter-day Laocoön.

Today was unbelievably warm, almost 70 degrees. I saw the first red-winged blackbird and a pair of mourning doves. Last week the snow was 3 feet deep and the woods were absolutely silent. Now the brook is roaring, and we've lost more than 2 feet of snow, gauging by how much of the burdock patch in front of the house is revealed. The broken windshield scraper I threw into the yard in a fit of pique two months ago also emerged today, along with a carpenter's square lost in the first snow last fall.

I went into town to get copies made and to give blood. Then I came home and spent hours sorting through all this artwork I've agreed to donate to various causes for their annual fund-raisers. I started feeling resentful. Maybe it was because I'd already given away a pint of blood. Parting with all this ink and sweat on top of it made me wonder if I was being too generous.

I'm feeling very lethargic. I don't know if that's from the blood-letting too or if it's because it's time to start the next two episodes of my strip. I've noticed that my work cycle bears a striking resemblance to a manic-depressive episode. Or depressive-manic, to be more precise.

I had to lie down on the floor for a while, I was so tired. This has gradually become a strange, yet integral, part of my writing process. I'm not sure if it's just procrastination or if it's a normal response to the exhausting prospect of having to fill up a blank page. I don't sleep when I lie on the floor: I just kind of lapse into a semiconscious state for half an hour and then I'm refreshed. It helps if I have a piece of dialogue I'm working with to perseverate on while I'm lying there, almost like a mantra. In fact, as I drew

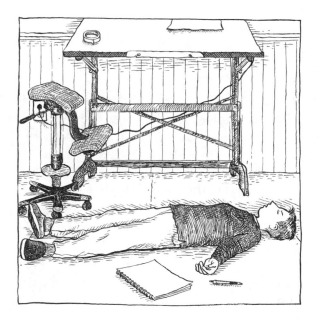

this picture of myself lying on the floor, I realized that this is the yoga position savasana, or the Corpse.

Another feature of the depressive phase of my cycle is this awful sense that my work really isn't very good. In my last trough, I was whining to Amy about how stale and irrelevant I thought the strip was getting. She reminded me that I say that every month and that by the time I make my deadline, I think I'm a genius. This unnerved me, because it probably means both extremes cancel each other out. I asked Amy if she thought that I was really just average, and she said she was getting fed up with having to reassure me.

Maybe it's masochistic of me, but thinking my strip sucks seems like another necessary part of the process. It motivates me. If I were feeling all smug and complacent, I don't think I could muster the momentum it takes to begin a new episode.

The road grader went by in the afternoon. It scrapes up a thick layer of rutted mud, rolls it along with its big blade, then smoothes it out behind like a fresh, blank page.

POSTED Thursday, April 2, 1998, at 4:30 P.M. PT

I got a call today from Chassman and Bem, the local independent bookstore. They've canceled the book signing I had scheduled this month — they're going out of business. I knew they weren't going to last much longer, but it still came as a blow. They've been struggling ever since Barnes & Noble came to town. But the nail in their coffin was the Borders Books and Music store that will be opening just up the block this summer. The woman who called me said morosely that a lot of the Chassman and Bem employees would probably try and get jobs there.

I've set up a similar scenario in my comic strip. Madwimmin Books, the women's bookstore where some of my characters work, has been losing sales to Bunns and Noodle for years, and now a

Bounders chain store is opening nearby. Stores that specialize in women's or gay or African-American books have slightly more of an edge against the chains than general-interest independent stores do, but they're still feeling the pressure. I hate the thought of closing Madwimmin down, but it's beginning to look like I'll have to eventually if I don't want my strip to become a complete anachronism.

A couple weeks ago Amy and I went to visit her sister and brother-in-law in Albany, N.Y. The four of us had some time to kill while their kids were at a play, so they suggested that we all go to Barnes & Noble. Amy and I demurred, but it was Friday night and there really wasn't any other quiet place to go. On the way I tried to explain the chilling effect these stores are having on the culture. I talked about how books are just commodities to the chains, and how if a title doesn't come with an author interview on the *Today* show and the potential of selling a zillion copies, they won't stock it. Or else they'll order two copies, shelve them spine out, and re-

turn them to the publisher when they don't sell. I talked about how this means books that can't compete against Billy Graham's autobiography just aren't going to continue being published. I waxed apocalyptic about censorship. They listened politely, but by the time we were standing in the mellow, cappuccino-scented glow of Barnes & Noble, even I had lost interest in my arguments.

The place was packed. People were lounging in comfortable chairs reading through entire books. They were sitting at tables blatantly copying information out of computer manuals. They were hauling stacks of magazines into the cafe and filling them with biscotti crumbs before returning them to the rack. The whole store had such a pleasant, populist atmosphere that it was hard to remember it's The Devil. Amy had to physically restrain me from buying a book. The spell was broken once we got back outside. I returned home and dutifully ordered the same volume from Chassman and Bem.

It rained all day today. The snow is almost completely gone, except for dingy little patches here and there. The traction of spongy turf is thrilling after months of inching gingerly up the icy path to the mailbox. I feel suddenly weightless without all the snow, as if I'd just taken off a heavy backpack. The Emergency Broadcast signal keeps coming on the radio. The first time I heard it I was envisioning clouds of anthrax before I realized it was just a flood warning.

Benazir Bhutto

*Benazir Bhutto is a former prime minister of the Islamic Republic
of Pakistan. She fled while serving as Opposition leader in the
National Assembly*

POSTED Tuesday, June 17, 1997, at 4:30 P.M. PT

My wake-up call goes off several times. I wish it would stop. It does
not. Another day has dawned.

I get ready and go down to the office. It is empty except for my
political secretary.

We go through the morning mail. The Portuguese ambassador
has sent me a book by their poet Fernando Pessoa translated into
Urdu. The Portuguese have done this to commemorate our golden
jubilee year, which is really thoughtful of them.

I flip through the pages. I see the poems about women and sad-
ness. I close the cover.

I jot down some additional points for my budget speech, slip in
an explanatory note to the office and leave.

As a Muslim woman, I cover my head with a veil, called a *dup-
patta*. It keeps slipping unless one has a beehive hairstyle. Every time
there's a big speech, I have to try and make it to the hairdresser's.

As a Muslim woman, I almost always go out accompanied by a
lady companion. Gone are the days when I could hail a taxi or drive
a car. I miss the informality of the past.

My political secretary Naheed accompanies me. I have two cups of tea at the parlor. Not good for my blood pressure, a little voice whispers, but I drink the tea anyway. You only live once.

We return to the house to find that the government has cut our electricity. It's boiling hot. The computers are not working. I make corrections with sweat dripping all over. It gets into my eyes and blurs the page. I am angry but I concentrate on the work.

We enter the National Assembly at 5:00 P.M. There are hardly any members. Good. There will be less heckling.

The speaker has broken with precedent and decided not to give the electronic media permission to film my speech. I get angry. Stop it, I say. That's what they want. You are not going to play their game.

"I call upon the leader of the opposition to begin the general discussion on the budget proposals," the gray-haired speaker intones.

Taking a deep breath I begin:

"Mr. Speaker, Sir, the budget proposals for 1997–98 presented by the finance minister are based on deceit, disinformation, distortion. This is a breach of the privilege of the House. The budget theme is to borrow. Borrow time and borrow money."

I notice the House is beginning to fill up. The back-benchers can hardly contain themselves when I speak. They start muttering.

The finance minister has admitted that the civil servants are in a deep crisis. I respond, "When customs officials are punished for performing their duties, when police officials are accused of extrajudicial killings, when senior bureaucrats are tortured into making false statements, there will be a deep crisis."

The Treasury benches start heckling. There are only 17 of us in the House and 160 of them.

I mention that the politics of revenge has frightened capital and paralyzed the economy. I begin to give a few examples. When I mention my political secretary, who has been imprisoned and freed on court orders three times, off-loaded from a flight once, tortured and asked to lie about me, the Treasury benches burst into an uproar.

I shout as loud as I can over the microphone, "Sir, why do they panic every time they hear the name of a woman?" That shuts them up. At least temporarily.

When I finish, the Treasury benches start discussing my speech. Their first speaker makes sexist remarks: "She is melodramatic. She should have gone to New York and performed in the theater. She would have been a prima donna."

Bored, I sit back and begin to read the "Tasbee," the Muslim rosary. When I finally get to my office in the Parliament I am too tired to meet the press. Instead I ask for water, tea, sandwiches, deep-fried chicken wings. I am rewarding myself for the one-and-a-half-hour speech delivered in a House where we have only a handful of supporters.

Now the work is done. It's time to go home.

I go onto the verandah and call the cats. One of them is from Maui. I got her in 1992 when I visited Hawaii. I gather their plates, wash them in soap and water, get a can of food, and put it into their plates. They are jumping and purring all over me. I love it.

Then I call Dr. Ashraf Abbasi, the former deputy speaker of the National Assembly, a remarkable lady. She worked with my father and gave me the love of a mother.

We go to the upstairs lounge, put on CNN, call for some green tea, and sit down to watch and chat.

Bliss.

Tomorrow is another day.

POSTED Wednesday, June 18, 1997, at 4:30 P.M. PT

Our electricity has been cut once again. No use moaning about it.

The good news is that our member in the Provincial Assembly of Sindh, Mir Hayat Talpur, who had been arrested last night, has been released. The bad news is that our deputy leader of the opposition and former minister, Pir Mazhar, who was kidnapped a week ago, has not yet been recovered.

The chief minister of Sindh does not like the deputy leader of the opposition. They both hail from the same home district. The chief minister began his tenure by filing a murder case against the leader of the opposition in the Sindh assembly. Then he ordered his minions to fabricate a case against the vocal deputy leader of the opposition.

Pir Mazhar always traveled with an overnight bag. He never knew when he would be thrown behind bars. But we didn't expect him to be kidnapped.

His wife was traveling with him when five armed men stopped his car. Assuming they were police and would fire, killing him and his wife for "defying arrest," he stopped. Both were kidnapped. The kidnappers didn't want the car, jewelry, or cash. The tearful wife was later left on the superhighway to find her way back. The police refused to file her report charging the chief minister with the kidnapping of her husband.

The chief minister has not even come to their house to shed crocodile tears. This morning he had the audacity to call the deputy leader of the opposition, grandson of a former chief minister, elected four times consecutively as the people's representative, a "corrupt," "abductor," "extortionist," "kidnapper," who had "staged the drama of his own kidnapping."

Meanwhile the leader of the opposition in the Sindh assembly informs me that the Sindh government has bribed three members of the Provincial Assembly to form a forward bloc. He has gone to the election commission seeking to unseat them.

But will the election commission act?

So far it has not disqualified a single member for floor-crossing despite laws to the contrary.

Two other former ministers from Sindh are behind bars. One of them, Munawar Talpur, is my brother-in-law, a sitting member who has been elected on five consecutive occasions. The other is Zafar Leghari, from the home district of the chief minister. Surprise, surprise.

One of our members of the National Assembly has hosted a lunch for me. I go to his house. It has lovely wooden doors. The guests are discussing the statement of the president. The president has criticized the credibility of the government's anticorruption drive.

Senator Haider walks in and briefs us about the proceedings of the Supreme Court. The former army chief of staff has admitted that a banker was asked to pay Rs. 140 million to the intelligence service to influence the elections of 1990.

I feel vindicated. I had always said that the elections of 1990 were rigged to make my party lose. I become confident that the day will come when it is proved that the elections of 1997 were rigged to prevent my party from forming the government.

After lunch I go upstairs and meet the family members. My host has two wives and three children. Both wives are sitting happily side by side. We chat and take photographs. Seeing the children makes me miss my own.

In the old days, most people had two wives or more. But now the old ways are giving way to new, and most people have one wife.

I recall another colleague inviting me to his wedding earlier in March this year.

"Sorry," I said, "I would love to come but I am in mourning for one year over my brother's death and, according to our family customs, not attending festive occasions."

"Then come to my wedding in November," he said.

"I beg your pardon!" I exclaimed. "I do not understand."

"Well," he explained, "I'm marrying my first wife in March and my second wife in November."

I tried to convince him of the merits of having one wife, not two. He agreed with all my arguments but said, "It's my father's wish."

Here parental influence matters a lot.

After lunch I go back to the house. The electricity, which had come back when I left, goes off again.

"Let's go to the Marriott Hotel," I tell my afternoon visitors. It seems as though the fly on the wall has heard for, as we are preparing to leave, the lights come back on. Hooray.

I catch a flight to Karachi. As I reach home, I shout, "Children, children!" They come rushing down the stairs with screams of delight, hugs, and shouts of, "Mama, Mama!"

Bilawal discloses that Bakhtwar's tooth has fallen out. She shows me the gap and says she's leaving the doors and windows of her room open tonight. Do I think the tooth fairy will come? she wonders.

It seems I have come back just in time.

Amy Bloom

Amy Bloom, a clinical social worker, is the author of Come to Me,
Love Invents Us, *and* A Blind Man Can See How Much I Love You.

POSTED Tuesday, July 6, 1999, at 7:42 A.M. PT

I have not found myself so often in wet and ill-fitting clothes and so
much in need of a drink by 6 o'clock for many years. We have a
Fresh Air Fund guest with us. Her name is K——, she's 7, lovely and
dark-coffee-colored, missing her two front teeth and capable of
great sweetness, sharp observations, and classic 7-year-old obnox-
iousness. (I have not had to see a cheeseburger chewed open-
mouthed or listen to people being called "doo-doo head" for a long
time, and I have not missed it.) She loved watching Wimbledon, especially the Venus-Steffi match, and for all that Venus Williams is
an extraordinary athlete and a singularly uncharming public figure,
we were glad to see her dark face and white beads exploding on the
screen. K—— did cheer for her (and was sorry to see those two exceedingly white players, Steffi and Lindsay, in the final) but, in fact,
delivered her allegiance solely based on whoever was leading in the
match. I wonder what her family in New York makes of our family,
or how much they've thought about it. Her foster mother and I
have chatted, with mutual grooming gestures and appreciation, but

I bet she has feelings of uneasy, regretful disapproval, just like I do. (How could you not send your asthmatic child's inhaler, and why does K— flinch when she spills two drops of orange juice? And she may think, *I packed those postcards for her to send home—why haven't you got your privileged ass to the post office, and by the way, why are you letting her call herself by something other than her given name?*) But in the midst of endless juice boxes (and occasional bouts of the kind of whining that makes you think that boarding school for 7-year-olds is not a bad English idea but a good one, unaccountably neglected by Americans) and huge, hot-bodied hugs and runs through the sprinkler and Reader Rabbit computer games and feeding grass to the horse on the corner and viewing blueberries with great suspicion and viewing the ocean with admiration and astonishment, replaced within two hours with a Connecticut kid's casual pleasure, we are in a very odd and happy and not-at-all simple time with this little girl and glad that her family sent her or was willing to have her sent, glad and proud and touched that my own daughter, the baby of the family, at 17, is willing to help, willing to offer her considerable warmth and nurturance and willing not to be too disheartened or permanently annoyed by bouts of bad manners on K—'s part, or by her sudden withdrawals, clouds in the midst of bouncing light.

I can barely get time on my computer—this is the one that works the best for all of K—'s programs. I guess I will never finish this collection of short stories...at least not in the next week. I keep playing with the last story at least, trying to get the main characters into focus—the mother comes in, the daughter slides out, and I better decide if the lover is, in fact, transsexual.

My one break today will be tennis doubles at 8 A.M. with players who range from arthritic, deaf 84-year-olds (with great drop shots) to stocky, powerful women in their 30s whose bad haircuts and bluff manners would spell lesbian in many places but here, in our little Connecticut hamlet, usually mean: married the high-school sweetheart, has three kids and an M.S.N. degree. The only

queer couples I know are the nice queer clergy-people, the two
pipe-smoking psychiatrists (guys), and a very sweet older lady
who organizes the church potluck and her much younger companion, who are both happy to refer to themselves as "dear friends"
and seem to not mind that Miss M.'s open and tender devotion to
Miss H. (I once saw one bicycle over to the tennis court with towels, to mop up the morning's rain for the other's match) is viewed
as something quite a bit less than Harry and Bertha's 25th wedding anniversary at the Grange.

   Still trying to nail down plans for my mother's 80th-birthday
all-family cruise, Joy's 50th-birthday party (still trying to get
Tracy Nelson to come and sing), and still trying to find a middle for
this fucking short story.

POSTED   Thursday, July 8, 1999, at 9:18 A.M. PT

K— had her first tennis lesson and her third meltdown (not bad
for 10 days) last night. The lesson was great—especially since our
friend, the best tennis player we know, slept through the scheduled time and gave us the lesson free. K— did well and then tried
to accelerate from ball tossed to her to ball hit to her and then had
a bunch of failures. I was afraid that it'd be like swimming, that
she would just announce, "I hate that. I don't want to." But she
said instead, "I'm not quitting," which is the kind of thing when it
comes out of the mouth of a little kid with a mane of black braids
that makes you hear swelling "God Bless America" music. At
least, it has that effect on me, which is why I'm not as tired of raising children as most normal people at this point (two launched,
one almost).

   The meltdown was over dinner. She was hyped up from the lesson and wanted to go back to the court to play. I promised we could
before dark, but after dinner. Joy made pork chops, at K—'s request. Excellent pork chops. (I don't have much of a standard, it's

true, having never eaten a pork chop until I was 18, and still never, for whatever odd reason, ordering pig in chop form — bacon, yes, Italian sausage, fabulous, Chinese pork anything, of course, but no chops, please, we're Jewish.) So she stuffed four pieces of pork chop into her mouth and just smooshed it around, as little bits bulged out. Disgusting, of course, also dangerous, also irritating, also wasteful. When I could not cajole or coax her into chewing and swallowing and she stuffed in a fifth piece of pork, I put her plate off the table. Terrible weeping, gnashing of teeth, head down, lamentations like you wouldn't believe. And not crocodile tears at all. I was accused of taking rice off her plate and eating it, under the pretext of removing her plate as an act of discipline. I defended myself (vigorously, insanely). We both sat with her, and Joy suggested that if she stopped crying before dark, there would be time for volleyball and fireflies. Joy went out to close the grill, looking sympathetic and concerned. More weeping, more recriminations. I didn't care. We could sit, weeping or not, till the cows came home. I think this must be the legacy of 24 years of child-rearing. I knew we'd ride it out and get over it and that she would be better off in the long run (forgetting, of course, that I am not raising her, and that we have no expectation of a long run, as much as we'd like one). Finally, dismally, she swallowed the stupid bits of pork chop and went outside. When they came back in, there were many hugs and big, smoochy kisses. One more meltdown to go, a last reading of *Horton Hears a Who*, a completely wonderful book, as good as the *George*s and *Martha*s (which are more clever, but less moving) and as good as most short fiction. I may teach *Horton* and *George* and *Martha* next spring at Yale.

Caught up with my ex-husband, home after a holiday, the tanned and relaxed-looking owner of the pool we tried to teach K— to swim in. I'm glad he lent us use of the pool, gave us the code to his house, glad I watered his geraniums, and feel deeply glad that after all our pain, I'm happy to see his face when I do and very happy that we have been and are parents together — just as

I'm so glad that Joy and I have spent this time with K—. It seems to me that although it is not always possible, if you can remember and even salvage some good pieces (even though they are not enough to make a marriage happy), you have not failed, you have suffered, but you have not given away your past.

I leave this afternoon for a couple of days of spa-going with my sister. We promised each other this time long ago, long before K—, and I feel terrible to be going. But Sarah and Joy have lots of stuff planned, and my sister and I have waited two years for this getaway. And, as much as I feel, *Oh, dear, too much for Joy? Oh, dear, how hard on K—*, I actually feel, *Rats, I'm going to miss the glow-in-the-dark fish at Mystic Aquarium and the Ferris wheel at Lake Compounce and K—'s wide-eyed delight*. And instead, I'll sit with my sister and play gin and laugh ourselves sick and wonder whether or not the three pounds we lose drinking juice for lunch will really make a difference, once we get home. (Just as I know that "please" and "thank you" are important things and that sticking K—'s braids back off her face—which I like and she doesn't— is stupid, I know that juice fasts are even stupider. Funny how that doesn't change anything.)

I miss my darling Joy, my beloved Sarah, and now my dear K— already.

Ron Carlson

Ron Carlson's most recent book is the story collection The Hotel Eden. *His novel,* The Speed of Light, *will be published in 2001. He teaches writing at Arizona State University in Tempe.*

POSTED Monday, Aug. 4, 1997, at 4:30 P.M. PT

Oh sing in me muse and through me tell the story of our road trip —or anything you feel inclined to type up while I drive.

This is a road trip in what we call a recreational vehicle, an RV, which means anything with wheels in which you can watch TV. We (two families) are rolling out of Phoenix in the long-awaited massive monsoon rain toward Cedar City, Utah, where we'll pick up the Nelsons' daughter Becky, who has been at Shakespeare camp for 10 days. Seven people going up, eight coming back. Three boys ages 12 and 13, two of them ours. The TV is on before we're out of Scottsdale.

Our family road trips, of which there are at least two every summer, are different endeavors. In the closer quarters, Elaine reads to us; in the last two summers we've had a dozen books.

By the time we're north of Flagstaff, all the characters in this vehicle have sorted themselves into the furniture. The three boys are in the far back, well into a cinema classic about a plane crash, snow—a film made five years after my one-minute monologue: "I

Ate My Best Friend's Brain." The first line there is: "Well, he wasn't my best friend, I mean, what's a best friend?"

Today our route is the great old Highway 89: Flagstaff, Page, Kanab, Hurricane, Cedar City, the little ship rocking through the Navajo Reservation, rain all the way.

After the first film and before the second, a feature about spiders, we consider a reading. The *Odyssey* is our next book, but there's some resistance. We're in an RV and Nick is lobbying. He says from the kitchen table, 10 feet behind the driver: "I already saw that show."

"It's not a show," I offer. There are seconds between every sentence in this huge noisy thing.

"He starts with the goddess," Colin (12) adds; he's always been an evidence man.

"It's not a show," I repeat. "It's a book."

"He tries to get home and he kills that one guy," Nick says.

"The Cyclops," Brian says. There's a reverential pause for one of the first great action sequences, and then Elaine reads the first page, which sets a different tone, kind of legal, and makes the story seem to be about property rights. It's relatively hard to hear. The boys hide behind the TV way back there.

Elaine does the pragmatic thing. She stands in the rolling ship and gives everybody a cup of pistachios. Immediately a fabulous moment of gratitude descends; we've got snacks — and the wonderful debris! We've got the open road before us, the spiders in the back, and we've got snacks. In 90 minutes we'll be in that American paradise — a motel!

I've always loved the invocation of the muse, however. I spend my life dealing with writers' tenuous confidence in their stories and there's something true right off the bat about writers nodding at the fact that they may have bitten off a story that may bear a dimension or two they may need help chewing. I'd like to bring it back; it would beat the heck out of acknowledgments and serve the same purpose.

POSTED   Tuesday, Aug. 5, 1997, at 4:30 P.M. PT

This morning we watch the student actors at the Shakespeare Festival here in Cedar City, Utah. The light rain has us in a bland classroom, which all these noble youth transcend with dexterity. These are mainly high-school students and they are good, every one of them ready for trouble, that is drama. For two hours, without hesitation, they sing, cajole, tease, declaim. Such language in such instruments is a ringing pleasure. I watch our boys, the seriousness they give to these performers, who are only two and three years older than they.

The actress Rebecca Nelson, 16, is fully surprised that her family and the Carlsons have come to retrieve her, and she grins and colors, and then, thank god, introduces us to all her friends.

Our family slips away and uses lunch at a Mexican restaurant to preview *Hamlet*, the play tonight, and as I tell the story, the boys light to familiar moments that they know from somewhere. When Nick expands the orchard murder, I ask him if he's seen this show before. The prince is still alive when the bill arrives.

Summers I find myself traveling in close quarters with my family, and there are surprises in such proximity. Throughout the lunch and our long walk afterward, we're talking, and as we talk, that odd thing happens with our names, that is, everyone uses the wrong name once or twice. Colin walks with me and he turns and commences some of his observations with "Nick" or "Mom." We do it when we start sentences. I remember my mother going through my brothers' names looking for mine as she stood before me with an instruction, and we all got so we knew that a revision of the name or an apology was unnecessary. And that is what has happened now in my family. Nick starts a sentence to me with his brother's name and he is undeniably speaking to me. It only means we've all created our code; we're in the circle.

In the last daylight we attend the outdoor "Green Show," watching these clapping gypsies sing and strut and tell fortunes and bad jokes. The lawns of Southern Utah University are filled with hundreds of playgoers. Two plays are performed every night.

Our *Hamlet* is indoors and it is absolutely off the charts. I won't review it but to say it has exactly the vital shadowed heart that I wanted the boys to see in their first production. It's been set somewhere between the World Wars—rifles, uniforms, European business suits—very classy. Fortinbras' soldiers wear smart red berets. Polonius steals the show, his two-thirds. Sitting in the theater I'm aware again that a thousand novels take their titles from the play, and I'm not sure there isn't a book of poems waiting for the Ghost's phrase, "The Porches of My Ear."

After the curtain call there's a little water in my eyes, but not for Hecuba, and as our group stands, Colin says quietly, "That was pretty good." On the way back to the motel, everyone tired and righteous (having sat still for three hours), I ask my friend Scott if he's got one of those berets somewhere. He's driving the motor home slowly under some leafy sycamores on a quiet street. The branches brush the top of the tall vehicle. He looks at me puzzled, then smiles. "That's right," he says. "They were Norwegians, weren't they?"

POSTED Wednesday, Aug. 6, 1997, at 4:30 P.M. PT

Certainly many of my most optimistic moments have been spent checking the oil of my car in motel parking lots early in the morning. There's a paper cup of coffee balanced on the bumper. A little packing, a search under the beds for lost treasures, and then: away! The world awaits! Today, we (all eight, two families) draw away from Cedar City under blue skies and head toward Phoenix.

Climbing east into the mountains, we tour Cedar Breaks State Park, a shocking panorama of red and white towers in a canyon that yawns from over 10,000 feet out over the good if not great plains. I've never been here. The nearly empty viewpoint itself is rustic, a huge log rail over the precipice, and there at land's end is a writer. Some kid, probably 15, stands on the wrong side of the rail with his notebook propped against it, writing. If he takes three steps backward, he'll be a scream and a memory. I watch my wife, Elaine, and our friend the novelist Barbara Nelson circle the area, pretending to take in the radical view, but they are watching all the children, thinking them away from the edge. The writer wants what we all want. He wants me to come over and ask him what he's writing and if he knows he's in danger.

Early afternoon we pull into the Kaibab National Forest and everyone climbs out. The ponderosas are huge and fragrant in the warm day. This is secret, one of my family's caches. Up a logging road and under a tree Colin digs up what we buried when we were here last, over a year ago. I can't say what it is, but we share a pungent and foamy toast. Everyone makes offerings for what to put back, and we gather more than five dollars and Elaine's bead necklace. Brian Nelson (13) hands over his ticket stub from *Hamlet* and it was headed for a scrapbook. There's more there right now, buried under a special marker that Barbara threw in a special place, after five tries.

We've always had caches. For years we had a jar of money buried by a fence post off Highway 40 in Utah near Starvation Reservoir. We'd dig it up each year and then simply add more cash. The bills in there were brown. Then two years ago we stopped and they'd widened the road for oil exploration and moved the entire fence. The boys walked in circles for a while.

Winding down the Kaibab Plateau, I pull off at the newly paved turnout. I've been worried about not being able to get any sex into any of this until now. We can see clearly to the red rock notch that cuts toward Page, and a 1,000-square-mile desert floor lies below us like just what it is: some primal thing, that eerie shadow snaking through it is the Colorado River gorge which 10 miles south becomes the Grand Canyon. This very turnout was the site of a magnificent tryst 30 years ago, and my associate in that tender endeavor is now 12 feet behind me in this vehicle reading. Our children and our friends sit between us. When I ask her if she remembers anything, if she remembers any particular thing about this particular place, she looks over her book, tilts her head, and says, "Can it, Ron."

Five hours later, we're throwing our duffels onto our driveway in the dark. Everyone is jangled, whacked out, splenetic. The hulking recreational vehicle hums ironically beside our farewells, as if it were innocent. I can see a FedEx mailer glowing by our door. It is too late to get the cats from jail, the kennel closed, and we four stagger inside. This building, we see by the mail, must be our home.

Tucker Carlson

Tucker Carlson writes for the Weekly Standard *and* Talk *magazines.*

POSTED Monday, Sept. 14, 1998, at 4:30 P.M. PT

Woke up at 8 A.M. when two Guatemalan guys carrying a sheet of drywall opened my bedroom door and gave me a long disapproving look. Still in bed, huh? they said without saying it. For a moment I felt totally confused. Who are these people? Why are they in my bedroom? And why do I feel so terrible?

Slowly I unraveled the mystery: I feel bad because I went to bed late. I went to bed late because I was writing a freelance piece about the 1998 congressional races. I wrote a freelance piece about the 1998 congressional races because...of course—the Guatemalan guys. They're "doing" our bathrooms. And I'm paying them. With money from freelance pieces about the 1998 congressional races. So they can come to my house and wordlessly insult me as I lie in bed feeling terrible because I stayed up late writing....The circular quality of it all made me queasy.

I'm going to be seeing a lot of the Guatemalan guys this year, and probably next. Last month we bought a new house. The fact that it hadn't been updated since 1906 seemed like a strong selling point at the time. "That way we won't have to tear out all those schlocky '60s renovations you find in most old houses," I said to my wife. She nodded in what I took to be agreement. We settled on the place, then left town for two weeks on vacation.

For reasons too complicated and embarrassing to explain, we never had the house inspected. Not that we didn't know it needed work—the dozen or so broken windows were a strong hint that it did—but somehow the place seemed more charming than decrepit. Getting some officious inspector in there to nitpick over every deficiency didn't strike me as worth the $500 fee. The house still seemed charming when we got back from vacation. Only it also seemed decrepit. The wiring, I noticed for the first time, was antique and cloth-covered. The water pressure was so weak it was impossible to wash the dishes and shave at the same time. The basement, on the other hand, had more than enough water— though only on the walls and floor—and smelled like an entire animal shelter's worth of cats had lived there for a decade or so with no litter boxes. The back stairwell had been boarded up since the mid-1960s after someone apparently fell down it and died. The main stairs were creaky and worn concave on every step. Many of the moldings had been smashed. Much of the woodwork had split into splinters the size of hatpins.

Then there were the bathrooms. A couple of years ago, I went to Philadelphia to do a story about crack houses. The anti-drug group I was profiling had decided to use the Roman siege technique to clean up its neighborhood. Rather than push the cops to close down a nearby crack house, it petitioned the local utility companies to suspend power and water service to the place. Then it waited. For months.

Crack-heads, it turns out, have a cockroach-like ability to survive in barren environments. By the time the addicts finally moved out and I toured the house, probably 20 people had lived there for several months with no plumbing or heat. There are two things I remember about the place. First is the floor, which was covered (don't ask me why) with hundreds of empty bags of Munchos, the repulsive fried-onion faux potato chips that probably aren't even made anymore. The second thing I recall vividly is the bathroom. Every tile on the floor and walls was cracked and smeared with what looked like a mixture of motor oil and bacon grease. There were a number of elbow-size holes in the walls. In the corner, next to the trash-filled bathtub, was a five-gallon bucket that had once held construction adhesive. It was overflowing.

Our bathrooms didn't come with honey buckets, but for suburban Virginia they were as close as you'll ever get to the feel of a Philadelphia crack house. My wife immediately declared them off-limits to the children, then called a contractor over to rip them out. That's when yet another myth from childhood died a hard death. All that chatter you hear from yuppie parents at the playground about how expensive it is to "do" bathrooms? It's all true. Every word, and worse.

That's what went through my mind at 8 this morning after my run-in with the Guatemalan drywall men. I got up and went to work.

POSTED Wednesday, Sept. 16, 1998, at 4:30 P.M. PT

Had the sort of day that gives magazine writers the reputation—entirely deserved—for being lazy and overfed: Played with the kids in the backyard after breakfast, wrote at home till noon, had an enormous lunch at the Palm, returned a few calls, then sat around the office listening to gossip, telling stories, and trading theories about Clinton's sex life.

At 6 P.M. I drove over to the Capitol for a reception Frank Luntz was having for himself. Luntz, in case you don't live in Washington, is a pollster who gives advice to Republican members of Congress. Or did. Luntz has announced that he is retiring from politics, hence the cocktail reception. (Of course, this being Washington, there were no actual cocktails, just wine and cans of beer.) The party took place in the same room where the Republican leader-ship often holds press conferences, which somehow seemed fitting. Luntz wandered through the crowd of a hundred or so, the only man in the room not wearing a tie. I found a beer and talked to a couple of lobbyists I know. What are you doing here? I asked one of them. "I used to think Luntz was a total fraud," he said. "I still think he's sort of a phony, except now I know how smart he is."

So do I. A couple of years ago I had a conversation with Luntz about one of his clients, a member of Congress named John. At the time I thought I might do a piece about Luntz, so I recorded the ex-change. "I look at John's head as something to fill with the best and the brightest," Luntz explained. "It's like taking all of the classics and getting them down to Cliffs Notes and getting them into his head so at least he knows something about it. The smarter they make John, the better John is, the better it is for me if I want to be part of John's world."

Wow, I thought, that's the most patronizing thing I've ever heard. John can't really be that stupid, that desperately in need of Luntz's help. Can he?

Sure he can, as I discovered several months later on a trip through Texas with another member of Congress, who as it hap-pens was also a Luntz client. The congressman in question was and is one of my favorite politicians in Washington. He's witty, smart, politically sensible, and loves dogs. He's also, as I learned one after-noon in Dallas, completely bonkers.

"Hey, there's the grassy knoll," the congressman said, pointing out the window as we drove through Dealey Plaza. "Did you see that British documentary about the assassination that came on the other night about 3? It was fascinating." I thought he was joking. By the time he finished explaining how Kennedy's autopsy photos had been doctored, I knew he wasn't. Over the next hour, the con-gressman proceeded to give me the full story. The assassination, he said gravely, was in fact a planned "coup d'état" staged by "rogue CIA operatives" who killed the president and framed Oswald in a diabolical attempt to extend the Cold War. Or possibly to end it. The congressman wasn't sure which, though he did seem to have just about every other detail memorized.

But what about the physical evidence? I asked. Hasn't it been proved that Kennedy was killed with Oswald's gun? He looked at me like I was an idiot. Speaking slowly, he explained the deception: Days before the assassination, CIA technicians fired a bullet from Oswald's gun into a pail of water. The slug was retrieved, coated with plastic, reloaded, and placed in a larger-caliber rifle, which was then used by government agents to kill Kennedy. The plastic coating disintegrated when the slug hit the president, leaving only the tell-tale marks from Oswald's rifle to throw off investigators from the Warren Commission.

Assuming of course that investigators from the Warren Commission weren't involved in the conspiracy, too. The congressman suspected they were. Just look, he said, at the FBI report on the TWA crash off Long Island. "The government claims the plane just crashed on its own. You think that's really what happened?" Sure, I said. He shot me another how-dumb-can-you-be? look. "I believed the Warren Commission, too," he said. "At first."

I never wrote up the conversation I had with the congressman —lucky for him, every word was, by prearrangement, on background—but I did take notes, mostly because I could hardly believe it was really happening. Could this be the same man I'd seen speak thoughtfully and coherently to rooms full of adults? Then I grasped the difference. Those had been speeches. Frank Luntz doesn't provide scripts for private conversations.

Leslie Carr

Leslie Carr is a school nurse in Pennsylvania.

POSTED Monday, Feb. 28, 2000, at 10:30 A.M. PT

When we were tykes, we would never go to the nurse for an itch due to a bug bite or for chapped lips. It was understood that these things were parts of life with which we coped. Now such visits are commonplace. What does it mean? I see it as one of my main functions to reinforce what these kids must already sense is reality in these cases. The child says, "I have a mosquito bite." I say, "Yup. (Pause.) You have a mosquito bite. (Pause.) It's gonna itch today, and it's gonna itch tomorrow. It will probably also itch the next day until it heals." Then, just so they don't think I'm a total meanie, I teach the little trick about scratching around the bite instead of directly over the bite. Dismissed.

I wish this school district allowed the regular administration of Tylenol or ibuprofen as needed. Or, in lieu of that, I wish I had some sort of placebo to give. They're so handy. True, they foster the simple-solution idea and promulgate the life view best put forth by the fast food chain "Hot 'N Now," but placebos sure would keep kids in class longer. Forty years ago, my nursery-school teacher had a sack of what she called "bump pills." They were Tootsie

Rolls. When we had a boo-boo we got one. Nice deal. One day she accidentally cracked me on the head with a wooden bench and gave me the whole damn bag.

I was a hyperaware child and a stutterer to boot, so being newly immersed in the elementary-school environment makes me more than a little uneasy. I see the kids in classrooms, seats arranged in clusters or horseshoe formations, chewing pencils, jostling in the cafeteria, Hula Hooping in the gym, and I am glad to be over 35 years old. Very glad. The nurse's office was a wonderful refuge for me as a stuttering little girl. I had to run from all the required speaking—from the What I Did Last Summer gig to the seventh-grade reading of *Romeo and Juliet* in which everyone had a part, up and down the rows of desks, taken in turn, until the turn was mine. I'd bolt when I saw it coming. Nothing like a good stopover in the nurse's office to eat up 30 otherwise most uncomfortable minutes.

Today, if someone similar to my past little self would show up in my office, I'd be likely to draw her a bubble bath and order room service. No matter that it would be cafeteria fare: Chicken Nuggets With Tea Roll, Hash-Brown Potatoes, Winter Mix, Peach Crisp, Milk.

POSTED Tuesday, Feb. 29, 2000, at 10:30 A.M. PT

OK. This is what and whom I saw today: Three fevers—two raging, one borderline. A principal who had stapled his finger and who proceeded to regress at an alarming speed once he entered my office. A sorry mixture of scabies and chicken pox. Three stomachaches. One old wound to be re-dressed. A diabetic on an insulin pump who became hypoglycemic. A child referred by her teacher because the teacher suspected that the child had not wiped her bottom properly after using the bathroom, and would I investigate that? A sore throat and a splinter. Glasses broken at recess. All the kids who receive daytime medications (only about 15 of them at this school). An asthmatic in distress. Three bumps on the head necessitating calls to the parents (school-district policy).

Calls to the parents can go several different ways. When I called the mother of the child who had broken his glasses, she was annoyed—presumably at me. I wanted to say, "Hey look lady, I didn't break his glasses. I'm letting you know what happened as a courtesy so you can plan your day better, not be surprised, maybe squeeze in a trip to the optician." I did not say this. Instead, I used my step-aside favorite, "Would you like to speak with Jake yourself? He's right here. . . . " Usually the calls go well, and I am received well. Maybe a school nurse is viewed as a benevolent force. People switch into the cooperative mode when they hear it's me on the line, even if they do not initially answer the phone that way. Maybe they are just so relieved that I'm not calling to say that their Chandler or Winston or Dakota just fell head first off of the monkey bars. Although sometimes I am calling to say just that.

I'll never forget when the school nurse called me at home some years ago and said (erroneously) that my sixth-grader had just had what looked like a seizure in class. The floor of the kitchen where I was standing rose up in one plane toward my knees and then tilted around. I heard my voice saying that I'd be right there. The floor settled back down so that I could leave the room. My walking legs were not my own, but they walked me to my car. I thought of that today when I heard a catch of panic in a parent's voice, and I rushed to the part in my message that described how absolutely okey-dokey the child in question was doing.

It was a busy day. On days like this I get all pumped up. I want the kids to remember me; I want to have an impact. A little girl in the hallway smiles at me like we share a secret, but I don't even remember her name. A child with whom I thought I had connected nicely looks past me when I greet her in the lobby. Did our encounter mean nothing to her? Am I one in a series of well-meaning nobodies to her?

I wonder if I am put together in such a way that I can give so much at work without being lauded. Or, put another way, I wonder if I have the inner-directedness to make it as a school nurse. There is no one to say, "Boy, you really sized up that situation with Jimmy." Or, "Wow, you did a swell job convincing that parent to get Mariah seen by a doctor!" It's an isolated position—not much adult company, no peers to bounce around with. There are no murmurs of approval, like from committee members when you volunteer to do something. No witnesses. Just me and the kids, mostly.

I stayed late today documenting everything and tying up loose ends. Driving home, the aromas of burning wood and manure blended in the cold air. The sky was filled with creamsicle-colored clouds.

POSTED Wednesday, March 1, 2000, at 10:30 A.M. PT

Today I am at my "slow" school, a quiet elementary that houses just two classes each of kindergarten through second grade. Here I have time to look up records, detect patterns of behavior in students, and write. It feels luxurious. A kindergartener today complained that he had worse itches than anyone who had ever gone to that school. He then revealed a 3-by-2-inch area of scaly pink skin beneath his sock. "How long has it been bothering you?" I asked. He replied, "Oh, just a few whiles."

I got out of the car upon arrival this morning and, as usual, was met by the wafting scent of the most delectable baked goods. There is actually a dog-food factory a half-mile away that is responsible for this. Things were not what they seemed inside the building, either. There was silence in the lobby and down the hall where I enter, like nothing was going on, like zero movement, no buzz. Turns out there was an ambulance behind the building already carting away a teacher who broke her ankle on the playground before my arrival. The district's head nurse (called to the scene) was out there managing things. This was the most serious health-related event at this particular location this year by far.

There is no medication parade at this school—just two Ritalin recipients and one inhaler on gym day. I am lucky in this regard. The middle-school and high-school nurses roll out carts like stewardesses to dose up the student body at lunch time.

I did height, weight, and vision screening of a first-grade class today and was struck by the lack of maliciousness among the children. We always hear (and often observe) how vicious kids can be, how unforgiving of differences and shortcomings. But it must start later than age 6 or 7. This group treated differences as merely differences ("We are the world....") and not opportunities for stigmatization. One chubby boy announced, "I'm the heaviest one here!" By God, he was. A markedly overweight human being if I ever saw one. However, his statement was not met with taunts, but instead, "My Dad's heavier than you!" "My Aunt Martha is really fat!" "Maybe you won't be next week!" It was downright inspiring.

The inspiration did not penetrate deeply, though, because later I did something, or failed to do something, that left me with a feeling of shame. An 8-year-old boy came into my office with a minor complaint, and right away I could tell he was a stutterer. I wanted to say, "I stutter too!" but I did not say it. I was afraid. Of what? I was afraid he'd have to realize in my presence that there was a strong chance he'd stutter all his life. I was afraid he'd be embarrassed. I was afraid he'd get attached to me and want to visit me every day. I was afraid he'd look to me for something beyond understanding. I was most likely wrong on every single count, and anyway what would have been so terrible if I were right? So much for my vision of rolling out the red carpet to greet my former self! Shame, shame. I hope he comes back again soon. I'll do better.

On the other hand, a victory was scored with a sick and sad little girl who is always sad even when she's not sick. But today she was afflicted, temperature 103, a certain sort of misery creeping through her bones. I was having trouble reaching her mother;

there was no father nearby; emergency contacts out of town. The phoning went on for 90 minutes or so, on and off. Finally, I did reach the mother and arranged for her to come to take the child home. I was relieved and happy. As I put down the phone, I spontaneously started to sing a simple song (with about six words) about going home. I did a jig to accompany this. I was having fun and expressing myself. Miss Misery was not buying it. As if she sees a school nurse singing and jigging around every day of the week! In her weary and laconic way she interrupted me asking, "Should I go to my classroom and get my coat and backpack?" Skipping just a beat or two, I said, "Not until I've finished my song," and then she smiled. Her face actually smiled and we *met*. I finished my song.

POSTED Thursday, March 2, 2000, at 10:30 A.M. PT

I arrived this morning to see both daybeds in the health room already taken—by girls who were pretending to be surfers headed out to catch a big one, paddling on their bellies, the beds as boards. I saw them before they saw me. When they did see me, I was embarrassed for them. They leapt into "sick" positions, and the moaning and groaning began. A pathetic display.

After the beach girls returned to class, I received a call from an irate and unreasonable parent. Last week I did vision screenings for a second-grade class. This mother reported that on the evening of that screening, her child had a headache at home. The mother took this to be entirely and absolutely my fault. She demanded to know why I wanted to blind her child. This was not asked rhetorically as part of a rant, but she really wanted my motivation explained. She claimed that if I said her son wore the convex lenses (part of the screening procedure for that age group) for 30 seconds, and her son said he wore them for "a while," then I was calling her son a liar. Wow. I remembered the boy as being very pleasant, cooperative, not irrational or looking for trouble. What would it be like to live with someone like his mother? Anyway, she did not make me cry (as I later learned she had done with another nurse and a teacher), but she did make me sweat.

The father of a first-grader who was pushed at recess happened to be in the building at the time of the pushing incident and accompanied the boy to my office. He had a bloody nose and scraped lips. Within three minutes, Dad said the same thing five different ways. "He's made of iron." "He's tough." "He's a stone." "He's a tough one," accompanied by the tousling of hair and a playful shove to the shoulder, "Right, Buddy?" "He's rock tough." Rock tough? All right already. We get the picture. This is a man who does not want his son to advertise his pain, his dismay. That would be unmanly or unrocklike. This irks me. Everyone, even tough little men, should be given the chance to say "ouch" once in a while and seek some comfort.

It is difficult to believe, but today was something called Slipper Day at my school. The theme has something to do with "slipping into the future" successfully or not letting the future slip away. I don't know. So all students and staff wore bedroom slippers in school. Fuzzy, floppy slippers. Kids are tripping on the steps in clusters. I saw six kids take sliding falls within a few hours, and my office is relatively isolated. I imagine other accidents occurred that I did not see. True, I actually treated only three slipper-related injuries today, and true, nobody asked me, but I vote against Slipper Day.

When I heard a floor-shaking crash this afternoon, I ran into the boys' bathroom in the hallway near my office. The commotion seemed to come from that direction. There I discovered that when a little Kosovar refugee (who can barely speak English) went to exit his stall, the 90-pound bathroom door fell off its hinges. Anyone would have been scared, but Luzim (not his real name) was crouched against the back of the stall beside the toilet, shaking his head back and forth, mouthing words silently, cheeks wet with tears. The door had hit his toe as it was settling (not a direct hit, but

I did not know that at the time). Luckily, he was not wearing bedroom slippers. Luzim was mostly shocked and confused, probably wondering what he did wrong or if other doors throughout the building were also falling off, remembering God knows what from his experiences in Kosovo, toe throbbing. It felt good to care for him almost wordlessly, to communicate through touch and facial expressions.

At the dinner table at home, my four children want to know all about my patients from school. I tell them about Luzim. There was also someone whose pinky finger was stepped on in the hallway and someone with a dental cavity resembling a mini strip-mine. I describe the technique for checking for lice, which I did twice today. A mother smacked her kindergartener across the face on the way to school, so I dealt with that person, her bruise, and the County Department of Children and Youth. I was actually inundated today with twisted ankles and stomachaches, urinary accidents and nosebleeds. Toward the end of the day, I did not want to see anyone else. I dimmed the lights in the office, but they kept coming. I closed the door, and that did stem the flow somewhat. My own kids are satisfied with these tales from the outside.

POSTED Friday, March 3, 2000, at 10:30 A.M. PT

There are field trips for the fourth grade today, thereby reducing the student population in the building for a while. I've learned to look forward to things like rainy days, which mean no outdoor recess, which in turn means a 75 percent reduction in injuries. I packed the backpacks of first-aid supplies and medications for the field trips. The student who came to pick them up wears a ponytail pulled back so tightly that she looks to be balding at age 10.

I kept a mature fifth-grader (whom I will call Julie) in the health room with me for much of the day. Her temperature rose approximately 0.5 degrees per hour. I was unable to reach her parents or neighbors to take her home. We shared clementines and Hershey's Kisses. I pressed her to drink water. She helped me unknot and tie the shoes of the 30 kindergartners I was measuring. It was rather nice. When she left me, she hugged me and said, "Thank you so much for taking care of me." This feels very much like a paycheck. It occurred to me that Julie seemed especially needy and especially grateful for the maternal ministrations, but I put it out of my mind until later, reading her chart, I discovered that her own mother has indeed been very busy. She was "supposed to die" of cancer six months ago but somehow did not.

Along this same sorrowful vein, one of the most worrisome students came to see me this morning. I was merely informed of his existence prior to this date. And suddenly there he was. He has a cardiac condition known as prolonged Q-T syndrome. People with this abnormality have a small but significant chance of developing severe cardiac rhythm disorders that are potentially fatal. It is a disturbance of the heart's electrical system. The Q-T refers to an interval measured on the electrocardiogram (EKG). This condition would explain why this student might complain of chest pain or dizziness. It would also explain why he might abruptly faint or die. It can be an acquired or a hereditary condition. So, I was kneeling down, jamming something into the file cabinet, when I heard a voice say this: "I have long Q-T syndrome which is what my mother died from last year. Now I'm feeling light-headed, and I think you'd better take my blood pressure."

I looked up over the edge of the desk and saw an adorable 9-year-old, dressed (by the grandparents who are raising him) in a plaid button-down shirt with solid matching vest, tailored pants, and shoes that were not sneakers. He was sporting a gigantic orthodontic appliance, spectacles, and a cowlick. My own heart felt peculiar — but nothing that would show up on an EKG. I didn't know which issue to address first. I slid my eyes over to the CPR cheat sheet hanging on the wall. Judging by his composure and overall lack of distress, I did not feel that I had an emergency on my hands. However, this kid is not known as a complainer, and I am not known for my cardiac expertise. I focused on the physical, checked him out, chatted a bit, let him rest while I observed him. I did not mention his mother again, but I will. First I will get to know him a bit, find out what it's like to be him.

Later today, I vaguely and gradually lost interest in what I was doing. I started handing out ice packs for everything you can imagine. An ice pack goes a long, long way with this age group. Although I usually leave my office windows open (no matter what the weather) to blow the bacteria out into the hallways and dilute the airborne toxins, I think I'm coming down with something. My thorax feels packed with wet cardboard. My eyes are sinking, and I feel lazy in the posture department. I've got a dense head, slight nausea, a feeling that I'm peering out at the world from an enclosure. Anyone who comes in looking like me in the next three hours gets sent home. No questions asked. I'll probably send myself home after awhile.

Randy Cohen

Randy Cohen writes "The Ethicist," a weekly column in the New York Times Magazine, *and "News Quiz" for* Slate. *He wrote this shortly after being fired as head writer of* The Rosie O'Donnell Show.

POSTED Tuesday, Jan. 28, 1997, at 4:30 P.M. PT

McD. calls with good news. He's the music director of *The Rosie O'Donnell Show,* where I used to work. "I'm putting the theme song up for a Daytime Emmy." McD. composed the music; I wrote the lyrics. Unlike most TV themes, ours is actually sung; the words are heard. Most opening themes are arranged as instrumental music, but nearly all have lyrics. Even if the words are never heard, the lyricist receives a royalty each time the theme is played. The *Star Trek* theme has lyrics; the executive producer, Gene Rodenberry, wrote them. In television, writing lyrics that will never be sung is regarded as a fabulous opportunity.

McD. isn't optimistic about our chances: "Patti LaBelle wrote that new *Oprah* thing." But a nomination would mean seats at the awards luncheon, which is sure to be attended by many soap stars. I'd go in a second. I'm disconcerted but not displeased that Patti and Oprah may have a genuine effect, if not on my happiness, at least on my lunch plans.

A phone call about a possible job. ABC wants to create a recurring segment to unify its miscellaneous Saturday-morning cartoon shows. This sort of thing is called a wrap-around. The producer says, "We don't know what it will be, except that it will have two kids and an 8-foot puppet and be shot at Chelsea Piers. Do you have any ideas?" No, I don't. And theirs seem prematurely specific, like a first-date discussion of where the kids will go to college. I'm just relieved I didn't suggest a 9-foot puppet.

Walked up the hill to Broadway to meet Sophie's school bus. In bad weather, we parents and caretakers wait in the cash-machine annex of the Republic National Bank. You need an ATM card to get in. There is no city bus shelter nearby. Some cities provide these, but we're in tune with the great forces of history: Our ad hoc privatizing of government services outpaces even Mayor Giuliani. And he's sold advertising space on the basketball backboards in city parks.

Next door to the bank is a hardware store, then a dry cleaner, then the Indian grocery with these three signs taped to the window, handwritten on Day-Glo cardboard:

BASMATI RICE ON SALE: BUY 2 GET ONE FREE
ON SALE CORONA BEER
XXX MOVIES ON SALE: BUY 2 GET ONE FREE (NO REFUNDS)

All in all, a rich, full evening's entertainment.

POSTED Wednesday, Jan. 29, 1997, at 4:30 P.M. PT

Looking out my bedroom window on this bright January morning, I see that the parking garage across the street has again deposited several cars on the sidewalk, using it as a kind of annex. Folks heading for work have to squeeze past the Toyotas. This is illegal, of course, as are many routine transactions of New York life, from running red lights to selling insurance to transit cops. B. told me that all the delivery men from all the Chinese restaurants bring you your food on stolen bicycles. Thieves sell bikes to restaurants at a price so low, their felonious origins are undeniable.

When I lived on 13th Street, there was a numbers parlor around the corner, halfheartedly disguised as a stationery store, with two packs of yellowing loose-leaf paper and a dozen Flair pens fanned out in the window. On summer days, the door was propped open; any passerby could see the counter shielded with heavy glass and the sign above it listing that day's winning numbers. I knew about it. The neighborhood knew about it. Surely the police knew about it, but of course did nothing. Corruption or incompetence? Indifference, perhaps.

New York is not Lagos or Mexico City. I needn't bribe the mailman to get my letters. But what I want to know is, when a firefighter genuinely risks his life to douse the flames at the fabulous apartment of a grotesquely rich man, does he slide a Rolex off the night table into his big black boot? I just want to understand how actual life differs from the official version.

New York is not Mexico City, but twice a year, we parents at the 96th Street school-bus stop collect money for Mr. R., the driver. "You have to give, or he'll drop your kid in Times Square alone," someone jokes. And it is a joke. New York is not Lagos, Mr. R. is a responsible man, and the money is a gift.

Picked up a flier at the Cinema Village for their Hong Kong Sexploitation series. *Naked Killer* sounds promising. "Kitty (Chingmy Yau) is a beautiful young woman painfully torn between heterosexual love and the heady kicks of blowing men away." Fortunately, we live in a country where you needn't choose between one and the other.

Douglas Coupland

Douglas Coupland lives in Vancouver. His most recent novel is Miss Wyoming. *He wrote this while on tour for* Girlfriend in a Coma.

POSTED Friday, March 20, 1998, at 4:30 P.M. PT

An eventless flight into Raleigh. Good.

Raleigh is one of those asteroid cities with no particular core. It's an enormous, rather pretty, paved Moebius of malls, gravel pits, cemeteries, pine forests, discount golf outlets, and cherry trees. High-tech research has moved in recently. There are huge IBM and Rhone-Poulenc facilities. And cigarettes, of course. I really wanted to see an ammonia tanker drive into the Marlboro factory.

I checked into the Asteroid Marriott with a room overlooking the parking lot, feeling as though I were in Kurt Vonnegut's Midland City. I asked the desk clerk if there was a Museum of Smoking, and he said he thought there was. And the big surprise is that there were nonsmoking rooms.

I had 90 minutes all to myself to make personal phone calls, and it felt so luxurious. I ordered macaroni from room service, because I just can't look at another club sandwich or burger, and all the other food on the menu was steak, steak, steak, or steak. Ugh. And the Americans are now wrecking french fries by batter frying. It's the one truly perfected food in the country, and now they're wrecking even this. What is going through their heads? Why are they doing this?

Oh—all this road food is making my stomach go Michelin, so it's The Zone for me as of next week. I feel like I'm made of pirogi held together with toothpicks.

Late in the afternoon there was this amazing rainstorm—rain unlike anything I've ever seen—and I grew up in Vancouver and I've lived in Hawaii. It was more like a huge wave lapping over the hotel. And then it turns out there were tornadoes all over the city and that the rain was a freak occurrence. The radio was telling everybody to stay indoors and go hide in the basement, and when I arrived at the bookstore, it was utterly empty and I felt like such a loser. And then a crowd showed up at the last moment—literally at the last moment—like the citizens of Whoville at the end of *The Grinch Who Stole Christmas*. And the reading was really magical.

Cruel punch line: club sandwiches for dinner. And then at 4 A.M. everything I'd eaten all day turned to battery acid in my stomach and I woke up sneezing vomit and it was so frightening. So I'm going to eat hippie food for the next week whenever possible.

What else?

Oh, nobody in Raleigh-Durham knows how to pronounce the city's name correctly. It's so odd. I asked everybody in the signing lineup after the reading. I heard about a dozen variations:

Rally-Durrum

Rawlly-Durrrrm

Rolly-Dirram

Rully-Dur Um

Rollyderm

Rowllay-Dihr-um.

Peter Desmond

Peter Desmond has been preparing taxes for 25 years.

POSTED Thursday, April 13, 2000, at 10:00 A.M. PT

More than 120 million individual taxpayers file returns every year.
Wednesday I meet with five of them, talk on the phone with a half-
dozen others, and get e-mails from three.

What's on the minds of American taxpayers with the filing
deadline only five days away? If today's sample of one 10-mil-
lionth of all individuals is statistically valid, some 25 percent are
perplexed by the proper tax treatment of investments.

I don't mean reporting interest on Line 8, dividends on Line 9,
and capital gains distributions on Line 13 of Form 1040. My clients,
at least, are not doofuses, and the statements from the brokerage
house marked "Important Tax Documents Enclosed" present this
information clearly enough. I'm talking about the tax consequences
of selling stock or shares in mutual funds—the reason four client
folders have been languishing for weeks on my dining-room table.

The problem usually arises when a client hands me the envelope from Fidelity Investments. All goes smoothly until I get to
Form 1099-B, which reports the proceeds of sales. I say, "I see you
sold some shares in a mutual fund."

"That's right," they answer. I continue, "You don't get taxed on the proceeds of the sale. You're taxed on the difference between what you bought it for and what you sold it for—the gain."

They nod in agreement. Next I ask, "How much did you pay for these shares?"

That's when they start looking concerned and say, "You mean that information isn't in there?" I suggest, "It may be in your year-end report from Fidelity. Did you bring that?"

"Well, no," they'll typically answer. "The envelope didn't say 'Important Tax Information Enclosed.'"

I'd like to nominate Fidelity as the most taxpayer-unfriendly brokerage house in America. What's missing from its client tax reports is the "average cost basis in shares sold"—vital information which other investment firms, including Scudder and Vanguard, painlessly provide right in their tax-time mailing.

Is this the result of some misguided cost-saving effort at Fidelity? All it usually takes is a phone call to get the missing information, but I'm billing the client for my time. And the voice-mail system on at least one of their 800 numbers won't even let you talk to a human being unless you enter a PIN. One might call Fidelity a brokerage disservice.

Shareholders' worst tax headaches occur when their account regularly reinvests dividends and capital gains in additional shares of the mutual fund. Then the investors' cost basis is no longer just $6.33 per share, or whatever they originally paid when they started the account. Each time a dividend is reinvested, the price per share can be different. And with every additional investment, the dollar amount of their basis increases and the eventual tax bite is lessened—if they can keep track.

That's why I've been getting so many phone calls from Bob, one of my table people. He's owned shares in a mutual fund since the early '80s, before the investment industry became fully computerized. The dividends were reinvested every quarter, as the stock market soared, sank, then soared again. Bob finally sold some shares.

However, the brokerage house's mainframe has no idea what his average cost basis might be.

Worse still for Bob, his doting grandmother more than once contributed gifts of shares in the same fund to his account. So, he has to figure out what *her* average cost basis was too, assuming it's legal for him to get copies of her year-end statements, which in any case may stretch back to the 1960s.

Bob is an honest taxpayer, trying to do the right thing. Should he take an extension, assemble the needed records, and devote his weekends over the next few months to figuring out exactly what his basis is? Or will he just call tomorrow and give me an arbitrary figure? And shall I pretend to believe he assiduously calculated it?

Debra Dickerson

Debra Dickerson is a senior fellow at the New American Foundation, a columnist for beliefnet.com, and author of the memoir, An American Story. *She wrote this while serving as a fellow at Harvard's Department of Afro-American Studies and a contributing editor to U.S. News & World Report.*

POSTED Monday, March 3, 1997, at 4:30 P.M. PT

Reader, I slept with him.

Coming back from the ladies' room at Dali, a trendy Spanish joint here in Cambridge, I steady myself with a hand on his shoulder to squeeze back onto my bar stool. Which is all it takes to decide.

I'd realized that dating a professional athlete (he's not famous —let it go) meant I'd be spending more time outdoors, that I might have to learn to interpret the sports page, that I'd meet people different from the asthmatic pointyheads I usually date. What I hadn't realized was what that might mean in terms of musculature.

"You lose something?" "Tim" asks. He's amused.

No, smart-ass. I found something. Smart, funny, educated, gentlemanly, close to his family, successful, well-traveled, multilingual, and best of all, not a neurotic, angst-ridden East Coast egghead. No résumé envy, no constant need for external validation. No using words like "problematic" when "screwed up" is meant. And did I mention that incredible body?

OK, then. It's decided: Debra has sex before the new millennium.

But this is problematic. Having spent so long waiting militantly for the right man, I've developed protective booby traps. Like not cleaning my apartment before a date, or not shaving for several days preceding, or wearing big, comfy Socialist-Realist panties that nearly reach my Afro'd armpits. I take mental inventory: Apartment? Neat. Armpits? Check. Legs? Thank God, yes. Drawers? None.

Back at my place, he toys with me. He aims for an armchair, I toss our coats on it. He asks to read my clips, I pretend not to know where they are. He keeps his hands to himself and makes conversation a Boy Scout could be proud of. No double entendres, no sweet talk. Just a knowing smirk. Just like Mr. Three and a Half Years Ago, he makes me do all the work. Then, I'd ended up climbing into the guy's lap and asking what a girl had to do to get laid around here. I have no intention of being that subtle again.

POSTED Tuesday, March 4, 1997, at 4:30 P.M. PT

I spend the entire day indoors wrangling with editors. It turns out that writing a "Diary" is a tricky proposition. I have now had someone find fault with absolutely everything about me—today, it's the way I record my thoughts. Eventually, that's done, and I have to face my *U.S. News* editor. Though I faithfully cash their checks, I have so far produced only one piece for them. When I was in the Air Force, we had what was called a "come to Jesus meeting" wherein I confess my sins, engage in ritual self-criticism, and get forgiveness. I lay out my ideas, he shapes them into good ideas. Then I agree to a production schedule that basically requires me to research and write three articles about five minutes apart. Now all I have to do is hide from my book editor for as long as I did from my magazine editor. Then it's dinner time.

I'm reading *The Giant's House* by Elizabeth McCracken and waiting for him in Grendel's, a mystifyingly popular Harvard hangout that legend holds was saved from extinction by Lawrence

Tribe (he defended it when the city tried to revoke its license). Weekends, people actually stand in line so they can sit on hard wooden chairs at cheap wooden tables and drink widely available beers. New Year's Eve 1994, I came here with a friend, two lonely women pretending not to be, and discovered that I had asthma. Party poppers and champagne corks exploded around us as Vicky watched me curled up in a fetal position concentrating on breathing through an esophagus the circumference of a drinking straw.

He's 10 or 15 minutes late, which concerns me not at all. The door bursts open and he hurtles through, jaw stern and worried. He's searching for me so intently, he doesn't actually see me. I find this hilarious, since I'm the only Negro on the premises. I don't call to him because I enjoy watching him move. One of my most cerebral friends, a writer and a Harvard Law student, had only this to say about him: "Look at the ass on that guy."

When he finally sees me, he's apologizing and explaining that he's double-parked, no spaces. Oh, I say, are we leaving? I'm used to overbearing men making unilateral decisions for us. But no. He just wanted me to know he wasn't lollygagging. But we could leave if I wanted to. This doesn't quite compute for me. Finally, I get it. You were being thoughtful? I say. He gives me a strange look and runs off to continue the search for a parking space.

POSTED Wednesday, March 5, 1997, at 4:30 P.M. PT

I finalize the arrangements for a two-week trip back home to St. Louis. I hate St. Louis. All right, I hate the gloomy weakling I was when growing up in St. Louis. Friends who attended Washington University, who fly in to consult at Monsanto or McDonnell Douglas, do not recognize the miserable city of my memories. The St. Louis beyond my working-class orbit remains a mystery to me, as does whatever was good within that orbit. I blow into town just long enough to witness kinfolk being either married or buried, and am out again on the first thing smoking. I will have to buy a map of my hometown. At the last wedding I attended, a niece imitated me by lobbing make-believe belongings into a paper-bag "suit-case" and Mad Max-ing her Hot Wheels full tilt for the airport "cuz that's where Debbie lives."

My newly cagey *U.S. News* editor sicced the photography guys on me. They call to coordinate the photos for the many simultane-ous articles I agreed to produce. Can't blame him. He gave me an inch, I took six weeks. If I fall behind now, I'll drag innocents with me. Even so, this development cheers me because the last photog-rapher was a hoot. We giggled for six hours. He'd spent the cam-paign watching endless showings of *Fargo* on the press plane and tormented me with trivia questions. My favorite: How many ponytail revolutions did the prostitute servicing Steve Buscemi perform? I forget how many, but he killed me imitating her.

Get a surprising call from an old acquaintance. We've never been close, so I know he wants something. He's just heard that my ex-boyfriend (we all worked together) has come out as a homosex-ual. I confirm that piece of intelligence and brace for the usual questions.

Gay men demand sympathy for my ex. Certain straight men (the kind who barely know you but ask personal questions) want to know first, whether he and I were having sex, and second, whether he was having sex with men while with me. Though they pretend to provide comfort (I don't need it—he's my best friend), what they really want is to know whether he was having sex with men while they were treating him like a heterosexual. They know this question is deplorable, they stammer and turn red in the face, but they can never control themselves. As ever, I refuse to answer the first question and refer my caller to the source himself for the second. Then I tell him never to call me again.

Women have two responses. They either murmur sympathy for me, or, more often, want to know precisely how furious I was when he told me and exactly how and where I struck him. When I admit that I did not hit him, they launch into furious pantomimes of their own hypothetical anger and graphically shadowbox the way they'd thrash such a creature. It's always fisticuffs, never tears, guns, knives, or hit men. Knuckle sandwiches. I offer up weak defenses of my friend and secretly enjoy their anger.

POSTED Thursday, March 6, 1997, at 4:30 P.M. PT

Widowed and 70, my mother scurries home before dark, asked for a security system for Christmas, sets booby traps for burglars. She agonizes over whether the porch light will attract or repel prowlers. Watching her scuttle fearfully from the car to the house is a sight I have to look away from. Both frightened and furious whenever someone is carjacked in her driveway or ambushed at midday, she recounts each murderous detail while I grope for words that will reassure her. "What are decent folks supposed to do?" she asks after each atrocity. My talk of decreasing FBI statistics held no balm, so she came up with her own. The cure for violence in America? A cell phone. No militia member ever wanted a gun as militantly as she wants a cell phone. In her mind, a bad guy will lunge and she'll speed-dial the police station to tell on him. He'll hang his head in shame as she conferences in his mother and his minister. Justice will take its course on speakerphone. I got her one and pray it gives her peace of mind.

She just picked it up and needs me on the line while she programs her secret weapon; it beeps and crackles while she half-listens to me. A former Mississippi sharecropper with an eighth-grade education, she's convinced she can't understand anything important. I have diplomas on the wall; I'm a genius. I have to stand near her while she uses an ATM; otherwise, she queues for a teller. Today, though, I have to chat since I'm invisible. So she presses buttons and I babble.

"Debbie, it says, 'Depress the PRGM key on left side of display.'" She reads haltingly since she thinks she can't possibly be getting it right.

"Yes, ma'am," I say.

" 'Depress.' That's just 'press,' right?"

"Uh hmm."

"The PRGM key—'program'?"

"That's right."

"It's on the left side?"

"Yes, ma'am. Do you see it?"

"Yes. P-R-G-M. There's a P-G-R button, but it's on the right side...."

She pauses hopefully. I say nothing. "They don't mean that one do they?"

"No, ma'am."

Long pause.

"Now, press it, Ma."

I hear congratulatory beeping.

"Ooooh," she croons, amazed.

If the phone malfunctions mechanically, she'll pry off its cover, tinker with its innards while making cornbread, and repair it with a crochet needle. That's manual labor, something she can do. But recording a voice-mail message? Not without prayer.

Now she's trying to make her inaugural cell-phone call, me in one ear, her safe new future in the other. She's excited and giggly. I cannot persuade her to ditch me and play with the cell phone without training wheels. So, I babble about O.J., a favorite subject of hers. This distracts her and she tunes in to hear her fancy lawyer daughter using words like "problematic," "evidentiary issues," and "money damages as a surrogate for criminal justice."

"That's right," Mama agrees energetically. I can see her head nod once, implacably. "He won't get into heaven."

Mark Doty

Mark Doty is a poet and memoirist. His latest book of prose, Still Life With Oysters and Lemon, *will be published in January 2001.*

POSTED Wednesday, May 3, 2000, at 10:00 A.M. PT

I didn't think I could get away with another day of saying "Well, I didn't write the poem again" without taxing my readers' patience or my own. And so today I was grateful I'd been keeping this journal, because it gave me a little bit of an extra push, helped me stay at my desk, wrestling the lines into focus. All this afternoon I worked and reworked, and though I felt as if the poem were just waiting there, right beneath the surface, waiting to be written, I was also surprised by where it moved, and a bit spun around by it —which is a good sign, that a poem takes its author aback, unsettles.

Showing you a poem at this stage in its development feels a bit like answering the door in my underwear: I don't feel presentable or put-together. The poem may well have gaffes and repetitions, or weak lines. I'll be fine-tuning it for a while to come, reading it aloud, listening for the weak spots.

But I can feel that it's substantively here, its embrace achieved. Or so I think just now, anyway—I may look at it in horror tomor-

row and decide a major overhaul's in order! But today it feels
right, and here it is.

ULTRASOUND

I'm ushering the dogs into the back of the car,
after our morning walk in the wet woods,
herding them in—Beau who needs his generous

attention brought into focus, his gaze
pointed into the tailgate so he'll be ready
to leap up, and Arden, arthritic in his hind legs,

who needs me to lift first his forepaws
and then, placing my hands under his haunches,
hoist the bulk of him into the wagon,

so that he growls a little before he turns around
to face me gratefully, glad to have been lifted—
and as I go to praise them, as I like to do,

the words that come from my mouth,
out of nowhere, are Time's children,
as though that were the dearest thing

a person could say, the most loving name.
Where did that come from, why did I
call them by that name? I know

they fly along that quick parabola
faster than we do, racing the arc
as though it were some run

they'd gone for, a jaunt in the best
of woods, so inviting they continue
in their dreams, paws twitching slightly,

sometimes even releasing little stifled cries,
—as though even asleep they must hurry ahead
in the motion of time, which doesn't go fast enough

for them already? Weeks ago
my good boy—patient, willing to endure
whatever we deem necessary for him—

lay on his side on the high table,
while the vet ran along the shaved pink
and blonde down of his belly a kind of wand,

pointing a stream of soundwaves
to translate the dark inside his ribs
onto a midnight screen, its pulse

and throb of storm systems
charcoaled, imperial black, his body
figured as a field of pinpoints

subtle as the faintest stars.
The wand slides, the unseen's made
—not clear, exactly, nothing like anatomy

as I'd expect it, no chartable harmony
of parts. Something more like a blackboard
covered with a dust of living chalk, feeding,

hurrying, a live chaos-cloud worried
by turbulence, as the rod glides ahead
and the doctor narrates these swoons

of shadow I can't quite force into shape:
The kidneys might . . . the spleen appears . . .
But I can't see what he sees, and so resort

to simile: cloudbank, galaxies. That's it,
the inside of a dog's body resembles the far sky,
telescopic space alive with slow comings

and goings, that far away.
The doctor makes appreciative noises,
to encourage me; he praises Beau's stillness.

I stroke the slope of face beneath
his open, abstracted eyes. I'd like to see
where a bark begins its urgent unspooling

up from the depths beneath the surface of his belly
—revealed now, blue-veined, gleaming
with an alcohol gel to allow the sound waves

to penetrate more precisely. Though they don't locate
the quick core of him, his alert responsiveness
to the world—rabbit, stranger, cat on the lawn—

how the impulse leaps out of nowhere
then swells as it unfurls beneath the spine,
past the lungs' sounding chamber,

saying back to the day anything at all.
You can't see that, nor the clockworks deep
in the wellsprings, or that fixed place

out of which the dog's long regarding
of us rises. We didn't see, really,
anything. It wasn't cancer, wasn't clear,

no diagnosis firm. He's having trouble
keeping up his weight, and he's lost
his old appetites, though he races the damp trails

as though there were no tomorrow,
still fire, the same golden hurry
I've loved these years. Imagine a sound

to read us, render us, this morning,
in the last of the April rain,
the three of us energized by duration,

bound by the firing and fueling
in our depths, penetrated
by a rhythm too swift for us to hear,

though we catch intimations
of that furious rush and ardor.
Would it be an endearment,

the sound time makes,
seeing through us,
ushering us through?

Larry Doyle

Larry Doyle writes for television and lives in Los Angeles. He is currently a supervising producer for The Simpsons.

POSTED Monday, March 17, 1997, at 4:30 P.M. PT

Saturday, 9 p.m.

I get my wife back tomorrow. We've known each other 18 months, been married seven, apart the last two, but already we've chalked up two deaths, two scary illnesses, two transcontinental dislocations, four careers, and five addresses. If my wife were here, I'm sure she would insist I add: *There have been many good things, too.*

I met my wife at the wedding of a good friend of mine and ex-boyfriend of hers. I had seen her perhaps twice before, several years ago, when she was not my wife but Miles' girlfriend. I don't remember thinking much back then other than that Miles sure had a swell girlfriend. But that Saturday afternoon, when a huckleberry Saab pulled up to a miniature golf course somewhere in western Illinois, the woman who emerged with cold beer was my wife. I figured Miles wouldn't mind, his marrying somebody else and all. A few hours later I proposed: *Becky,* I wrote on the back of a business card, *I will marry you at any time.* It was a joke, but not really.

I proposed, really, just after Christmas, in the Brooklyn co-op I had bought for us (I had never owned property, or spent more than

72 consecutive hours with a woman, before). Becky sold her house in Chicago, quit her job selling real estate, and moved to New York. A couple of days later, her grandmother died. A couple of weeks after that, I was hit in the head with an oar and subsequently developed a form of aphasia in which I often cannot recall common words like "soft" and sometimes accidentally call tables "plateaus" and eyes "balloons." Two weeks before our wedding, my father went in for a checkup and got a quadruple bypass instead. An hour before we left on our honeymoon, we were told that my Uncle Joe in Ireland had died suddenly. As luck would have it, that was where we were going on our honeymoon. The day after Uncle Joe's funeral (I had promised Becky a raucous Irish wake, but everybody drank tea and wept quietly), I got a call from work: My boss had been fired. I decided to quit my job the moment I got back, then I decided to wait until I found another job, then I decided to quit via telegram right that second, and so on, for the remainder of our honeymoon.

(I've just read the above to my wife over the phone. "Jesus," she said. "Write some *nice* things.")

My post-honeymoon unemployment and job search were very nice, made all that more pleasant by the fact that Becky hated selling real estate in New York and consequently didn't do it anymore, so we had plenty of time to hang out in the house together and compare levels of hysteria. Just before Christmas, Becky got an exciting new job in public relations; then about 5 P.M. on Jan. 2, the night before her first day, my agent called to ask if perhaps I wanted to move 3,000 or so miles to write for *The Simpsons*. My wife gave notice on her second day of work. A week later we were in Los Angeles finding me a temporary apartment. Four days later we discovered we had somehow bought a supercute house in the Hollywood Hills. Becky went back to Brooklyn and sold our co-op in two days at a tremendous profit. Then a week later, the sale fell through. A day later, Becky sold the co-op again, for almost as much.

As Becky would say, a lot of it has been nice. But all I know is, it has been a lot.

POSTED Thursday, March 20, 1997, at 4:30 P.M. PT

Our dog is arriving today. He didn't want to fly out with Becky and so decided to drive cross-country with two friends. Last night, my dog was in Las Vegas.

I've never been to Las Vegas.

We got Beauregard a year ago this week. He was called Serpico then, by the guy who found him in Prospect Park. He doesn't look much like a Serpico. He's about the size and shape of a beagle and has the coloring of a Rottweiler. He has huge paws and, in repose, a look of general confusion. I came up with the name Slurpico, but we resisted the urge.

I have not seen Beauregard in nine weeks, though I have been kept abreast of his bowel movements. I told Becky yesterday that in a way I missed Beauregard more than I missed her, because, after all, I got to talk to her on the phone every day and—well, I was trying to make the very interesting point that the bond between man and wife is essentially a higher meeting of the minds while the bond between a man and his dog is a more primal, physical one, but Becky didn't find this very interesting.

I tried talking to Beauregard on the phone a couple of times, but when he heard my voice, he would run around the apartment frantically looking for me, Becky says. Though now I wonder if she was just saying that to make me feel better.

I can't wait to feel him.

People keep asking me what it's like to write for *The Simpsons*. I don't really know. Mostly so far I've watched other people write for *The Simpsons*. But I've learned this much:

- No joke is so funny that it can't be thrown out.
- It can always be funnier.

The way the process works, basically, is that you sit in a chair all day saying funny things. And if you have nothing funny to say, which for me is most of the time, you just sit around.

I thought I knew some funny people. I've worked at the *National Lampoon*, *Spy*, and *Beavis and Butt-Head*; I know *New Yorker* writers, Letterman writers, and at some point or another have been cornered by every one of Manhattan's young wags. But I've never been in a room with this many funny people (I am not stupid enough to try to provide an example here).

Back in New York, I was the sourpuss, the guy who never cracked a smile, never laughed at anything. Now I laugh all day long. I've never had so much fun.

It's the hardest thing I've ever done.

The most common phrase heard in *The Simpsons* writers' room is "We already did that." I pitched an idea a couple of weeks ago, and one of the writers said, very nicely, "Actually, we once did a joke about Homer inflating a pig by blowing in its ass."

Phone message from Becky: "It's 3:15. Beau doesn't even know me. I think I'm going to cry."

I can't concentrate for the rest of the day. If Beau could forget Becky in a week, I'm thinking, he's going to bite me. My mind drifts off. I'm remembering that when Becky and I would go out for the day, Beau would steal our shoes and underwear and we would find them on the floor in a pile, undamaged. I realize: Instead of barking at him on the phone, I should have FedExed him my underpants.

Becky and Beauregard arrive to pick me up from work. For weeks I had been imagining him leaping from the car and jumping all over me, like he used to when I had been gone only a day. He sits in the front seat and stares at me.

Out of the car, he walks right past me to some bushes. He sniffs around and eventually wanders over my way. He lets me pet him, but he would let anybody pet him. (Note: Call about security system for the house.)

He is so cool. He is acting almost exactly like the scariest kind of ex-girlfriend of all. She doesn't still love you. She doesn't hate you. She hardly thinks about you.

It will take some time, I console myself. My dog will have to learn to love me all over again.

Roger Ebert

Roger Ebert is a film critic for the Chicago Sun-Times *and co-host of the television program* Roger Ebert & The Movies.

POSTED Monday, April 6, 1998, at 4:30 P.M. PT

For the last 29 years I have been coming here to Boulder, Colo., for a week every spring for the Conference on World Affairs. It is like no other conference I can imagine. More than 100 members of the chattering classes buy their own airplane tickets to fly here, are paid no honorariums, sleep in guest bedrooms, eat lunch at the student union, and appear on three or four panels every day—panels not of their own choosing and often not on their specialties. Newcomers are recruited because veterans bludgeon them to attend. Friendships have ended because people were not invited back.

I do a shot-by-shot analysis of a film for two hours every afternoon, 10 hours in all, in Macky Auditorium. For years we used a 16-mm projector with a freeze-frame attachment, but now laserdisc has made it easy to stop, advance one frame at a time, back up, and subject a film to group analysis. "Democracy in the dark," we call it: Anyone can shout out "stop!" and then talk about what's on the screen. This year's film is *Dark City*, by Alex Proyas, about a city operated by aliens as a workshop for experimenting on human behavior. It is visionary and bold, and opened to a fourth as much business as the clunky *Lost in Space*. Have audiences lost their will to be shown something new?

The conference was run for 48 years by the loud, impossible, insulting, tyrannical Howard Higman, who was beloved. He chose the speakers, ran roughshod over the committee, made the rules, and infuriated the University of Colorado by using its facilities and yet paying little heed to its requests. He often wore a sport coat that looked like an explosion at the Tibetan rug factory. When Higman died two years ago, I suggested the coat be preserved and given to each year's keynote speaker, to wear as a talisman. The coat was feared lost, but this year it miraculously reappeared, like the Shroud of Turin, and will be offered to Studs Terkel when he delivers the 50th anniversary speech on Wednesday.

There was no conference the year before Higman died; the old curmudgeon and the university had arrived at a furious standoff. Now the conference is finding a new footing in its third year under the direction of Professor Sven Steinmo, who has made needed improvements but raised some eyebrows by inviting Marianne Williamson to deliver the opening day plenary address. "Howard is looking down in disbelief," I told David Finkle, the critic and satirical singer who is back again this year. We ran into each other in the Stage House, a used-book store on the downtown mall. We decided that if there is a heaven, Howard will know Williamson is right, and if there isn't, he'll have the last laugh.

Over the years here in Boulder I have been on a panel with the Greek ambassador to the United Nations, about masturbation; heard Ted Turner outline his plans for CNN; and attended a Betty Dodson workshop on turning Polaroids of vaginas into watercolors. I have learned that I can draw, been debriefed by a former priest, visited the Internet for the first time, and watched a communal family living on the stage of the auditorium. I heard Buckminster Fuller speak for three hours (his voice carried by loudspeakers to those who could not get in) and saw Chief Fortunate Eagle, who led the sit-in at Alcatraz, walk out of a panel in protest after it was picketed by topless lesbians.

Boulder is how America would be if the 1960s had prevailed. I cannot imagine this conference existing anywhere else. Allen Ginsberg died while I was here last year, and of course there was a reading of his work in a coffee shop, right down the street from the Beat Bookstore and across from the Zen restaurant with the barbecued tofu I like so much. When I come here time stops, and this year is like last year, and I have always been here, and it is the rest of the year that is an illusion. On Tuesday I will order one of the famous burgers at Tom's Tavern, and at Jane Butcher's party on Thursday night someone will tell the story about the British ambassador who said he was staying with some lovely people who lived on Baseline Road, and rhymed it with Vaseline.

POSTED Wednesday, April 8, 1998, at 4:30 P.M. PT

The Conference on World Affairs was holding a program at the local high school, and Mary-Ellis Bunim and I were the panelists. What is this? The students of Boulder High are orderly, attentive, and intelligent? I'd seen too many news reports about modern American high schools and was surprised to find no metal detectors at the doors, no armed security guards roaming the aisles, just nice kids at a school assembly.

Mary-Ellis Bunim talked about her daily MTV soaps, *The Real World* and *Road Rules*: how they got started, how they cast the shows with real kids and were in fact casting in Boulder even as we spoke. The students lined up at microphones and asked us if we didn't think the ceaseless violence on television was slopping over into American life, and if the news wasn't too sensationalized, and if we agreed that Jerry Springer and his clones are degrading the quality of our civilization. I felt I should apologize for the world we had prepared for them.

"What Is a Classic?" was a panel at which we agreed that in modern America, hardly anyone knows and fewer care. Wendell Harris, emeritus professor of English from Penn State, observed sadly that we do not have a generally shared American culture. Sayre Sheldon of Boston University, president of Women's Action for New Directions, read the titles on the current *New York Times* fiction list and asked who thought each title would be remembered as a classic. Toni Morrison did well. Robert Parker didn't do badly. Jingalu, a 25-year-old aboriginal artist from Australia with wonderful curls spilling down her back, wondered if traditions such as the aboriginal initiations into manhood and womanhood could be called classics. We thought perhaps they could, since they're an art form passed down through the generations as bearers of style and values. Paul Kolsby, the playwright and actor, read a list of things that are classics and turned it into a comic performance. I said I didn't want to know anyone who didn't know who Dr. Johnson was. Accused by an audience member of being an exclusivist snob, I amended: I didn't want to know anyone who was not at least willing to know who Dr. Johnson was.

Then to Macky Auditorium for Cinema Interruptus. We will take eight hours to go through *Dark City* using a stop-action laserdisc player. Many of those who saw the movie yesterday agreed with me that it is a visionary achievement. I predicted that, like *Blade Runner*, it will pass directly from box office disappointment to cultural touchstone, without passing through the intermediate stages of success.

We started looking at the film. Ninety minutes later we had made our way through only six minutes. Not in 25 years of Cinema Interruptus at Boulder has a film inspired such intense scrutiny. We froze frames to speculate about special effects, matte shots, models. We wondered if the round window in the black space in the hotel wall was intended to mirror the leather headbands with holes in their centers that were used by the Strangers to guide their injections of fresh memories. A woman seated near the front offered a complex theory involving the Third Eye. We looked again and again at the skillful editing of a brief scene in which a knife is knocked from a table and spins to the floor.

Afterward, Andy Ihnatko and I went looking for the Tuesday night buffet dinner. Andy, the Macintosh expert, bills himself as the 47th most beloved figure in the computer industry. A storm dropped a screen of thick, wet snow. We couldn't find the University Club. We couldn't even see the two high-rise dorms it was allegedly behind. We went instead to Video Station, and I bought a DVD of *Amarcord*. The guy told me DVDs are "growing exponentially." We ate at the Mongolian Stir-Fry House. We were the only customers. We talked about how Apple should have sold the eMate to newspapers to replace the obsolete Tandy 100. The red-hot Mongolian sauce in the curious little bottle sent a convincing warmth to every corner of my body.

David Edelstein

David Edelstein writes about movies for Slate.

POSTED Tuesday, May 13, 1997, at 4:30 P.M. PT

It is the loveliest day of the year, I have been married a month, and everything is birdsong apart from the jackhammers that are ripping through the foundation of a building next door. I fetch a Tab from the refrigerator. People grimace when they hear I drink Tab in the morning, but that first can of the day tastes sharp and fruity and has the added benefit of eating the plaque right off my teeth. The kitchen is in a shambles. In a moment of grandiosity, I volunteered to furnish the cake for the wedding of my wife's best friend, Erik, in Toronto next week, and my education in baking has turned our small Manhattan apartment into something out of *Independence Day* after the aliens have moved on. I am on my eighth trial cake and my third chin. The good news is that I'm closing in on a final recipe — a golden, white-chocolate butter cake with lemon and raspberry mousseline buttercream. The bad news is that I don't know what will happen when I multiply the recipe by a factor of 10.

With my Tab I eat a slice of wedding cake and make a note in my lab book to reduce the proportion of rose water in the fondant.

Now, being a famous film critic, I must sit down and do some real work. This morning, I will type up my notes from a Sidney Lumet movie I saw on Friday. I can't say whether my thumb is up or down because the picture doesn't open until next week, but it is puzzling that the very Latin-looking Andy Garcia has been cast as a man named Sean Casey, and that his dad, an uneducated Queens cop, is played by Ian Holm, currently howling into the winds as King Lear in his native England. As always, my greatest challenge as a film critic is trying to decipher my handwriting, which, even when I haven't been scribbling furiously in the dark with my eyes fixed on a screen, resembles Hebrew.

At lunch time, my lovely new wife, Rachel, and I head out to look for a bigger apartment away from the jackhammers. We'd like to move to Park Slope, Brooklyn, where people pushing baby carriages make nice-nice with hand-holding lesbian couples. Dreaming of a more civilized place to raise my children, I swerve to avoid a cab that stops short to pick up a passenger, whereupon a bicyclist calls me a cock and accuses me of trying to kill him. Meaning to explain that I had narrowly averted an accident and to inquire after his welfare, I say instead, "Fuck you, asshole, I wish I had killed you." Rachel finds my behavior disturbing and wonders if I see too many violent movies. I am convinced it is the sugar from all those wedding cakes, or possibly the Tab.

Park Slope has become nearly as expensive as Manhattan. The so-called third bedrooms of the three-bedroom apartments we view are too small even for a young child, unless one wanted to do some sort of Skinnerian experiment in sensory deprivation. Yet, wandering through Prospect Park on this gorgeous day, my spirits pick up, and I buy some soft-shell crabs for dinner. As it will be several hours before I can cook them, I take them home alive, thinking it will be a cinch to "clean" them myself. It turns out that to "clean" a live soft-shell crab, you must first take a large pair of shears and snip off its face. It gets worse after that. Meanwhile, the crab continues to wriggle madly, albeit minus a face and innards.

Using tongs, I roll one in flour, then in a beaten egg, then in bread crumbs. Still, its body moves, while, from the sink, its face and the faces of its fellow crabs stare up at me in mute reproach. What have I done? Clearly, the fastest way to end its misery will be to slide it into the hot butter—where it unfortunately continues to wriggle. After what seems an eternity, I serve up four amber, lightly crusted crabs, which Rachel pronounces the best she has had this season. I pray, as I cut into mine, that it won't let out a yelp.

It's odd that my empathy does not extend to humans on bicycles. Or on the screen. After dinner, I head out to catch up on what I missed while eating *vongole* in Venice on my honeymoon. *Breakdown* is a *Straw Dogs*-issue yuppies-besieged-by-rednecks picture that exploits class hatred in a country that claims to be above such things. Kurt Russell wears a lavender alligator shirt, but he covers it up with a dirty windbreaker when he must become a man and save his wife (Kathleen Quinlan, who looks awfully good in ropes). The working-class-white-trash-sumbitch bad guys think he deserves to die simply by virtue of his shiny new sport utility vehicle with its Massachusetts plates. The movie is well made, but it seems to me that when the bad guys get it, they don't get it good enough, so that they really, really suffer. (In *Cliffhanger*, for example, the bad guys not only die in agony but are shown, just before the light goes out of their eyes, to recognize the innate superiority of Sylvester Stallone.) Rachel worries that soon all I'll want to see are movies like *Make Them Die Slowly*. But there's no time to discuss this tonight, as I must rise early to bake a wedding cake. As we fall asleep, the garbage trucks come.

POSTED Wednesday, May 14, 1997, at 4:30 P.M. PT

My wife and I go to *Austin Powers* primed to laugh, but after a lively opening the picture tanks. It's rife with overextended gags, but the strange thing is that the gag is not the gag, the gag is the overextension of the gag. The terrible, flaccid timing is what's supposed to be funny. What does it say when a gifted performer like Mike Myers sets out to make a "bad" movie, the kind of cheeseball, '60s Bond imitation that untalented people made by accident? Bad movies, even Ed Wood's consummately bad movies, give me claustrophobia—they shrink your sense of what's possible. Art is supposed to expand that sense, to teach you to make imaginative leaps under even the most hopeless conditions. These movies—the ones that spring from the minds of people who watch too much television, that hold to the *Mystery Science Theater 3000* aesthetic, in which viewers cultivate a sense of superiority—they make me despair of seeing anything on-screen that hasn't been done a zillion times.

As if to reinforce this, we see, as we leave the theater, Fifth Avenue eerily lit up around the Flatiron Building, with a kind of luminescent geodesic dome on the north side of 23rd Street. *Godzilla* is being filmed—another American original! The avenues are closed, so we stand and gawk and scan the skyline for the giant, fire-breathing lizard. Then my wife says, "Godzilla's probably on a computer in Los Angeles." I remember going as a kid to the old downtown Strand in Hartford to see *King Kong vs. Godzilla*, the one where King Kong wins in the American release and Godzilla wins in the Japanese release. How weird that nationalistic pride extends to the monsters who destroy our cities. "Gojira," of course, was originally a thinly veiled metaphor for the A-bomb, but after many cheap sequels (which came to look more and more like pro-wrestling matches), he evolved into Japan's protector. They really did learn to stop worrying and love the bomb.

Rachel goes to bed but I have a Tab and stay up to roll out a giant layer of fondant for her best friend's wedding cake. Tab, by the way, is a big joke in *Austin Powers*—Austin being from the '60s, he still thinks it's groovy—but I think it's the only diet cola with the courage of its convictions. Diet Coke is syrupy-sweet; it tries to disguise what it is. The flavor of Tab is sterner, with inky depths; it carries with it the tragic awareness that to keep from being overweight, we must sometimes imbibe carcinogenic chemicals. We Tab drinkers are a breed apart, nodding to each other in the street the way homosexuals did in the '50s. Our eyes are trained to spot the steely pink can. At a deli the other day, buying a Tab, I stood next to a woman with a can of her own. We smiled at each other in silent understanding. Then someone else said, "Tab. Do they still make that stuff?" I said, "If I had a can of Tab for every person who asked me if they still make that stuff...."

"You'd be in heaven," said the woman.

POSTED   Thursday, May 15, 1997, at 4:30 P.M. PT

Triumph! I've made a test version of the bottom layer of my wife's best friend's wedding cake, and it's so good that I believe I'll have another piece. That was yummy; I'll have one more. Now, just a sliver, to scrutinize more closely the raspberry buttercream, the lemon-infused fondant. Damn, I'm one hell of a cake baker. Sugar high! Adapting the original recipe to serve 75 people was quite a task, but with the help of Rose Levy Beranbaum's *The Cake Bible*, a calculator, Microsoft Excel, and several calls to the math department at Princeton University (which, curiously enough, has a cake-recipe hotline), I have arrived at the perfect proportions. Tomorrow, I'm going to teach myself to pipe icing.

After less than five weeks of matrimony, it sounds strange to write "my wife," and I still suppress an urge to put her in quotation marks. In truth, there have been one or two occasions when I've wanted to put her in quotation marks, add some parentheses, and drop her in a bog. But we can usually laugh at ourselves, even when our hands are around each other's necks. We instructed our rabbi to adapt the marriage vows so that we promised to love, honor, cherish, and amuse each other—this in a marvelously egalitarian service that had my brother, firmly Orthodox, whispering darkly into his beard. On honeymoon in Italy, I'd always mispronounce the phrase for my wife—mia moglie—as "me emollient." Then, when I thought about it, I realized that she is me emollient. She softens and soothes all the rough patches.

Of course, she now and then finds my sense of humor crass, and she has had to police my comments on our joint wedding-gift thank-you notes. (She did like the tag I appended to the cousins who sent us the Wusthof knives I'd coveted: "Thank you also for the knit cap and the Bruno Magli shoes.") She finds my Tab drinking "disgusting" but is otherwise good-natured about it, especially as I have no other addictions, having given up alcohol approximately 417 days, 11 hours, and 32 minutes ago, along with a gig as the "beer critic" for *New York* magazine. (She's grateful that she no longer has to phone me at some bar at 3 A.M. and have me holler at her, "Leave me alone, I'm *working*.")

But she draws the line at Leno tonight, when I choke with hilarity at a bit about children's books you might want to keep away from your kids, especially the one called *James and the Giant Canker Sore*. We agree on the classic movies, though, which is the real litmus test: *Notorious; The Godfather; Truly, Madly, Deeply; Dumb and Dumber*. I once dated a woman to whom I eagerly showed *The Lady Eve*, and she groused that slapstick bored her and besides, she didn't know what the film was "about." I stammered something about things that men project onto women, but I wasn't very convincing, and by then my faith in the relationship's future had sunk. To me, the joy of *The Lady Eve* is irrational, and if you don't get it, you don't get it. Besides, if you can sum up what a movie is "about," chances are it's *Volcano*, which is about a big fucking volcano under Los Angeles that wastes a lot of Angelenos.

The emollient and I see *Volcano* and have a pretty decent time. The crack director, Mick Jackson, knows how to move masses of people across the screen. He's great at drawing out those eerie moments preceding an eruption, like the sizzling stillness before the popcorn pops. (One lyrical touch: a seismographic needle intercut with an old black man drumming in MacArthur Park.) The lava looks cartoony, though, like the monster in *The Blob*, and the climax is blown—too much emphasis on Tommy Lee Jones saving his daughter in slow motion, not enough on the gusher being diverted. And the brotherhood-of-man, anti-Hieronymus Bosch theme is a tad hypocritical: If man does not "incline toward sin in defiance of God's will," he certainly loves watching fellow humans get royally wasted in disaster pictures like this.

Mostly, we goggle at Anne Heche, who is more alive (and sexy) on-screen than any young actress I've seen in years. If her recent disclosures about her private life end up limiting her roles, it will be a terrible waste. Then again, *Volcano* doesn't exactly stretch her. It wouldn't be the worst thing if she made a "girl" movie with, say, the Sichel sisters, whose *All Over Me* I caught in a matinee yesterday while waiting for my fondant to harden. The story of a teenager separated from her best friend by a thuggish boy, and her subsequent coupling with another girl, the film paints a portrait of heterosexuality-as-slavery that I found hard to stomach (and me emollient had better agree). But it does an amazing job of capturing the visceral intensity—the rawness—of adolescent friendship.

Walking back from *Volcano*, Rachel and I find 23rd Street shut down again by the filming of *Godzilla*. This monster really has paralyzed a major city. In the morning, the police have moved to the streets around my apartment, immobilizing Washington Square Park and its environs for New York University's graduation ceremonies. As I write this, I can hear the voice of New Jersey Gov. Christine Todd Whitman giving the commencement speech. Where is Godzilla when we need him?

Dave Eggers

Dave Eggers spent 11 years as a makeup artist in the Golden Age of Television, when people really cared about quality makeup. He is an editor for McSweeney's, *a journal and Web site for children, and the author of a memoir,* A Heartbreaking Work of Staggering Genius.

POSTED Monday, Dec. 13, 1999, at 10:30 A.M. PT

Today or yesterday:

2:14 P.M.: Seen, on the sidewalk: a rubber glove, yellowed. Unremarkable but for this: It had landed or was arranged with all fingers but one folded under. The middle finger erect on this rubber glove, soiled, imbedded into the sidewalk in Brooklyn, N.Y. It symbolized nothing.

3:11: This from Alexander Johannesson's *How Did Homo Sapiens Express the Idea of Flat?* (H.F. Leiftur Publishers—Reykjavik, Iceland, 1958):

> By moving the jaws from the back-position forwards to the lips and at the same time producing sounds of the type kap-; in such word-forms we see many variations of k, such as q, g, gh etc., and of the labial (p) such as b, bh, m, w (u); the interjacent vowel may have been a or e or have had another form (we know very little about the vowels in prehistoric times). I have shown this very clearly by a rich collection of examples in six "unrelated" languages, viz.

Indo-European (as seen in the construed IE. Roots), Hebrew (as representative of the Semitic group), Archaic Chinese....

You get the idea.

5:14: The sky is that blue that can only be called "electric," darkening, and this evening there are nine. Five of them are wearing matching hats. They are all on their knees, and through a small speaker set up on the sidewalk, their prayers can be heard. Visitors to the museum, in black-framed glasses and faux leopard-skin coats, leave carrying gifts and souvenirs in large bags that say "Sensation" on them. The praying people continue to pray. There is a poster standing on the sidewalk. It says: "The Virgin Mary Speaks to America. 1-800-345-MARY." Three of the nine are holding rosaries, and all of them chant the same words at the same time: "In the name of the Father, the Son, and the Holy Ghost...." They are bundled up—the wind is abrasive—and periodically they rise from their knees, stand up, while continuing to chant the same words in unison. They kneel again. They rise. The road is just behind them; cars and their red and white lights pass and inside one of the cars there is a woman going home, where she will take her small child in her arms and squeeze her much too much because she is tired and cannot believe that they are both alive after all these years.

5:44: Intermission.

5:54: There is nothing quite like the thrill of a presidential race.

6:10: The woman at the Seventh Avenue Copy Shop sometimes looks happy, and sometimes looks sad. Once, a few months ago, it appeared that she had cut her hair. When she was asked by a regular customer if her hair had indeed been cut, she said: "Oh you haven't seen this yet?" while fluffing it with one hand, much like Charlie Brown's friend does—she with the naturally curly hair. These words and this gesture made the regular customer feel very connected with the woman at the copy shop. The regular customer wondered if he would come to know the woman's name, and if they would someday talk about things unrelated to stationery. But the next time the regular customer visited the copy shop, he could not pick up the thread of connectivity begun during his last visit. This time, after selecting his items and bringing them to the counter before her, she rang up the items and put them in a white paper bag, and when she gave him the bag, instead of asking her name or whence she comes, he gave her a smile of satisfaction. The satisfaction of a satisfactory purchase.

7:12: Louis Prima. Clark Gable. Maude Adams. You know what I mean.

7:16: Let us say, hypothetically, that there are two men, one a decade or so older than the other, who live together and who are related. At home, when work must get done, things usually work very well between the two, because when one is working on his computer, the other also works on a computer, albeit a different one. Then, when the first man decides he would like to take a break and watch the television, the other ceases working and watches, too —which is fine, because television is even more enjoyable when watched with a friend or loved one. After some time watching a show together, the two men will turn it off and then go back to working on their computers. But then something happens. Sometimes the second man, the younger man, will enter the workspace of the first man, who is working on something that must be worked on, and, while standing in the doorway, he will say something. Here are some of the things he might say:

"Hey pussyboy."

"Hey dumbass."

"Hey stupid rockhead ugly man."

Sometimes the work-interrupter will have with him a basketball, which he will bounce repeatedly on the wood floor of the workspace of the worker. "Is this bothering you?" the work-interrupter will ask. "I would feel terrible if this were bothering you."

And all the first man, the hard-working man, can think is: Why do such things happen? Why, in a country where we can find just about any submerged space capsule we want, any time we want, should something like this basketball-bouncing and name-calling be allowed to happen? And, perhaps more importantly, when is someone going to have the courage to finally do an all-black *Wizard of Oz*?

8:21: People ask David Gergen what he thinks about things. But people who really know David Gergen know that the only thing that David Gergen really knows for sure is that if he doesn't dance better and faster, and with great style and passion, the world will fall. As we speak, there is a small crowd, standing below David Gergen's window in the nation's capital, and they are watching David Gergen as he dances, alone in his apartment, in a V-neck cotton sweater and plaid pants, dances feverishly, so that the world might be saved.

9:00: It's actually 9:23. Sorry.

Tomorrow: Suspense.

POSTED Tuesday, Dec. 14, 1999, at 10:00 A.M. PT

12:40 P.M.: The flag of Grenada is really something. It is bright and optimistic; though some of its parts symbolize blood. It has a red border, and imbedded in the red border are six yellow stars, three on the top, three on the bottom. Inside the red border, in the flag's central area of play, are two yellow triangles and two green ones, the yellow top and bottom, the green left and right. In the middle of the flag is a red circle, with a yellow star inside it. Then, in one of the green triangles...man, this is pretty hard to describe. Do you have a book of flags? Look up Grenada—it's probably in there.

12:43: Advice for those of you hiding terrible secrets: Carry your secret with you somewhere where you can access it easily. Front pocket or purse. In general, be happy and laugh at the jokes told by friends and the stars on television, but sometimes take your secret out and look at it to remind yourself of what it looks like and how it feels in your hand. It feels like a burr. It is small and has a soft center, but if you squeeze it, it will puncture your skin, even if just a little. Do not give your secret to anyone else. Do not show anyone your secret and do not let anyone touch it. It will not feel the same to them. To them it might feel furry; it might even tickle. And if your terrible secret is tickling the hand of someone else, where will you be?

1:20: Ty Cobb. That guy had some amazing numbers. 45, 3, 67, 9, 83, 892, 4, 34, 1611. Incredible.

1:34: Advice for those who have seen things they should not have: Remember seeing that thing very clearly, but at the same time, with no clarity at all. Forget whether it was a dream or it was real, or whether it happened in a book or in a movie. Forget the people who starred in the thing you should not have seen. Remember the colors, and remember the things that happened just before, or just after. Add people to the scene who were not there but should have been there. If it was light in the room, make it dark. Add a range of burgundies. But never, ever, tell anyone about what you saw that you should not have seen. Instead, talk to people about Jon Cryer, of whom we surely have not seen the last, and John McCain, who just might give George W. a run for his money!

1:43: AN ABRIDGED HISTORY OF HAND-HOLDING

- 890 B.C. Only men hold hands.
- 28 B.C. Men sometimes hold hands with children.
- A.D. 77 Children begin to hold hands with their mothers.
- A.D. 230 Hand-holding banned, except between wealthy people. Wealthy people do it like it's going out of style.
- A.D. 235 Hand-holding goes out of style.
- 240–1245 No record of hand-holding.
- A.D. 1412 The elders of a small Inuit tribe try to hold hands but cannot, due to bulky mittens.
- A.D. 1877 Holding hands underwater invented.

- A.D. 1999 Pete Rose appears on *The Martin Short Show* and wows 'em.

5:37: HEROES OF CAPITALISM (a short docudrama, based on the real events of today)
"Hi."
"Hi."
"Is one of you Michael?"
"Yes, that's me."
"Oh, hi. I talked to you on the phone."
"Right."
"I have a painting that needs to be shot."
"Right. How many slides do you need?"
"Oh, just a few."
"And this is the painting?"
"Yes. I didn't stretch it. Is that OK?"
"Sure, sure. OK. When do you need the slides? I can get them back to you by Thursday...Friday at the latest."
"Oh. Um. I'd really love to have them by Wednesday, actually. I'll pay extra, if that would help."
"Hmm. OK, we can do it. No extra charge. How's Wednesday afternoon?"
"Great, great. Thanks."
"No problem."
"Thanks. So I'll just come by on Wednesday?"
"Yep."
"Great."
"Great."
"OK. Bye now."
"See ya."
"What?"
"I said 'See ya.' "
"Oh. Oh. OK, bye. Thanks."

James Fallows

James Fallows wrote this when he was the editor of U.S. News & World Report. *He is now the national correspondent for the* Atlantic Monthly.

POSTED Monday, Oct. 27, 1997, at 4.30 P.M. PT

The big difference between weekly newsmagazines and other parts of journalism is the tyranny/oddity of the weekly schedule. At a newspaper, the tension rises during the day, but then it's over, and the presses roll, and you can go home and have a beer. At most monthlies, you're working on articles at different stages of completion for a couple of forthcoming issues at the same time, and no one week is that different from another.

At a newsmagazine, each day of the week has its distinct personality, dictated by how many hours are left until press time. *U.S. News* goes to press on Friday night, so from Wednesday afternoon on, activities like "planning" or "extra reading" or "physical exercise" or "seeing the family" melt away, in favor of whatever is necessary to get pages off to the printer. Monday and Tuesday are the days when the pressure is off—and the trick is to avoid the temptation to blow them off altogether. Anyone who's worked for more than two months at a newsmagazine has seen at least one case of an issue being completely remade on the last day because of breaking news. Knowing that you could do the whole issue at the last minute, if you had to, can make it tempting to wait until the last minute for the always-vexing work of writing or editing or making big choices. One of the standard jokes of newsmagdom concerns a different national weekly (OK, *Newsweek*) where no writer wants to see his story on the lineup at the beginning of the week. Since everyone knows the plans will be torn up on Thursday, writers type away at Potemkin stories, like Jack Nicholson in *The Shining*, until the last day—when the adrenalin surges and they really try for the stories that will actually appear.

But it's Monday, and we're trying to use it to think ahead. The different sections of the magazine have their 10 A.M. staff meetings, throwing out ideas and possible assignments. We have a grand nearly-staff-wide planning meeting at 10:30, talking about the issue just behind us and hearing about stories lined up for this week. From then until 3 P.M., the kind of activities that get shoved to a Monday because there is no time on other days of the week: recruiting efforts for new staff members; resolving turf wars among existing staff members; lunch with four of our librarians, as part of a rolling meet-and-dine-with-the-staff project; discussion about new computer equipment we need. Half an hour of the work editors theoretically spend all their time doing: reading a projected cover story and suggesting changes.

And then...the stock market crashes! Actual news! If this were a Thursday or Friday, the solution would be obvious: Rush it on the cover. Now the drama of the next week is set, as we decide how to cover what is obviously real news—and cover it in a way that will still seem compelling a week from today, when our issue appears, and people have a week's worth of TV and newspaper reports behind them. Stay tuned.

7 P.M. Drive home from work, find something from the refrigerator for dinner, warm it up and eat it while watching the TV news about the crash—I mean, "correction," as the president and all the newscasters say. My wife and younger son, a senior in high school, are away on a college visit. Plate on my lap as I sit on the

couch, I think of Humphrey Bogart's line from *The African Queen*: "A man lives alone, he gets to living like a hog." Fortunately they're only gone for three days and get back late tonight.

8 P.M. Take out my beloved laptop—the ThinkPad 560, first portable since the Radio Shack Model 100 a decade ago to show complete elegance of design—and plug into the ISDN line that connects me with the magazine's central computer. Spend the next two hours "top editing" a couple of articles from what we had been planning, until midafternoon, as the cover-story package for this upcoming issue. This assortment of stories will still run, unless in the next four days the San Andreas fault opens up and every famous person with an in-the-can obituary dies, and similar unignorable news pops up to complement the financial news of the week. But it will run inside, and might as well be taken care of before the end-of-the-week closing rush occurs. "Top editing" means going through a piece and asking all the "hey, wait a minute" questions that the writer and story-editor have not gotten around to dealing with, but of course always in the supportive and constructive spirit for which editors are famous.

10:30 P.M. Get a call from *U.S. News'* owner, Mort Zuckerman, inquiring about how we're planning to cover the financial chaos. Ask him for market tips.

11:00 P.M. True to spirit of advance planning, work through investigative piece planned for two weeks from now. Send back many supportive suggestions to the writer. Look through proposals, now appearing on the computer, for how to cover the financial story.

12:30 A.M. Wife and son arrive. Happy family reunion. And so to bed.

POSTED Thursday, Oct. 30, 1997, at 4:30 P.M. PT

Tonight, none of that annoying waxy buildup. It's 1:35 A.M. I want to get out of the office; so here is the way the last 18 hours have gone.

8 A.M. Up. In the background hear my son driving off to high school. Really try to look at papers this morning—last night didn't get to them until nearly midnight. Market news, China news, AIDS news, Nixon news—plenty of stuff to bear in mind as we get through the next two days.

8:20 A.M. Log on to magazine's central computer through the ISDN line. (Subject for student essay: Modern communications systems—threat or menace? Discuss.) Promised to look at a story that one writer and two editors had been working on until nearly 2 A.M. Looks fine now! They stayed awake that I might sleep—last night at least. Get the final comments plugged in before they log on at 8:30 A.M. Get dressed and all of that.

9:00 A.M. Go through the motions of collecting e-mail. Wonder what really is the point. Several months ago I realized I might as well stop even looking at paper mail, since I would never answer it. Knowing that it existed would only make me worry. Same has happened with phone calls from anyone outside the direct chain of command here. I still limp along with e-mail—but each week the unanswered backlog grows. Maybe this weekend I'll answer them. (Oh sure.)

9:15 A.M. Go to bank to put in checks that have been sitting around for 10 days, waiting for me to "have time" to deposit them.

10:00 A.M. Arrive at work! Ready for the final two days! Read through all the comments and reports and complaints about stories that should be closed (i.e., sent off, electronically, to the pre-press operation and then the printer) today.

10:15 A.M. Say hello to Mort Zuckerman, in office next to mine. Admire his fit and rested look.

10:30 A.M. Booking meeting! This is where we do actual journalistic business, taking story proposals for next week's issue from the various sections of the magazine, matching them against the space available, and deciding what we should "book" (schedule) and what we should kill, postpone, or ignore. Oops! Stories to be booked for this issue exceed available pages by 13 pages. Certainly better to have this problem than the reverse. (Problem in this case caused by two contending cover stories fighting it out for primacy in the same issue. Again, right kind of difficulty to have.) Hear descriptions of the various stories, reserve judgment in front of large group. Retire to executive chambers with Lee Rainie (managing editor) and Steve Budiansky (deputy editor) to carve up the pie.

10:45 A.M. In theory it is time to start down the Sign Off Trail, known as the Trail of Tears in difficult weeks. This is the process of giving a final read to upcoming stories before sending them off to press. As the clock ticks between now and tomorrow night, story names appear in a special SIGNOFF file, various "top editors" work them over, and they leave the building—assuming they also make it through the fact-checkers, the proofreading room, the lawyers, the ever-surprising computer system, and so on.

11:00 A.M. One of three-dozen talks during the day with Lee Rainie, coinciding with one of a dozen with MaryAnne Golon. MaryAnne, the photo director, had commissioned a big-name, big-ticket New York fashion photog to do a special cover for us this week. This is the cover that, because of breaking news, will never appear. (I am revealing no secrets here. All newsmagazines will have covers on the same news-related theme next week. I have no inside sources at *Time* or *Newsweek*, but I'm sure it's true. Check it out next Monday.) MaryAnne brings along Jerry Sealy, our cover-designing whiz, to show the cover we will actually use, which is fine—and then, just to make us wince, the one we paid for, but must keep to ourselves. On one wall of my office I have the nearly 60 covers that have appeared in my time here. On another wall, the covers we loved but for some reason couldn't print.

Time for an executive decision! For the cover we will actually use this week, two serious contenders for the main cover line. (You know, the huge type saying "More About Diana!" and so on.) One is artier in its phrasing; the other is more direct in telling people just what we have inside. Art is fine, but this week we have to be direct.

Noon. An unbelievable surprise! I see my wife, Deb, on one of the last two days of the week! She is downtown and stops by. I say hi, say "this will just take a minute," and sit at the Atex. She wanders down the hall. (I find her later on.)

1:00 P.M. Back to the Sign Off Trail. Working yet again on the same Big Piece that occupied so much of my time—when was it? — two days ago. Seems like last month.

2:00 P.M. Mmmmmmm! Time for lunch! I walk outside the building to the hot-dog cart run by an Ethiopian woman and buy a delicious pork product. This is not the way it worked in Henry Luce's day, I suspect. Our building cafeteria is being converted to other uses; I don't feel like walking to an adjoining one we are allowed to attend. Construction in our building may subject the hot-dog woman to a windfall-profits tax.

2:10 P.M. While still savoring the taste of pork and ketchup, get a visit from Bill Cook, our science writer. Hot tips on new software and other topics of mutual interest. Discuss what we would do if we owned our own airplanes.

2:15 P.M. It is a beautiful day in Washington. Go downstairs, change my clothes, and head out for a run in Rock Creek Park. Decide after two miles that I probably should turn around and come back. Change and shower in the basement. Come upstairs feeling chipper.

3:00 P.M. Energetic and talented young reporter shows up to apply for/be recruited for a job. Tell him that the newsmagazine life is stress-free and almost like a paid vacation. Detect skepticism on his side.

3:45 P.M. For novelty, decide to return a few phone calls. Then sign-off reading on two medical-related stories for this issue. Erica Goode (culture and ideas editor) detects my need for emotional lift and passes me a copy of a very good article she has booked for next week. Read it and feel emotionally lifted.

4:15 P.M. Back to sign-off reading. Think of Bill Whitworth, the *Atlantic*'s sainted editor, going through long galley proofs of articles and asking the right, penetrating question at the right place. No illogicalities could hide from him. Try to ask questions that would crop up in the reader's mind — consciously or unconsciously — and distract him from what the writer was trying to say. Try not to ask so many as to prompt staff revolt. Also bear in mind that the minutes are ticking away until press time.

5:00 P.M. Sign-off reading of the lead essay of the issue, called "One Week." This one, by Gregg Easterbrook, actually has a surprising twist halfway through, like a short story! Impressive considering that it's just one page long.

5:15 P.M. through 6:30 P.M. Glued to the phone on secret activities. To be revealed only when Bob Woodward tells us who Deep Throat is.

6:30 P.M. With Lee Rainie again. Budget questions, decision for cover stories over next two weeks, personnel redeployment, other stuff.

6:45 P.M. MaryAnne Golon and Jerry Sealy reappear. Moral decision. Do we use a little tiny part of the previously scheduled gorgeous cover on our breaking-news cover? We make a decision. See the results for yourself on the newsstand on Monday.

6:50 P.M. Ten more minutes of secret activity on the phone.

7:00 P.M. Read one of the stories contending for extra space in next week's issue. Decide that this is one that can be held. Pick up the phone to call author and tell him — naaah, will do it tomorrow.

7:10 P.M. Pick up a meal ticket and join the Chow Line — the queue of people who will be working late into the night and thereby qualify for a gala free meal brought in by a local restaurant. While looking over the array of sandwiches, wonder if Henry Luce ever ate dinner from a plastic box. Compare notes on corporate dining habits with Damon Darlin, "News You Can Use" czar.

7:20 P.M. Settling down for serious Sign Off Trail traveling, sandwich on my desk, Beach Boys playing on the CD. Comforting sounds of my youth.

Through 10 P.M. One story after another on the Sign Off Trail. Hope that endless exercise of the critical faculties ("What exactly is the point here?") does not permanently stunt creative ones.

10:00 P.M. More good news! Another delightful story for following week pointed out to me. Feel happy. And a good one for this week too! Joy knows no bounds. Phone call from a prized employee who has decided not to take attractive job from rival organization. Hallelujah. Rumor that someone else we want to keep is being recruited by alien forces. Write note to myself to send out truth squad tomorrow. Phone call to publisher, Tom Evans. Phone call from owner, Mort Zuckerman. Goodnight call to wife and son. Feel well connected to all significant figures in my life.

10:30 P.M. Signed off on everything that is signable at the moment. But then — the ever-changing life of the news hound! — there is a story that needs some more substantial changes. And it is . . . the Big Piece I know about so well. Discuss it with Jim Impoco, business editor, who is lurking in New York. Decide that I am the guy to make the changes. And that is what I have been doing until . . . midnight.

Midnight. Linc Caplan (special projects editor), signing off the last of his articles in what would have been the cover package, appears at door putting on his sweater, asking how much longer I will be. Interest is partly humanitarian; partly, he wants a ride home. I suggest he take a cab.

1:55 A.M. The present. I will leave the building by 2 A.M.

(Picture of person asleep at 2 A.M.) This is your brain.

(Picture of person with raccoon eyes sitting in front of Atex terminal at 2 A.M.) This is your brain at a newsmagazine. Any questions?

One more day.

David Feige

David Feige is a criminal defense lawyer at the Neighborhood De-
fender Service of Harlem, where he represents indigent defendants in
serious felony cases.

POSTED Monday, May 5, 1997, at 4:30 P.M. PT

Robert was sentenced today to seven and a half years to life. He
wore a nice black shirt and a restrained camel-colored blazer to
court, and shook his head respectfully when asked if he had anything to say before sentence was imposed. I think he would have
made a good impression on a jury. Since he decided to take the
plea, I've spent a lot of time wondering whether I did the right
thing.

Robert admitted to selling just over two ounces of cocaine to an
undercover police officer just around the corner from my office on
125th Street. In New York state, selling two ounces or more is a
class A-1 felony—like murder—punishable by a minimum of 15
years to life. People doing "life bids" seldom get parole their first
time up, so Robert, who is 27, may be doing close to 10 years. We
were about to pick a jury when he and his three codefendants decided to get out of the case. I pushed them to do it.

The morning they copped out—after the hearings, after we had
arranged ourselves at the table, and after I bought a new pair of trial
shoes—that morning, I really believed we could win. I was ready to

try the case, eager, in fact, to do it. I was past the gut-numbing fear, the feeling that I was an imposter who was not competent to stand in front of a jury and try a case with the rest of my client's life in the balance. Past the part where I stride around my studio apartment practicing opening statements on friends over the phone. I had my trial bag. My case was organized and coherent. I was ready.

I think that having trial experience means being able to step back and tell a client to plead, even when you're in that gung-ho state of mind. As much as I wanted to go forward, it didn't seem like the right thing to do. We had a tough judge who could easily have sentenced Robert to the full count of 25 years to life if we lost, and although the entire case hinged on the word of an undercover police officer, 18 years is a lot to risk on a Manhattan jury not used to the realities of the streets and unlikely to question police-officer testimony. I don't know. Robert wanted to take his shot. In the three weeks between the plea and today's sentencing, I've wondered about it every day.

It is not the first time I've taken a life sentence, nor will it be the last. But I am always struck by the stoic reserve of my clients as they turn away from their weeping mothers, away from the nearly empty courtroom, away from the judge, and away from me. Usually I see them again in a cell downstairs to make sure all the loose ends are tied up, but sometimes the last time I see them is as they are walked toward the door at the back of the courtroom that leads to the cells and, via a long series of barred corridors and mesh-covered bus windows, to prison.

There are only certain places where a lawyer gets to see an incarcerated client. Holding cells behind the courtrooms, visiting rooms at the jails, sometimes the large holding pens at the courthouse. Beyond these is an entire world of iron bars and petty regulations I have little access to or comprehension of. But even this limited exposure changes me and most of the people I work with. As clichéd as it sounds, it's unsettling to walk away, back into my own terribly different life.

I have to go hear a reading at the Mark Hotel, the kind of swank Upper East Side place I usually avoid. I know I am going to have that sensation of dislocation that sometimes comes over me after a case I've been involved with ends, I move on, and my clients go to prison. I know I am going to look around at the faces of the people —mostly white and well-to-do—have a drink, and wonder at the growing void between the halves of my life.

POSTED Tuesday, May 6, 1997, at 4:30 P.M. PT

I saw Kaleh today. He'd been rearrested, and I had him brought to the courthouse from Rikers Island. He just looked at me with that weird mixture of toughness and embarrassment and said, "Hey Feige. What's up?"

I got Kaleh out of jail about three months ago. He was in for violating his probation, which stemmed from an old robbery case. I handle heavy cases, people looking at a lot of time, and I seldom wind up as emotionally involved as I was with Kaleh. He is young and smart, handsome and mischievous. Ask this guy who is looking at four years in prison what he wants to do with his life, and he cocks his head and smiles and says aeronautical engineering. He could do it too if he had the discipline to stay in school. I tried three times to get him out of jail, and when the judge finally relented, I wept openly outside the courtroom. Rebecca, my caseworker, didn't quite know what to do.

Kaleh's mother and I were pretty hopeful back then. We talked about getting things together at home—family counseling, curfews, school, and a job. Kaleh can't really get a job though. A few months after I got him out, his father kicked him out of the house. He crashed on my floor, and I tried to get him work. Along with the usual applications, I asked all of my friends to help him out. Maybe it's my friends, but I think the reality is that there are not that many jobs out there.

Kaleh stayed with me for three days. He is the only client to have slept in my home. I have a studio apartment and things got cramped. I set him up with transitional housing. He didn't have proper papers so he had to go to a shelter before they could place him. But he refused to go to Covenant House, a shelter for troubled teens. He had been placed there once before when the city took all the kids out of the home after a family incident, and he swore never to go back. We talked about it for hours, and finally, armed with some of my clothes and the good-luck watch I pulled from the surf off the coast of Puerto Rico, he headed downtown. Covenant House never saw him.

I didn't hear from him for a while, though I got word of him. When he was rearrested last week, his Legal Aid lawyer called. She said I must have had a good relationship with him, since when she went to talk to him the first thing he said was, "David Feige is my lawyer," and gave her my office number, home number, and pager number. His mother also told her to call me right away. When we get back to the judge who let him out, who took my word and said that on this one he'd trust my judgment, I am going to get that disapproving stare, the implicit accusation that I have failed in my duties as an officer of the court, the slight adjustment in courtroom credibility. I'm still glad I got him out.

POSTED Wednesday, May 7, 1997, at 4:30 P.M. PT

It is a rainy day in Harlem, and I am in the office for the first time in five days. Because the office is uptown on 125th Street and the court is downtown on Centre Street, I wind up dividing my time between court days and office days. I come to work in jeans and a floppy sweater hoping to write some motions and return some phone calls. Unfortunately, my team is on intake today; any case that walks in or calls in goes to one of the eight people on my team.

The morning goes by smoothly. I get a long letter from a client on Rikers who needs to get into a drug program in order to avoid going to prison. I put in a call to the assistant district attorney on the case. He explains that while he is in favor of having the guy get into the drug program, he is only allowed to consent to a placement made through his office. Unfortunately, the budget for the placement coordinator in his office may have been cut, which means that placement—and treatment—may no longer be possible. I tell him my social workers can place the guy in exactly the same programs as the ones approved by his office. He tells me he won't consent. I call the placement coordinator of his program and leave another message. She hasn't returned my previous four calls.

It is still pouring so I run across the street to Mity Fine for some home cooking. Back at my office, I am just polishing off lunch when the phone rings. The woman calling is distraught; her brother and son were just arrested on a shooting. I find out where they are being held and call the precinct. It is a murder case. The assigned detective is Jones. I get him on the phone and invoke my client's rights (I'm representing the brother). I tell him that K. is represented and to cease any questioning and inform me if there are going to be any identification procedures. The DT knows the drill. While I'm still on the phone with him, my phone goes crazy —five calls in less than two minutes. Two of the calls are from relatives of other people arrested in connection with the murder. I explain that we will not be able to take their cases since we already represent one of the defendants but that I will invoke rights on their behalf. I do. I arrange to have my client's family come down to the office immediately.

Ten minutes later I am in the van headed for the 24th Precinct. Detective Jones is pleasant and professional. He shows me to my client, who is in the squad-room cell, and he gives us some space. I don't talk about the case—plenty of time for that later in more private quarters. Instead, I calm him down and explain central booking, arraignment, bail, and other facts of life in the criminal-justice system. I do the same with the other two, but I don't discuss anything about the case itself lest I be removed for a conflict of interest. One kid is in the small room next to the cell—he seems to have been heavily questioned by the detectives. He is shaken and confused. I try to calm him down, too, though I can't let him talk about the case either. The third guy is downstairs in the main cell —a smelly, charred, filthy cage without benches that you'd expect to find in a Burmese prison camp, not Upper Manhattan. Third guy has been shot, and his bandage shows signs of being bled through. He is in a lot of pain, and I assure him I'll try to get everybody downtown fast.

It is 5 already and I call from the pay phone outside the precinct and relay everything back to the office. David, my team leader, is already sitting down with the families to explain what they can expect. I head back to the office.

After a quick case conference, Sylvia, my investigator, and I head out to the scene. We ask people hanging around if they heard about the shooting, and get some good information. Near the spot where we are told the murder victim, a teenager, died, we find a small shrine. It is made of votive candles and flowers arranged beneath a small picture of a kid who looks no older than 15. A baseball hat and other small personal items are there too, along with some graffiti. It's not really legible—the dead kid's street name or tag appears to have been something like Sky.

Weeping near the shrine is an eyewitness. We have a brief conversation. We'll have to speak again at length. There is also a self-styled minister who seems to have a good relationship with the residents. I give him my card and ask him to call me tomorrow. He points out the dead kid's family walking up the block toward the shrine. Though I'd like to talk to them, I decide that now is not the best time.

It is nearing 7:30 and I am getting cold. Sylvia drops me off at home. I manage 10 minutes of quiet time before the pager goes off. NDS has a lawyer on call 24 hours a day, and today is my day. The first call is a live one—a first-degree rape. The arrest was less than two hours ago. I start the whole procedure again. This time the detectives are from the sex-crimes unit, and less pleasant. I invoke rights with them and arrange to have them page me if a lineup is going to occur. I talk to some colleagues about the investigation in the murder case and start dinner. It is nearing 9.

10:10 P.M. My pager just went off. They are going to do a lineup on the rape case. I gotta go up to the Two-Eight.

11:50 P.M. Just rumbled home from the precinct in a gypsy cab. My kid was picked in a bad lineup. The detectives did a good job of keeping me away from the fillers, I think because they suspected that this was not the world's fairest lineup. To compensate for the fact that my client had huge bushy hair while most of the other fillers had shaved heads, they put silly hairpieces over everyone's head, which hid nothing. My kid was five years younger, six inches shorter, and 30 pounds lighter than the closest filler.

I spoke to the family across the street from the precinct, got contact numbers, and told them I would call in plenty of time for them to be present at his arraignment. I like my client's mother. She is sweet and feisty.

12:30 A.M. A narcotics case comes in. I invoke and get some information from the sergeant at the Street Narcotics Enforcement Unit. It is not worth a precinct run.

It is 1 A.M. and I need to sleep.

Bruce Feiler

Bruce Feiler wrote this soon after the publication of his fourth book, Dreaming Out Loud: Garth Brooks, Wynonna Judd, Wade Hayes, and the Changing Face of Nashville. *His fifth,* Walking the Bible, *will be published in spring 2001.*

POSTED Monday, June 15, 1998, at 4:30 P.M. PT

All my boots are packed.

Packing for Nashville has always been tricky for me. The first time I went to town, in 1995, I took my most conservative attire — olive green slacks, paisley tie, penny loafers. Growing up in Savannah, Georgia, I had always thought of Nashville as being full of preppies and socialites. There was Vanderbilt — a UVA-type bastion of pink and green (those were the days of *The Preppy Handbook*, a *Let's Go* for the social climbers at the Savannah Country Day School). There was Belle Meade, the Palm Beach of the landlocked. There was the Swann Ball, a white-tie affair that would have made even Whit Stillman wish he were from Tennessee.

But all during that week, a week devoted to interviews with executives and managers for a book I was writing on the country boom of the '90s, the only necktie I saw was mine. In fact, in most conversations, I was the only Southerner in the room. While most people dressed in country casual — boots, jeans, and polo shirts (no hats) — a surprisingly large number were decked out in three-button, free-hanging Armani suede and blunt-toed, high-heeled Manolo Blahnik leather. If I was going to write about Nashville, I would need a new wardrobe.

When I did move to town, the first thing I did was get myself a pair of boots—black, ostrich, around $450. (I wonder if this is what my mother meant when she said to me as a kid, "I hope you can grow up to afford your own taste.") But they were the only "country" thing I bought. Everything else was strictly L.A., such as the three-button Hugo Boss jacket I bought in Beverly Hills on a trip with Wynonna that I ended up wearing in my book jacket photo.

This had always been my philosophy of clothes: slightly altering what I wear with each new world I entered—lots of red ties when teaching in Japan, brown shoes as a grad student at Cambridge. But while my hip bizzer wardrobe worked perfectly in Nashville (helped by a late for L.A. but just right for Nashville goatee; Garth and I, for example, once bonded over what our mothers thought of our facial hair), it seemed to confuse everyone else. This weekend I was visiting an old friend in Putney, Vermont. He took one look at my vintage black shirt with white stripes (à la Kramer; I'm late to that trend as well), and said: "Are you putting on weight? Or is that Garth Brooks crap you got on?" Now I was confused. Garth would never wear something this self-consciously urban retro, I told him. He's self-consciously rural retro. Don't you get it: In Nashville, lots of retreads from New York and L.A. work to sell cowboy retreads like Garth to hippie retreads like you.

Plus, nobody in Nashville dresses like Garth. Even Garth only dresses like Garth when he's in public.

Which brings me to the issue at hand. Packing. I'm going to Nashville in an hour for Fan Fair, the annual backstage festival cum family reunion in which 24,000 die-hard country music lovers flock to town for the chance to rub cheeks with their favorite stars. I'm going for the industry hang part of the week (for that I'm taking that black shirt, even though it wilted a bit in the three days of rain in Vermont). I'm also going to witness the gothic spectacle of the fans (for that I'm bringing T-shirts, including my new white Krispy Kreme number—even vintage Southern is chic). And finally I'm going for some interviews about my book. For that, of course, I'm taking my Hugo Boss.

I do have this question, though: When does it get too hot for boots?

Stanley Fish

*Stanley Fish is dean of the College of Liberal Arts and Sciences at the
University of Illinois at Chicago. His latest book,* How Milton Works,
will be published in late 2000.

POSTED Monday, Jan. 10, 2000, at 10:30 A.M. PT

I have just returned from the AALS (American Association of Law
Schools) meeting in Washington, where I was a member of a panel
considering the state of legal theory at the beginning of the new
century. I gave my standard stump speech (called "Theory Mini-
malism"), which always makes the same three points: 1) if by theory you mean the attaining of a perspective unattached to any
local or partisan concerns but providing a vantage point from
which local and partisan concerns can be clarified and ordered, the
theory quest will always fail because no such perspective is or
could be available; 2) the unavailability of that supra-contextual is
in no way disabling because in its absence you will not be adrift
and groundless; rather you will be grounded in and by the same
everyday practices — complete with authoritative exemplars, understood goals, canons of evidence, shared histories — that gave
you a habitation before you began your fruitless quest for a theory; and 3) nothing follows from 1) and 2); knowing that resources
of everyday life are all you have and knowing too that such resources are historical and therefore revisable will neither help you

to identify them nor teach you to rely on them with a certain skeptical reserve; the lesson of 1) and 2) goes nowhere; if grand theories provide no guidance (because they are so general as to be empty), the realization that grand theories provide no guidance doesn't provide any guidance either. End of story, end of theory as an interesting topic.

I like this argument because no one else does. Those on the right don't like it because they have a stake in believing that without the foundations of fixed and absolute verities, the world will go to hell in a handbasket. Those on the left don't like it because they have a stake in believing that in a world where truths are always being revised and authorities dislodged, we can sweep old structures away and begin from scratch to build the just society. This means that I am never in danger of persuading everyone or even many; and that means that I'll never have to give up the argument because there will always be those who don't get it and complain (as did two members of the audience) either that I have undermined certainty and stability, or that I haven't.

I have to say, however, that the pleasures of performances like this one grow thin, in part because the act is getting tired after so many years, in part because the minimalist lesson at its center is empty (of course, that's what it's supposed to be) and the satisfaction of preaching it doesn't last very long. I find this to be true of the entire conference experience. A conference is a piece of theater; you are always on display, in the hotel lobby, at the book exhibit, on the dais, in the bar. In Washington, I catch myself worrying about how long it's been since anyone recognized me. I hang around the Harvard University Press booth to see if anyone will pick up my book. I wonder if anyone will ask me to dinner. (I get very lucky when a former colleague treats me to a magnificent meal with friends.) I recall a conference a year ago in Atlanta, when after giving a paper (basically the same one), I lingered in conversation before going out to the cocktail party. No one acknowledged me or commented on my talk or broke away from a group to say hello, or even greeted me on the drink line. What was happening? Was I becoming invisible? And suddenly I realized that I was at the wrong party (there were two conventions at the hotel), and I hurried down the hall to the right one where I was immediately surrounded by familiar faces and everyone knew my name. A narrow escape, but I realized then (though I pushed the realization away) that the escape was to something artificial and ephemeral, and that what was real or at least more enduring than brief moments of academic theater (also a description of the classroom) were all those moments when you were alone and had to make do with the resources inside you, if any.

That is the reason that (after an early experience in Boston) I never stay to the end of a conference; the letdown is too great, the hollowness of the event, and perhaps of yourself, is too apparent. And so this morning I got up at 6:30 and missed the all-star (without me) panel discussing and rewriting *Brown vs. Board of Education* and came back to Chicago where I was met by a slightly injured dog and an empty apartment. My wife is in California visiting a seriously ill cousin, and I am in my most vulnerable position, alone. I am responding in my usual way, by cleaning up, doing errands, making phone calls, checking e-mail—by doing any number of small things that protect me from thinking about the big ones.

POSTED Friday, Jan. 14, 2000, at 10:30 A.M. PT

A generally pleasant day gave me two moments of particular pleasure and I'll try to figure out whether there was any relation between them as I go along. (I couldn't come up with one.) The first came to me as I was reading through the journal *Heterodoxy*, which describes itself as offering "articles and animadversions on political correctness and other follies." Its editor and creator is David Horowitz, one of those '60s lefties who has turned on his former views with a vengeance and, accordingly, is now doling out vengeance to anyone who says anything that he might have said in 1964. What caught my attention this time is a long piece discussing the many times conservative students, and especially conservative students who work on campus conservative newspapers (usually not really campus newspapers since their funding comes from wealthy outside foundations), are disdained, mistreated, loathed, ignored, and even threatened. (Poor babies!) In the course of the piece, its author winds around to the founding of the *Duke Review* in 1989, a time, he says, that marked a "low point" on the campus because "Stanley Fish, the communist English professor, was in top form" and was "gutting the English department" by bringing in "revisionists such as Henry Louis Gates and Frederic Jameson." This is so looney tunes that I hardly know what to say, but I will say a couple of things. (Actually, it turns out, four.) First, Jameson and I were hired in the same year so I couldn't have brought him in. Second, the correct spelling of his first name is "Fredric." Third, I did hire Henry Louis Gates and would certainly do it again today if I thought I had the remotest chance of succeeding. And fourth, the idea that you gut a department by bringing in Fredric Jameson and Henry Louis Gates—two guys who will certainly merit chapters of their own when the history of 20th-century scholarship is written—is truly bizarre; it is easy to think of hundreds of departments that would line up for the chance to gut themselves in that way. I won't even bother with the "communist" bit.

The other moment of pleasure came to me when I was listening to a lecture by a job candidate, a statistician so sophisticated that I barely understood a word he was saying until he turned his attention to the thesis of another scholar. So and so, he said, says this, "but then he caveats it all over the place." Here was a double pleasure: first, in hearing someone transform a noun into a verb at once casually and effectively (everyone understood what he meant; so and so said something, but then qualified it so many ways that the assertion became exceedingly thin); but second, and even more pleasurable, a recognition that this wonderful piece of grammatically wayward prose accurately named what scholars in every discipline routinely do. We hazard a bold assertion and then we surround it with reservations, footnotes, acknowledgments of alternative hypotheses, and other varieties of waffling and weaseling. In short, we caveat it all over the place. In the space of about 20 seconds, I became so enamored of this phrase that I decided to invent a new school of criticism, the caveat-it-all-over-the-place school, already of course the school every one of us belongs to, but not yet, till this moment, properly labeled.

In between these two moments has been the usual administrative day, made up largely of meetings. First, a breakfast meeting on a matter so delicate and political that I cannot identify it here. Second, a meeting with another dean to discuss teacher education and the state of writing instruction on the campus. Third, a meeting with a colleague to discuss the progress of two search committees. Fourth, a meeting of a committee charged with overseeing the redoing of the plaza in front of my building; here much talk of soil borings, timelines, excavation with relation to underground tunnels, and most insistently, charettes (don't ask me what a charette is; someone told me but I still don't know). Fifth, interviews with two job candidates, usually the most fun part of any day because you are likely actually to learn something.

That's the end of the day and the end of the week of diaries and the beginning of a week in which I and a host of others will be celebrating my wife's birthday. A good way to start the millennium.

Mavis Gallant

Mavis Gallant is a writer who lives in Paris. She has written 11 books, including Across the Bridge.

POSTED Monday, Aug. 11, 1997, at 4:30 P.M. PT

I live in a narrow street on the Left Bank, in Paris, closer to Montparnasse than St. Germain des Prés. We all look into the rooms of near neighbors, know the programs they watch, the musical instruments the children play, but we never acknowledge one another in the street. We do, however, nod and smile (but never speak) if an encounter takes place at Le Midi, the café-bistrot at the corner, on the Rue du Cherche-Midi. So much for local customs. In an apartment just across from mine, a distraught, lonely, barking poodle has been keeping us all awake at night. Like half the quarter, the owners have vanished, probably for the whole of August, leaving just one of the sons—he looks 17 or so—to mind the flat and the dog. Alone at last, he seldom comes home. The dog, alone and dismayed, lets the world know. Yesterday I met them both, boy and dog, in the street. Nothing was said, but he stopped, pointed to the poodle, raised the leash, as if it were evidence in a trial, and gave me a look that conveyed apology, bewilderment, and gloom. If I were not constrained by local etiquette, I'd have said, "Yes, I know. You don't want your parents to know. Yes, I am one of the people who complained to your concierge. But I am not the one who made threatening phone calls or said the word 'police.' I am the one who said to the concierge, 'If he wants to stay out all night, tell him to take the dog.'" That may be what he is doing, because last night the street was as still as a village. It is a village, in fact. There used to be a writer nearby, a woman, who was an old friend of François Mitterrand. Everyone knew when he paid the neighborhood a visit, because she would order duck with orange sauce (a favorite of his) from Peltier, the wonderful *traiteur* on Rue de Sèvres. How did the story get around? By midafternoon, every storekeeper knew and had told every customer. He died, she moved away, and duck-with-orange-sauce has moved into the limbo filled with dead gossip.

My birthday. What occurs on one's birthday sets the tone for the next 12 months. So far, so splendid. The apartment is like a garden and smells of lilies and roses and even sweet peas. I had a successful tussle with French bureaucracy and left them smiling. (The trick is to say, "I knew this was going to make me miserable," and just stand there, looking as agreeable as one can, under the circumstances.) My German publisher has issued a friendly press release, announcing my birth date, with a photograph in which I look like nothing so much as a boiled potato with earrings. Inland Revenue, the British income tax, has refunded me a sum I never expected to see again. I shall be dining at a place where there aren't too many bright lights, so that I can see the August shooting stars. That ought to make for a fine year.

POSTED Tuesday, Aug. 12, 1997, at 4:30 P.M. PT

I'm in the Paris phone book, which means I'm a sitting duck for strangers, most particularly in summer. Some want to talk. Most want to write. What they expect from me is white magic, the revelation of a secret, the wizardly formula they think writers keep under wraps, and now and then bring out for an airing. Several airings should produce a book. A few still take me for a kind of literary travel agent. The other day I was asked, in all seriousness, where one can see authors at work in cafés. It sounded for all the world like watching chimpanzees riding tricycles: both are unnatural occupations. I have only one friend who still writes her novels in notebooks, in cafés. She chooses cafés that are ordinary and charmless, favoring one for a time, then another, as one does with restaurants. Some are near home, many involve a long bus trip. If anyone she knows discovers the café, she changes at once for another, more obscure, hard to get to. About café writing, in general, old legends and ancient myths die hard. Think of the way we touch wood—the sacred oak—to guarantee safety, even when we live in streets without trees.

A young composer, in Paris for the first time, told me how he heard Paris, rather than saw it, how he envisioned Paris sound in all its shapes and forms. The shape of the sound of Paris traffic is different from the sound of New York and Toronto. He drew or shaped those sounds in air with his hands. Since then, it was just a few weeks ago, I have been listening to familiar street noise and trying to see what he meant, but I attach words and images to sounds. Cars moving along Rue de Vaugirard are like gushing water, turned on and off. But a work site with a drill sounds like a work site with a drill. In Paris, streets are torn up in August, when most people are supposed to be away. The street next to mine, as well as the next one over, is closed to traffic. One is being destroyed for an underground garage, which no one wants—everyone in the neighborhood signed an anti-parking-garage petition—and the other for God-knows-what. All petitions are filed in cardboard boxes and thrown in the Seine, weighed down by dug-up concrete blocks.

Today, August 12, is the opening of the grouse-shooting season in Scotland. Pronunciation on the BBC is increasingly inventive. One can hardly keep up. This occasion is announced on the news as the start of "grace shooting." Either it has a metaphysical significance or they are setting sights on anyone named Grace. Either way, I'd as soon not consider it.

Bill Gates

Bill Gates filed this when he was CEO and chairman of Microsoft.
He now serves as chairman and chief software architect.

POSTED Wednesday, March 4, 1998, at 4:30 P.M. PT

When we got off the plane from D.C. yesterday afternoon at Teter-boro Airport, there were two cars waiting. One was a white stretch limo, so I got into the other car instead, since I think large cars like that are pretentious. Went to my hotel off Central Park, where I changed into my tuxedo. I don't wear them very often—not since I was at Harvard in a men's club where they wore them all the time. Melinda helped me with the cuff links, they're so hard to get on.

The car that *Time* magazine sent to pick me up for their 75th anniversary dinner pulled past the entrance to Radio City so you have to walk down about 50 or 60 feet of red carpet in front of the press. There was a huge bank of photographers and TV cameras like they have at the Oscars. And there were nearly as many movie stars at this dinner as there are at the Oscars.

This next part will sound like I am a real name dropper, which I don't like, but it's hard to describe this dinner without being guilty of it. I must have met more famous people in one place at this event than anywhere I've been.

Raquel Welch came up and wanted to meet me. I chatted with Kerri Strug, the Olympic gymnast, and ran into Senator Kennedy, who had been at the Senate hearings earlier in the day. Muhammad Ali was there. He came to campus a year ago when I was out of town, and left me a pair of autographed boxing gloves, so it was fun to finally get to talk to him. I talked for quite a while with Steve Jobs, and with John Irving, whom I have met before and whose books I love.

I thought the launch party for Windows 95 was a big deal. The *Time* dinner cost somewhere between $3 million and $4 million to produce. For one night! They covered all the seats on the entire main floor of Radio City Music Hall with tiers of tables. It was just incredible.

My table included Melinda and my father; Bruce Hallett, president of *Time* magazine, and his wife; Dr. James Watson, the Nobel Prize winner who discovered the structure of DNA, and his wife; and actress Sharon Stone and her husband, Phil Bronstein, an executive with the *San Francisco Examiner*.

The focus of the evening was paying tribute to people who really influenced the 20th century. Toni Morrison honored Dr. Martin Luther King. Steve Spielberg recognized the film director John Ford. President Clinton talked about FDR and Teddy Roosevelt, and I spoke about the amazing things the Wright Brothers did to figure out flight, and how that has changed the world for the better.

Even though I've spoken to thousands of people at hundreds of places before, I was kind of nervous before this event. This wasn't a technology crowd and I wasn't talking about computers. People didn't come to hear about anything I know anything about. I'm really into the Wright Brothers, but I wasn't sure if I could get the audience interested. It seemed to go well, though. The president was in fine form. He is a great speaker, and talking about FDR and freedom is something he was clearly excited about.

When the dinner was over, we waited on the curb for what seemed like forever to catch a cab back to the hotel, but it was fun because Tom Hanks was waiting too, so we had quite a long chat.

Melinda and I got back to the hotel room about midnight and considered calling Jennifer at home (there's a 3-hour time difference). She is almost 2 and we can ask her exciting questions over the phone now, like "What sound does a cow make?" I love the way she says "Moo." However, we decided it was too late to call.

This morning I went to Mott Hall, a public school in Harlem, with Tony Amato, head of District 6 in the New York schools. I met with sixth-graders who are using laptop computers in a program that is looking at whether giving each kid their own PC makes a difference in stimulating them to get excited about learning. You have to see it to believe how these laptops have really brought the classroom and learning to life. These kids have such enormous potential. They're even using PowerPoint to do class presentations.

There was one kid, Luis, who asked how hard it was to port 16-bit apps to 32-bit apps. I thought that was a great question from an 11-year-old. I also explained to the students how Senate hearings work and what it was like in D.C.

I then went to the New York Public Library for a question-and-answer session with TV interviewer Charlie Rose. He asked some pretty tough questions about the competitiveness of the American software industry and the future of the Internet. Melinda and I have been doing a lot of work with libraries, including the New York library, so it was fun to do an event there.

This has been a very exciting week. Intense, but exciting. It's had a little bit of everything. Testifying before Congress for the first time. Attending a glitzy bash in New York. I was very glad my father and Melinda got to be at both of these events. Then the meeting with kids in Harlem and the event at the library. I'm looking forward to getting home and seeing Jennifer, and, of course, catching up on my e-mail. I probably have 1,000 messages to answer by now.

I had a burger and typed this before getting into the car to go to the airport. It's going to be nice to sleep in my own bed tonight.

Atul Gawande

Atul Gawande is a surgical resident in Boston. He wrote Slate's
"Medical Examiner" column and is now a staff writer at
The New Yorker.

POSTED Monday, June 2, 1997, at 4:30 P.M. PT

I am a resident in surgery — two years down, five to go. I'm not allowed to make excuses. If a patient needs something done, I can't
say, "But my shift is over," or, "I'm too tired." With 100-hour
workweeks and many nights without sleep, I'm also trying to learn
to be a surgeon.

This weekend I was on duty, which means starting work at 5
A.M. on Saturday and not going home until Monday night. My
service, cancer surgery, had a handful of patients. A frightened college student had a lymphoma that triggered his spleen to sponge
up his platelets, which you need for blood to clot. We had to take
out his spleen before any unstoppable spontaneous bleeding
started. An irrepressibly cheerful woman in her 50s had a cancer in
her thigh. We excised all her quadriceps muscles and then replaced
them with some of her hamstrings so she could get out of a chair
or walk up stairs again.

My other patients came in for mastectomies. Breast cancer really is different. Not only is it cancer, but your breast has to come
off. (Testicular and prostate cancer are similar, I suppose.) Women
choose different ways to remake themselves. My patients include a

39-year-old who preferred no reconstruction, a 75-year-old who took a saline implant, and a 37-year-old who wanted the most realistic-looking breast possible, one rebuilt from her abdominal muscle and, for the nipple, a skin graft. I had one young patient with bilateral mastectomies who wanted to be the first Playboy pinup with wholly reconstructed breasts.

Everyone was recovering uneventfully. There are few emergencies on a cancer service. My sleep was disturbed only occasionally.

The last time I was on weekend duty, I was at another hospital and it was far busier, more like usual. Fifty pager calls a day. Four patients in intensive care needing to be checked every three hours. Midnight Saturday. I need to go to the bathroom. My pager goes off. An obese man in the ER has a rectal abscess I figure that can wait. I get paged again. ICU needs me stat (like yesterday, pal). A patient can't breathe. Pager goes off again while I'm fixing the problem. A Jehovah's Witness is bleeding from his colon. He's already lost half his blood volume. He refuses a transfusion. I consider going to the bathroom but think better of it. I go talk to the patient. No surgery, no blood, he says. He knows he could die. We hook up monitors, intravenous lines, a bladder catheter. We give fluids. The bleeding stops. I talk to my boss. I fill out the inevitable paperwork.

I go to the ER. The fat man is angry I took so long. I give him numbing medication and use a knife to open the abscess. Pus pours out. The stench is fearsome. He feels better. More paperwork. Three A.M. I finally go to the bathroom.

The Jehovah's Witness checked with his church. He can have surgery, but no blood. Then he has another bloody bowel movement. His blood count drops to 15 percent (normal is 45 percent). Surgery or not, he will die. Amazingly, at 12 percent, he is still alive. Stone-faced, scared, he changes his mind. He wants blood. Later, having revived him to a count of more than 30 percent, we took out his colon. He made it home the next week.

POSTED   Tuesday, June 3, 1997, at 4:30 P.M. PT

The first hour or so before sunup is a pell-mell scramble to see all the patients. This is "pre-rounds." I check lab results, vital signs, how everyone's feeling (they hardly ever know, since I have to wake them up to ask), and then wangle them around to check their lungs, bellies, hearts, wounds (now they're awake). Then I join the other juniors to round with a senior resident. We whiz by everyone again, the senior double-checking that we didn't miss anything and giving us our orders for the day. Some patients are to go home. They need prescriptions, instructions, visiting nursing, follow-up appointments. My young splenectomy patient has a fever. I'm told to get a chest X-ray, blood and urine cultures, and to get him out of bed more. I'll keep a close eye on him today.

I continue in a controlled frenzy to do everything by 7:30, when operating begins. I am assigned to four breast cancer operations. The senior keeps the more difficult cases for herself. I make it downstairs just in time to catch my first patient before she goes into the OR. She's having a breast biopsy.

"I'm Dr. Gawande. I'll be assisting your surgeon. Is everything going all right so far?" I extend a confident hand, give my best you're-in-good-hands smile, make sure to pose my empathetic question. But she gives me a withering glare.

"No residents are doing my surgery," she says. I try to explain that I just assist, that her attending surgeon is always in charge.

The whole edifice of medical training is based on subterfuge. I know I'm not just an extra set of hands. Otherwise, I'd never learn to be a surgeon. Two years out of med school, I hold the knife in most of today's cases. I have the table raised to my six-foot-plus height. I struggle to get a breast cancer out through a tiny incision without violating the mass or burning the skin with the electrocautery. I remove the lymph nodes from an armpit and avoid damaging critical nerves or puncturing delicate nearby arteries. The attending surgeon leaves to talk to the family while I sew the skin closed.

Yet it's not as simple as that, either. There's a distinction between pilot and navigator. A pilot needs a modicum of skill, but beyond that, the navigator is in charge. The attending draws the dotted line where I am to cut. She warns me if I'm too close to the cancer or too far. She tells me how she wants the skin sutured. Many cases are too complex to do without both of us playing our roles. And if she loses confidence in me, she utters the dreaded words — "Switch sides" — and I slouch shame-faced and silent away from the operator's side of the table. In the end, for a given attending, the quality of surgery varies little despite the variety of residents who help him or her.

To this first patient of the day, however, her surgery is more like the NBA Finals than like steering a submarine. She wants Jordan shooting the ball. She is unrelenting. The surgeon caves in, dismissing me since she can handle a biopsy without extra help.

POSTED Wednesday, June 4, 1997, at 4:30 P.M. PT

Let's talk money (I got my pay stub in the mail yesterday). I make $33,000 a year. The last year of residency that increases to $41,000. My fellow residents, scrimping to pay off their $100,000 loans, chafe at this. Fortunately for me, my parents are doctors and put me through school. Even with two kids and a high-maintenance wife, I've got it better than most.

When this is all over, though, you're talking big bucks. New general surgeons start at more than $100,000 a year. The average doctor makes $180,000 a year (so why does Dr. Mark Greene on *ER* still have that crummy apartment?). In the late 1980s, cardiac surgeons made the most — $675,000 on average, with the top 10 percent making a million bucks. People say managed care has slashed this by half. Still pretty freakin' good, though.

My son, Walker, needed cardiac surgery my first year of residency. His surgeon was incredible, operating on him in the day and then again in the night. Walker survived a condition that until recently killed most children. I'd pay his surgeon a million bucks myself. But I wouldn't do cardiac surgery if you paid me. After finishing general surgery residency, cardiac fellows put in more than 120 hours a week (that leaves only 48). I'd be 40 years old at the end of the training. And once in practice, I'd still have to work like a dog. I want to see my kids some day.

I'd also like to stay married. I've watched too many residents' marriages fall apart. Spouses have to be pretty independent, and put up with moodiness, 2 A.M. phone calls, and dashed weekend plans. The female surgeons have it worst. How well do you think men tolerate all that? Surgeons divorce nearly twice as often as the average doctor. (Can you believe there's a study on this?) For those of you looking for a doctor to marry, psychiatrists have the highest divorce rate (surprise, surprise), pediatricians the lowest. Oddly, doctors who had a parent die while they were in medical school also have a low divorce rate.

I also know two residents who killed themselves this year. But this is getting too grim.

This morning, my twenty-something splenectomy patient was combative and talking nonsense. His fevers were worse. His oxygen levels were low. This made him confused. Since he was confused, he wouldn't keep an oxygen mask on. I got angry with him, and he finally kept it on. An X-ray showed he had pneumonia. I hadn't prodded him out of bed enough. That would have made him take full breaths and cough up the junk in his lungs. I had the nurses bang on his chest to loosen up the pneumonia and browbeat him to cough. I started antibiotics. If he gets any worse, he'll need to be put in intensive care. I hope he turns the corner.

POSTED Friday, June 6, 1997, at 4:30 P.M. PT

Another night on duty. The day was like usual. My first case was an operation on a woman with escalating attacks of belly pain. Gallstones were causing the pains, so we removed her gallbladder (chock full of stones) using a small camera and long instruments inserted through tiny incisions in her belly. In my first year I'd stare at the TV screen, trying to keep the camera still with one hand while picking at the gallbladder with the other. Move one way with your hand and the instrument moved the other way on the screen. I thought the operation was maddening, and the attending surgeons thought I was. Their patience would soon give out, and they'd take the reins. Like learning a new video game, though, I eventually got the hang of it. Today, I got it done in an hour, and the attending only had to give me a few tips here and there.

By the end of the day's surgeries, I am puffed up and gleaming with self-satisfaction. Don't "Mister" me, buddy. I'm *Doctor* Gawande. The nurses, sensing my growing smugness, set about bringing me down to size.

7:00 — Rounds are over. One team member is still operating. The others fill me in on their patients. Things seem under control and they head home.

7:01 — Page. "Your new patient's here." What new patient? I meet him, and he's yellow as a banana. Turns out to be pancreatic cancer. Inoperable. I figure it'll take an hour working up his problems. But I'm hungry.

7:25 — I rush downstairs before the cafeteria closes. Dinner is fried chicken and mashed potatoes. (The hospital cafeteria manager must get kickbacks from cardiology.)

7:27 — Page. A nurse says there's a man on the phone who's furious that we're sending his wife home tomorrow. I say to make him wait, but she puts him on anyway. "This is crazy," he says. "In Russia, she would get one month in the hospital." I note that she's eating, walking around, and taking only pain pills. He vows not to pick her up until he feels she's ready. Whatever. My chicken's waiting.

7:29 — Overhead speaker blares, "Code Green on the seventh floor." This means someone's stopped breathing. I abandon dinner and join a platoon of residents descending on a man who had a lung removed because of cancer. One resident inserts a breathing tube through his vocal cords. Another puts him on a respirator.

7:45 — I'm back to my chicken. Another page. "Mrs. Z is itchy all over." I ask if she has a rash. Put on hold.

7:48 — Still on hold. I hang up and call back. They forgot me. Yes, the patient does have a rash. I figure she has an allergy and change her antibiotics.

7:50 — Page. "Mrs. B isn't making enough urine." I head for her floor. This time I bring the chicken. She's pale, dizzy, and dehydrated. Her blood count's low. I give her some blood.

8:10 — Page. My young splenectomy patient has a fever running to 102 and is throwing up. Damn it. I thought he was on the mend. I go see him. The pneumonia is still festering. I give him Tylenol and anti-nausea medicine to make him feel better. With my ego back to shrunken, resident size, I sneak off to my "call room" — a closet with a bed and a desk. I finish off the chicken and call home to see how Kathleen and the kids are doing. Another page. I gird myself for the long night ahead.

Masha Gessen

Masha Gessen is the chief correspondent of Itogi, *the Russian partner of* Newsweek.

POSTED Wednesday, March 31, 1999, at 11:30 A.M. PT

To be reduced to sleeping on the floor with all my clothes on, struggling to use a light jacket as a blanket, in an apartment that has intact windows, hot water, and an Internet connection—that sums up the Belgrade war game in which I am now undeniably caught. In every other war I have covered, it was the normalcy that struck me. I remember confessing this to a Warsaw friend six years ago, when I was returning from my first visit to the disintegrating Yugoslavia. "I know," she responded. "I used to beg my mother to tell me about the war, until she finally said, 'What do you want me to tell you? I took the tram to work every day....'" I have since observed the many different ways in which people reach for their routines, setting up candlelit marketplaces in bombed out city blocks, holding discos in temporarily vacated bomb shelters, and insisting on having a civilized cup of tea by the window while drunk soldiers shoot their fear off just outside.

Belgrade, of course, has to be different. I have seen no evidence of bombing within the city proper. Acts of war have been limited to Serbian vandalism of the American Library, the British Council offices, the French Cultural Center and Air France, and all the

McDonald's in the city. But the atmosphere of war as one might imagine it—a cinematic sense of crisis—has been perfected. Milosevic has been accused of being the aggressor so often he must be relishing this opportunity to play the victim. Nobody gets to do what he used to do anymore. Many nongovernmental organization employees do not go to their offices for fear of an official crackdown; in several cases, people who used to do other things have taken their place. The university is shut, and final exams, which generally occur in April, have been canceled—the better to staff the daily patriotic concerts. There are even shortages: Cigarettes have all but disappeared. I came here with three cartons of Lucky Strikes, which struck me as a questionably tasteful brand choice—but this was what my friends requested. Today a feminist anti-war activist friend told me that "women from Bosnia are sending us Lucky Strikes and Nescafe." Is there no coffee? "To be honest, there still is coffee," she laughed. "But just in case."

Now that news of NATO's third-phase bombing plans has trickled in, all this war preparation has shifted into an even higher gear. The organization where I was staying until last night has decided to vacate its premises, which are a couple of buildings away from Serbian military headquarters. I have moved to the office—a converted apartment, actually—of another group, a couple of streets over. We have removed the inner window frames so we have something to put back in and shield us in case the outer glass is shattered by the bombing expected overnight. Of course, this is the first night since the bombings began when the air raid alarm siren has not sounded. So the crowd here—about a dozen people, mostly idling university students—are waiting with varying degrees of tension. Two guys are sleeping on the floor in the room where I am working. Most are sitting at a long conference table playing preference, a watered down version of bridge. Two are playing virtual soccer on a computer.

A couple of guys occupying the other computer have been logging on and being kicked off for the last six hours, downloading and printing CNN reports. This is, they claim proudly, "a digitized environment"—in fact, I met a couple of the core members of the group four years ago when I was doing a story on e-mail in the Balkans. Like many local intellectuals, these guys don't have a television. "It's dangerous these days to watch TV," said one of them, a 24-year-old who escaped from Sarajevo eight years ago. "It can make you go nuts." Sanity, of course, is relative. When they are not passing around printouts from CNN's Web page or tuning into the BBC via RealAudio, they get their news the old-fashioned way: by telephone. Someone called and said the Vatican was sending a peace envoy to Milosevic. Someone else phoned in the news that NATO head Javier Solana and Gen. Wesley Clark have had a falling out and Solana has resigned. We're not sure about Solana, but the Vatican visit was confirmed. Of course, the confirmation came from official Serbian radio, which can also make you go nuts.

One thing featured prominently on the radio lately are so-called "locators," mythical objects supposedly dropped by NATO planes. They are said to be Styrofoam boxes that enter buildings without breaking glass and allow NATO to home in on its targets. Persons who find these locators in their homes are asked to disarm them by removing the battery or to report them to the police. I hope they use AA batteries like my flashlight. I also hope they really don't break the windows, because I'm freezing under my jacket as it is.

POSTED Saturday, April 3, 1999, at 10:30 A.M. PT

BELGRADE, 2 A.M.—Loreena McKennitt and bombing go perfectly together. Whoever she is, she has a beautiful soprano voice, and she is singing on the tape someone has put on. Here's how the bombing went: I was in the office of a women's organization. Everyone seemed relaxed after two nights in which Belgrade didn't get bombed. "I now don't think it's going to happen," one of

the women told me. For no better reason than that it hadn't happened yet, but that's good enough. "It's when you don't think it's
going to happen that it hits," I said, just in case. I meant myself—
getting caught "practicing journalism," that is—more than the
bombing. I too had come to believe that good sense had prevailed
and someone up there in the skies of NATO had decided not to
bomb a densely populated residential neighborhood, especially
now that the police and army have had ample warning and time to
relocate. The army has taken over at least one school building in
Belgrade, and the police have moved into the offices of a friend of
mine's father's business.

So we sat in the kitchen drinking cheap, light, and fresh Serbian
beer. Tired of a conversation I could barely follow, I went into the
tiny computer room off the kitchen and logged on, sort of. It was
taking forever to load, and I was going through the organization's
English language library when the bombs went off. One, two,
three, no more than 500 meters from here. The conversation in the
kitchen halted. I closed and shelved the book. I always do these
sorts of things in moments of mortal danger, exhibiting an otherwise entirely uncharacteristic love of order and organization. One
of the women came into the room and said, "That was here." I
think she felt avenged for a few nights ago, when she was terrified
of an explosion miles away.

In a few moments, we all somehow ended up crouched in the
hallway, which was the place farthest away from the windows.
Everyone looked at me. "You've been in wars," someone said.
"What do we do?" I asked if there was a basement in the building.
No. Where is the nearest bomb shelter? About five minutes away,
someone thought. Someone else thought fifteen. She also thought
she would never, under any circumstances, crowd into one of those
panic havens, with people who supported the regime that has
brought this upon us. Fair enough. More to the point, we probably
couldn't get into a shelter. The places are quasi-private enterprises,
heavily guarded against outsiders who might take advantage of all

the civilians crowded helplessly into an enclosed space. I declared no one was going out into the street.

By the time we were having this conversation, we were already in the kitchen. I heard a plane flying low overhead—low enough to bomb—and, using the authority bestowed upon me by my war experience, herded everyone back into the hallway. Then we decided to sit in the bathroom, which has a light. It was fun for the first few minutes, while the women were arranging themselves on the toilet, on the washing machine, and in the bathtub. Then one of the women tried to hang a flannel shirt over the mirror. "This mirror makes me crazy," she said. She is very butch and tough, and I think she wanted us to think she hates mirrors in general, but she was really afraid it would shatter. But I didn't want her to cover the mirror, because we Jews do that after someone has died, and I hadn't seen a covered mirror since my mother's death.

This is no time to say that it's the waiting that kills you, because it's not. But waiting for other bombs to drop gets very tedious very quickly. We started wandering around the flat. The phones were ringing off the hook—people checking to see if we were still intact. The police headquarters half a kilometer from here are burning magnificently, sending up huge clouds of smoke and tiny star-like balls of fire. We have opened the windows because someone thinks that this way they are less likely to shatter. The fresh damp air provides a good excuse for shivering. Two women defied the voice of my reason and went out to get more beer, which I am decidedly looking forward to drinking. Loreena McKennitt is singing. Another bomb has just dropped, about an hour after the first three. The women have come back and reported what they saw on the street: ambulances and water-main-repair cars rushing around, and not a whole lot of people. It's definitely the police headquarters that were hit. They have been cordoned off and there's a sea of shattered glass in the streets.

The Interior Ministry was still burning when the birds started singing. Then in a few minutes the pink glow from the fire faded and a bluish light came into the room. We were drunk and punch-drunk, and we felt safe in the light of day—as though NATO missiles were street hoodlums who sink back into their hiding places when night fades. Two of us left the office and grabbed a cab to the Interior Ministry before going back to the place where I had my sleeping bag and my friend T. had left her bike. The buildings of the federal and Serbian interior ministries are directly across the street from each other. The streets are blocked off in every direction, but after some complicated maneuvering our cabby managed to drive right past them. The federal building, a seven- or eight-story 1930s structure, was still standing, apparently gutted by the fire. From what I could see, it had no windows left. The Serbian ministry was a more dramatic sight: A low modern structure of steel and concrete, it had folded into itself like a crushed Coke can.

I guess this is what you call a surgical strike. I felt a little embarrassed at having been scared last night. Maybe those guys really do know what they are doing and won't hurt us thrill-seeking reporters and other helpless civilians. Then I remembered the missile that landed in a friend of a friend's yard.

"I thought there would have been more damage," T. said wistfully. She may be against the bombings in general, as all of us who hang out here are, but it's hard not to revel in the destruction of the buildings that command the Serbian police in Kosovo.

At the same time, T. is sad about the bridge in Novi Sad, blown up two days ago. It was a beautiful structure, over 100 years old. And it's not just that. Many of our friends have developed what we call "the fear of bridges." That is, the fear of being on a bridge when it's bombed. So the issue of going back and forth between the old town and New Belgrade on the other side of the Danube, where many people live, has become, well, an issue. But last night T. and I were going to do just that: go over to her place in New Belgrade and take a television set to put in the office where I am staying. But then her brother said he'd drive the television over himself the next day —somehow he was convinced he would get the mythical gasoline tickets supposedly reserved for civilians—and not to bother coming. And then, about half an hour later, the bombs came.

The first thing that S., the cyber maven from Sarajevo who also sleeps in this office, said when he woke up was, "Did you hear about Iraq?" He thinks those missiles must have been launched at the same time. He also thinks there is something funny about them hitting just in time for CNN prime time.

How do you pinpoint the moment when war has started? It creeps in on you, and after a while you start to recognize the feel of it. I think that's a sign that you've been to too many. Almost exactly a year ago I was in Kosovo with a horde of other journalists, all of whom had covered Bosnia or Chechnya or both. We knew the feeling, but the local residents—with the exception of the several thousand Serb refugees from the Krajina who had been re-settled in Pristina—could not recognize it yet. It was a very uncomfortable knowledge to be saddled with, this vision of what would happen in Kosovo.

Today the feeling came to Belgrade. As a friend of mine put it today, people have stopped feeling fear and started feeling panic. Fear you can counter with rational arguments; panic you can't. There's a feeling of total overwhelming helplessness—either people think, I've got to get out of town, or they think, just shoot me now, because I can't take the waiting. The city teems with armed policemen and army men in camouflage. The residents talk about the bomb that's sure to drop tonight. Everyone seems convinced it will be the General Staff building, a few streets over from the Interior Ministry buildings destroyed in last night's attack, and just a block from the place where I spent last night (this evening I am at a different office, five or six blocks away).

Overcoming my fear of bridges, I went over to New Belgrade today to deliver a package a friend sent to her grandmother here. The friend, whom I'll call Maria, is a journalist now posted in the city where I live. She holds two passports: Yugoslav and Polish. This just had to start less than two weeks before Poland joined

NATO. Thursday after the bombing began, Maria couldn't get her grandmother on the phone. Crying on the line to me, she said, "It's a horrible feeling—knowing they may bomb the people I love, and at the same time thinking, 'At least finally someone has done something.'" The next day, the two of us were at the Yugoslav embassy—Maria was helping me get my visa—and, whiling away the wait, started talking about whether NATO could have come up with a better solution. We decided it would have been better to assassinate Milosevic. And Sesel, as the most dangerous possible successor. We were discussing the fact that the two often go places together and could be taken care off with a single, well-placed explosive device. Then we remembered we were at the Yugoslav embassy.

I took a flashlight, batteries, and money to Maria's grandmother's sister's apartment. The sister, a youthful pensioner with dyed-black hair and a prominent moustache, gave me juice and said how scared she had been the night before.

"Maria wants her grandmother to go to Bosnia," I said.

"I know."

"Is she going to?"

"No. We keep waiting for this to stop any day. But there is no end in sight," she said, apparently undisturbed by the contradiction between their plans and their fears. "They are going to bomb the General Staff building today."

Then she added that Maria had phoned and said she was going to Macedonia. At some point you just grow incapable of staying away, which is, I suppose, why I am here.

On the way back over the bridge, I suddenly saw Kalemegdan—a Roman fortress rebuilt by the Byzantines in the 12th century and later modified by the Turks, the Austrians, and the Serbs into a magnificently weird labyrinth—and I remembered that I love this city. Scurrying from house to house for the last week, I had lost sight of the place. I remember reading years ago—I think it was Misha Glenny's book about the disintegration of Yugoslavia—

that Belgrade was a hideous city. He seemed to hold this to be self-evident. But to me, Belgrade has the kind of eclectic beauty that makes a city. Narrow winding cobblestone streets straight out of Istanbul lead up to grand buildings with clearly Parisian aspirations. State buildings make one think of the Habsburg Empire, and Orthodox churches look like retrofitted mosques. And then there is Kalemegdan, overlooking the rivers Danube and Sava.

Last year, on the way back from Kosovo, my photographer and I spent a couple of days in Belgrade. He had never been here, and I had told him the city would be our reward for nearly getting executed in Kosovo, which is a separate story and the reason I swore never to return there or to any other war zone. I broke the war zone promise because I could not stay away, but I have definitely lost Kosovo, and now I fear I will lose Belgrade as well.

That sunny day last year the photographer and I ran all over Kalemegdan, stopping to drink beer at outdoor cafes and otherwise celebrate our return to civilization. So today, going over the bridge, I decided to pause and treat myself to the comforts of the city. I had a piece of pizza, which is the first hot food I've had since Monday. Then an Irish coffee at an outdoor cafe. Everyone around me was talking about the General Staff building, and by 6 P.M. the cafe was closing. I walked over to the Internet cafe in the House of Youth off the main square, but it was closed. I wouldn't be surprised if it is shut for good. The Internet and cellular communications may be the last of the joys of civilization that we will soon have left. It's also what allows me to file these dispatches, and it is very easy to cut off. The authorities did cut off all mobile communications in the Kosovo region right after the bombing began.

The radio newscaster has just announced that the NATO forces stationed in Bosnia have blown up the part of the Serbia-Montenegro railway line that cuts through Bosnia. It's closing in on us.

The air raid alarm siren just went off. It's 8 P.M.

Malcolm Gladwell

Malcolm Gladwell is a staff writer at the New Yorker *and author of*
The Tipping Point.

POSTED Monday, Nov. 15, 1999, at 10:00 A.M. PT

The last time I did one of these "diaries" was close to three years
ago, and as I recall, I spent very little time being diarylike. This
time around, though, I have been instructed to actually talk about
what happens in my day, which has thrown me for something of a
loop, because I don't actually do all that much — at least as compared to the super-achievers who usually people this particular section of *Slate.* Today, for example, my chief accomplishment was to
wake up at 10:30 A.M. and somehow make it downtown in time for
the one o'clock kickoff of the Buffalo Bills–Miami Dolphins game
at the Riviera. In New York City, as many of you are no doubt
aware, the fact that there are two local football teams — the Jets
and the Giants — monopolizing the local television stations means
that it's virtually impossible to follow any other team unless you
have a satellite dish. Since I don't, that means my friend Bruce and
I have to go to sports bars to follow our beloved Bills.

Does that seem odd, that I would use the word "beloved" to describe a football team? I thought of that today, watching all the
young men (myself included) testify to their affection to their

team at the sports bar. I fell in love (there I go again) with the Bills of the 1980s, who were a high-flying, offensive juggernaut, who threw long and often to a fleet of extraordinary receivers. Had you asked me in, say, 1989, why I liked the Bills so much, I would have gone on and on about how they were the highest-flying offensive juggernaut in the league. Now, by contrast, the Bills play a careful, conservative, painstaking ball-control game that is the absolute antithesis of their old style. So, why do I like the Bills so much? Because I think they play the most enthrallingly careful, conservative, and painstaking ball-control game in the league. Now in that same period—1989 until today—I would not say that my attitudes towards, say, women or literature or movies have changed at all. I like now, as then, dark-haired Jewish girls, spy novels, and thrillers. Does this mean my love of the Bills is somehow more pure than my love of all else— since it can survive even the complete transformation of the object of my affection? What makes this whole thing even more strange is that I don't actually like Buffalo, the city. Bruce and I grew up near Toronto, and we generally regarded Buffalo with something bordering on contempt. I like Buffalo, in other words, even though I don't like Buffalo, and even though the Buffalo I used to like (to the extent I actually liked Buffalo) no longer actually exists. Who says men are incapable of unconditional love?

Actually, what I like is watching football with my friend Bruce. Bruce and I met on the very first day of first grade in the little Canadian town where we grew up, and we've been best friends ever since. Perhaps because of our long history—or perhaps because of some other peculiar and unfathomable aspect of the male psychology—I have the curious reaction to Bruce of always agreeing with what he says. If Bruce says the receiver was in, and I initially thought he was out, well then, by golly, he was in. If Bruce thinks that story in *The New Yorker* was perfectly awful and the whole problem was that the part at the end should have been at the beginning, then immediately I think back on that story and, by golly, the end really should have been at the beginning. I wonder sometimes whether there are other people out there who are as much under Bruce's sway as I am. Maybe someday I'll be at something like Bruce's wedding, and I'll be standing around with a group of Bruce's friends and someone will mention that particular *New Yorker* story and we'll all nod and blurt out simultaneously that the whole problem was that the part at the end should really have been at the beginning.

This is the part in the Diary entry when all the super-achievers grab a quick snack, sing a lullaby to their triplets, and then get back to writing their screenplay, or comic novel, or IPO prospectus. Me? I went shopping at Staples for those really, really awesome uni-ball Deluxe Fine Points (I bought six) and then went home and watched more football. Did I mention the Bills won their game? That made me really happy.

POSTED Wednesday, Nov. 17, 1999, at 10:00 A.M. PT

I talked to my father today. My book is in the absolute final round of preparation, and one of the copy editors questioned the seemingly improbable answer to a little mathematical puzzle posed in the introduction: "If you folded a piece of paper 1/100th of an inch thick over and over 50 times, how high would the pile of paper be, in the end?" (If you want the answer, I'm afraid you'll have to read the book.) Now, I haven't the slightest idea how to solve that problem. But my father, who is a mathematician, certainly does, and when I talked to him, he did that mathematician thing of making it sound like you could actually figure out the answer if you imagined, in your mind's eye, that you had four apples and little Johnny, your friend, took away two of them.

It used to make me feel sort of guilty that I have no interest in things mathematical, particularly since all the prevailing cultural explanations for why a son would reject his father's vocation —

He is competing for the attention of the mother! He is staking out his independence from the paternal model! — make it sound like I don't think that what my father does is deeply cool, which I do. Then I ran across the wonderful work of a psychologist at the University of Virginia named Daniel Wegner. (My life is entirely governed, in case you hadn't noticed, by what I read in psychological journals.) Wegner points out that much of what we "remember" actually isn't stored in our own memories. What we remember is where we stored that piece of information. So, you actually "know," in a roundabout way, what the capital of Madagascar is, because you remember that you can find that information in an atlas. Mostly what we do, though, is store information with other people: We develop what Wegner calls transactive memory, which is that we distribute responsibility for knowing things among our family and friends. That's part of what it means to be intimate with someone: that you know what the other person knows, so you can always access that knowledge when you need it, and you are relieved of the responsibility of knowing it directly yourself. In my book I talk about this in the context of organizations, because obviously any company that needs to communicate properly and be intellectually efficient must develop the corporate version of a transactive memory system. (If you want to know how to do that, once again, you're going to have to buy my book.) But, do you see? This explains why I didn't go into math and went in another direction. It's not that I'm rejecting or competing with my father. It's just that I realized very early on that it would be unnecessary. In my family's transactive memory system, we've got math covered.

It occurs to me now that I do the same thing with my friend Jacob (OK, OK: *Slate*'s very own Jacob Weisberg). I stopped reading virtually anything about politics right around the time I met Jacob, since he knows so much about the subject that it struck me as a far more efficient use of my time to "store" my political knowledge with him. What this means, of course, is that the nature of my intellectual relationship with Jacob has changed. Instead of arguing with Jacob over his support for the capital-gains tax, for example, I now come out strongly for the capital-gains tax but worry about whether Jacob has done the necessary research to properly make up my mind for me. Sometimes when I go over to his apartment, I look through the books on his night table, just to make sure he's not reading, like, Marx or something. Jacob's in Italy right now, and I'm suddenly struck with a panicked thought. Jacob—are you getting the *Times* over there? What if you miss something critical? Remember—you're thinking for two now.

I'm going home to Canada tomorrow, because my father is getting an award for his mathematics. The ceremony is in Ottawa, and my mother and I plan to get very dressed up for the occasion. (Whether my father will do the same remains to be seen.) My comments in Wednesday's entry notwithstanding, it's actually quite a strange thing to have your father be honored for something that you don't understand. It's more than that actually: It's not just that I can't follow the mathematics that he does, it's that I don't know what it feels like to do mathematics. My mother, for example, is a writer and I think I have a basic understanding of what it means for her to do what makes her happiest professionally. What part of attacking a math problem makes my father happy? How do the pulleys and levers in his brain move when he figures something out? I have no idea. When I write something I really like I usually get up and dance around my room and watch ten minutes of ESPN as a reward. As far as I can tell, my father does not do this, but even if he did, it really wouldn't answer the question. I remember as a child my father coming home from work and telling us that he solved a problem that day that he had been working on for 15 years. Could anyone ever adequately explain to anyone else the particular feelings of joy and accomplishment that must come from doing that?

This is always the stumbling block I hit when I try to write a profile. I want to try and understand that feeling—but of course you never can. The closest I came was with Charlie Wilson, a man I wrote about earlier this year, who is one of the world's great neurosurgeons. Somehow Wilson immediately understood that's what I wanted from him, and after we met he began to send me a stream of e-mails—each one more fascinating and articulate than the last—in which he came closer and closer to a description of the emotional state he reaches after a successful operation. It wasn't boastful or arrogant. It was just beautiful, in the way that all perfectly true writing is beautiful. Wilson may be the smartest person I've ever met, or at least he seemed to have a better understanding of how he was and what he did than anyone I've ever met. Of course, fool that I am, I spent the story giving my understanding of Charlie Wilson. I would have done better just quoting his e-mails. Oh well, everyone has a bad day sometimes.

Ira Glass

Since fall of 1995, Ira Glass has been host of Public Radio International's This American Life.

POSTED Monday, June 7, 1999, at 8:38 A.M. PT

I've flown to Los Angeles today to meet with network executives about doing a version of my radio program on television. Meetings are set up over the next two days with impressively high-level people at ABC, NBC, HBO, WB, Showtime, and Fox. A&E has also expressed interest.

I and my colleagues will be pitching the show. What is striking about this experience is how familiar it is, even though I've never done it. Like most anyone else who grew up in this country, I've seen pitch meetings in movies and TV shows about Hollywood. I've heard actors and directors and writers chat about them on talk shows. I've read—well, no, I haven't read the many *You'll Never Eat Lunch in This Town Again* tell-alls or the many novels about the customs of Hollywood, but somehow it feels like I have. I have read all those Doonesbury comic strips making fun of this process.

About a week ago I was on network television for the first time. I made a brief appearance on *Late Night with David Letterman*. It had this same *déjà vu* quality, and for the same reason. By the time we get to be adults in America, by the time we actually appear on

David Letterman's program, we've seen so many hundreds of hours of talk shows that, essentially, we have been there before. Simply from watching television, I knew that I'd be pre-interviewed before the show, that the questions and my answers would be roughly planned out in advance, but that David Letterman in particular likes to diverge from these preplanned moments to wander down paths unknown. Simply from watching television I knew the set where they tape *Late Night* would be very, very cold, because that's the way Mr. Letterman prefers it.

What I didn't know is what a strange physical space it is, the actual *Late Night* set, in the Ed Sullivan Theater. There's a live audience but they feel very far away. The cameras hover and surround in a way that makes you feel as if you're in an oddly cozy space, more cocoonlike that I'd have imagined. The band is very close to you, but the acoustics of the room are so strange that you can actually talk and be heard while they play. But most surprising of all: When you sit in the guest's chair, Mr. Letterman is sitting very close to you, closer than it looks on television. Or maybe he just seems unusually close because it's unusual to see him in three dimensions.

Interestingly, one of the greatest pleasures of appearing on *Late Night with David Letterman* actually happened the week before my appearance. It was this. Several times I simply declared to strangers at checkout lines that I was going to be on David Letterman's show Friday. Each time it was like saying "I appear to be one of you mortals, walking here amongst you, but in fact, I'm one of the gods!" As if I had this secret superpower I could reveal to anyone, anytime.

I only tried it three times, and each time it was followed by a rather delicate human moment, in which the person to whom I delivered this important news paused, and then very politely, with quiet tact, summoned the energy to ask the question, "Who are you?" At which point I'd have to say, "Well you know how on these talk shows there's always a bunch of famous people and then there's the guest you've never heard of? I'm the guest you've never heard of!"

That was my role. I was the farmer who grew a potato that happens to look exactly like Pamela Anderson Lee. I was the kid who won the science fair by exploding an ordinary pickle using static electricity.

As to my present mission, I'm here in Los Angeles to sell a one-hour television special/pilot of *This American Life*. The TV show, if it happens, would have the same form as the radio show: We'd choose a theme, do four or five stories on that theme. Each story would be filmed in a different visual style. It would look like nothing else on TV. The idea is that the stories on the TV program would be the kinds of narratives that we try to do on the radio show: Characters and conflict are introduced fast, and you keep listening because you want to find out what happens. Our hope is that the narratives will be so fiercely compelling that we can be less traditional in the way the visuals work. In many stories they'd be more impressionistic, more like a great rock video, more like Errol Morris, than anything on the TV newsmagazine and documentary programs. The visuals would work the way the background music works on our radio show—to intensify the feeling in the stories.

With me on this little adventure: A TV producer named Jed Alpert, filmmaker Bennett Miller (whose documentary *The Cruise* is one of my favorite films and very close to the spirit of *This American Life*: It's funny and moving and surprising and just beautiful to look at—black and white, shot on the cheap with all natural light on digital video, incredibly), and Ann Blanchard, who's an agent from William Morris, a woman I've met only over the phone but who seems to understand *This American Life* as well as I could ever dream.

We've all talked a bit on the phone about how to structure our pitch. Ann and Jed are pushing toward high-concept ideas like "It's the next step for reality programming on television" or "It's reality programming, done with the compelling narrative arc of fictional TV dramas." All true enough, I guess, though I suppose we should come up with a snappier way to say that second idea, before our meetings start at 10 tomorrow.

When I arrived here in L.A. tonight, I was picked up at the airport by a man who met me at the gate and drove me to the hotel. This is not the way I usually live. He wanted to carry my bags to the car, and I was so stunned by this that at first I didn't let him. Then I let him carry one. I carried two. I know that's completely idiotic, but I couldn't help myself.

His name was Lionel, and he's just moved to L.A. from Hawaii this year. At first it was hard to adjust, he said, he was so used to "island living." That's his actual phrase. I pressed him for details on "island living," but all I got out of him was that he used to go to the beach every day to run and work out, and that he has this huge and I mean huge family that got together most weekends to hang out. Hawaii, though, is like a small town. You get to a certain age and you want to leave. It's too dull. Before he moved here, he'd visited L.A. on vacation. The thought never occurred to me before: Where do people who live in Hawaii go on vacation? What is the even-more-like-paradise place they'd go for a break from all that lush loveliness and perfect weather? The answer, according to Lionel, is often Vegas.

We talked the whole ride. He never heard of my radio show and asked if it was like Howard Stern and I nearly told him it was, not wanting to disappoint him with the truth. I asked him what celebrities he'd had in his car, and because he's so new at it, all the names were TV producers I'd never heard of. He did seem to have some inside information on *Baywatch* moving to Hawaii, but after a while, talking about this stuff reminded me of the only thing I don't like about Los Angeles. I find the business side of movies and TV—the grosses, the ratings, the stories about how much stuff costs and how much it makes, all that stuff that fills the pages of so many magazines and so many hours of TV time—I find it all completely boring. And here everyone's always talking about it.

I have to admit, though, I did enjoy chatting with Lionel. And as I got out of the car, I thought about something Matt Groening, the creator of *The Simpsons*, said years ago somewhere. He said he realized he'd made it when he no longer felt obliged to make conversation with the limo drivers.

I cannot imagine that ever happening to me.

POSTED   Tuesday, June 8, 1999, at 7:43 A.M. PT

Over breakfast, our little team reviews what should be said in what order at the four pitch meetings we have scheduled for the day.

Ann, the agent from William Morris, tells Jed and Bennett and me that some execs at these meetings will have actually prepared for the meetings. They'll have listened to tapes she's sent of *This American Life* and watched Bennett's film. But many of them won't have prepared. It's our job, she says, to politely ignore it if they know nothing about our work.

Ann explains: The way one handles this situation is to tell them everything you think they need to know about your work, prefaced with the phrase "As you know already."

"*Everything* in this town is pitched with the phrase 'as you know already,'" Ann declares, between bites of omelette.

We talk about what each of the networks we're pitching is probably looking for. The WB only wants a younger demographic. A third of Showtime's audience is African-American. This goes on for a while and finally Bennett pipes up. "Not to be crude, but isn't there some part of their brains that's concerned with winning awards and getting critical acclaim? Wouldn't they view this as an opportunity to buy themselves some integrity?"

That's the spirit.

At our first network meeting, the execs all start to lose interest when I say the word "pretty." This is Ann and Jed's diagnosis in a coffee shop afterwards. They could feel the mood in the room change, and soon execs were talking about programming the show at midnight on Sunday night, if at all. That is the power of the word "pretty" to strike fear in men's hearts.

I used the word in response to a direct question. An exec who listens regularly to *This American Life* talked about the fact that one thing that's exciting about the radio show is that one doesn't see the people in the stories. One is left to imagine moments that are described. Could we retain that feeling in a television version of the show?

I replied that I thought we could if the pictures for some of the stories were more impressionistic, more suggestive. If they were more like a rock video, more pretty, less like *60 Minutes*.

That scared them, Ann said afterwards. It made it sound too arty. Arty is bad. By the end of the meeting, she and Jed turned it around, mostly by talking emotionally about making something entirely new on television, something as compelling as a great TV drama, with the irresistible narrative arc of a TV drama, but that happens to be nonfiction. Bennett argued that the current TV newsmagazines all seem to have a rather moribund and formalized sense of how to tell a story. I talked about a TV story I saw on Civil War re-enactors. The researchers who worked on the story had found interesting people to interview, but none of these interviewees stays in the report for very long. The story just flits from person to person. Incredibly, they even found an African-American woman who joins the Civil War re-enactments as a slave. But even she gets only a few moments in the report. There's no space for us to actually get to know anyone, and hear the real story of what happened to them and how it changed them. We never get to know anyone well enough that we can imagine what it'd be like to be in their situation. We never feel much empathy at all.

We continued on these lines for a while, then Ann brought up the idea of winning lots of awards, and soon the meeting was at an end.

Afterward in the coffee shop, we reworked the pitch. Ann told me that like anyone else, these execs need to be spoken to in their own language. That we need to compare what we're proposing to 20/20 and *ER* and *The Sopranos*.

So, what to do about "pretty"—the word that nearly scotched the deal? How to avoid the word "impressionistic"? What should we say if we're asked again what the show will look like?

We brainstormed, all of us, for a while, five minutes or so.

Finally here's what we came up with. Instead of saying the shots will be pretty, we'd say: "In contrast to TV newsmagazines, this show will not be shot on video but on film. We'll have a real director of photography, just like a movie has, to create more dramatic effects."

"Say 'more dramatic,' not 'more artful.'" Ann and Jed warn me. "Say whatever you want. Just don't say 'pretty.'"

Three hours later we're driving across town to another pitch meeting, and we pass the Will Rogers Park. It's all palm trees and bright, gorgeous flowers under a perfect sky.

"That's pretty," I say.

From the back seat Jed declares, "Ira! That word!"

In the driver's seat, steering gently, not moving his eyes off the road, Bennett gently suggests, "I think what you mean to say, Ira, is that the park's shot on film."

POSTED Wednesday, June 9, 1999, at 8:18 A.M. PT

We visit six networks and two production companies. I'm struck by how normal most of the people seem, how unlike the Hollywood stereotypes, how similar to my colleagues on *All Things Considered* and *Morning Edition*. At least on the surface.

The money in Hollywood—and what it buys—is sort of stunning. At dinner my first night in town I meet a screenwriter I like very much who seems like any of a dozen magazine writers I know in Chicago and New York. I'm told later that he's one of the many people who make a living here writing screenplays that never get made into movies. The price for his last screenplay? A quarter-million dollars.

The number is hard to fathom. The year we put *This American Life* on the air (just four years ago), my staff and I did an entire year of shows for less than that: $243,000 covered all our expenses — outfitting the studio, paying freelance writers and reporters, buying satellite time to distribute the show to stations, all our meager marketing costs, and our four salaries. It was bare-bones, even by public radio standards, but workable.

When I describe this budget to Ann and Jed, they ask me not to mention it in any meetings with anyone in the state of California.

For the record, Showtime's offices aren't as nice as NPR's in Washington. New Regency's digs — including the production offices for its hit show *Buffy the Vampire Slayer* — have the friendly handed-down-furniture, makeshift air of a not terribly well-funded congressional race in Iowa. Bare linoleum floors. Fluorescent light.

Everywhere else is lovely, and you feel the wealth that permeates it all. At every meeting some assistant offers us a choice of beverages, a custom I did not observe once in a decade at NPR's headquarters in Washington. There's beautiful original art on the walls and valet parking downstairs. When agents at William Morris park their cars in the agency's lot, attendants wash the cars, handle maintenance, fill the tanks with gas. An agent recently ran out of gas on the freeway simply because he'd been running from meeting to meeting for two days and hadn't stopped in the office. He'd apparently fallen out of the habit of pulling over at a gas station.

It is my second day in Los Angeles, and I'm called by a reporter from *Entertainment Weekly* who wants to possibly include me in the magazine's annual list of "The 100 Most Creative People in Hollywood." I've been here for less than 48 hours. Word travels fast. I tell this story to Doug Herzog, the guy who picked up *South*

Park for Comedy Central, who recently moved out here from New York to head the Fox Network, and he says that for the first week you're in Hollywood, everyone thinks you're a creative genius. Then everyone decides you're just like them.

POSTED Thursday, June 10, 1999, at 9:20 A.M. PT

The network where we had that glorious second meeting called. They want to make a commitment, have another date, move to the next step. No word yet from anyone else.

I flew back to Chicago on the red-eye, got into work late, met with the staff about whether we should construct an entirely new Father's Day show this year, or build one out of a combination of new and old stories. We have nine days to get it together, whichever we decide.

Tonight I moderated an event at the School of the Art Institute of Chicago featuring Lawrence Weschler and J. S. G. Boggs. Weschler's a friend; Boggs is the subject of his new book. Boggs is an artist who draws money. He draws only one side of a bill. But he doesn't sell these drawings. Instead, he takes a drawing of, say, a $20 bill out with him to a restaurant, and when it comes time to pay the check, he tries to talk the waitress into accepting the drawing of $20 as his payment. He explains that the value of any work of art is set arbitrarily, so he's decided to set the value of the drawing of a $20 bill at $20. If she accepts the drawing she'll have to give him change and a receipt.

Many people don't accept the drawing. Some do. If they do, the next day Boggs provides a copy of the receipt to one of the many people who collect his work, and that person will come hunting down the drawing. The collector will pay hundreds or thousands of dollars for the little drawing. The waitress will clean up.

What I love about this is that it's a con game, run in reverse. If the person falls for the game, they come out of it far wealthier than they went in. As Weschler puts it in his joyous little book, Boggs operates "a sort of floating aesthetical ethical crap game. Or else a sort of fairy-tale virtue test, in which the worthy agreed to sacrifice and [are] subsequently rewarded a hundredfold."

At the beginning of our presentation at the Art Institute, Boggs produced a copy of the Chicago yellow pages. He asked the audience for the name of a local pizza place. On his cell phone he called and ordered some pizzas. When they arrived at the theater, he asked the delivery guy up onstage, and tried to pay for the food with a drawing of a $50 bill. It was, frankly, a little uncomfortable. The guy delivering the pizzas suddenly found himself standing on a stage, lots of people watching, being asked to make a decision: Did he want Boggs to give him $50 in real cash—or did he want the drawing instead? He broke out in a sweat. All the poor guy knew is that if he didn't show up back at work with real American currency to cover those pizzas he took out, he'd be in trouble. He turned down the deal. It was hard not to jump in and just tell him: "You can make a thousand dollars here! Take the drawing!"

In retrospect, I realize I should have altered the game a little, still within Boggs' rules. I could've pulled a $10 bill from my wallet, got three people from the audience to pull 10's from their wallets, and suggested to the pizza guy that if he had $10, we could buy the picture together. He might've been carrying $10 on him. I think Boggs is completely original and inspiring, but asking the pizza guy to front $50 for a drawing might've been a lot to expect. I mean, *I've* never paid $50 for a drawing.

Boggs' signature at this point is worth a fair amount of money to collectors, when affixed to the right objects. You can download a Boggs bill from his Web site for free and, if you find him, he'll sign it and you can sell it for more than $300 to collectors. After the evening's presentation, many people came up to him asking him to sign this or that. Boggs has a strict policy: He charges $10 per autograph.

A 9-year-old boy in the crowd named Chris Meskauskas really

wanted an autograph and invented a scheme to get one. As we adults yammered on during the lecture, Chris got an Art Institute brochure and drew his own $10 bill on the blank back side of it. He copied from a ten-spot he borrowed from his dad. His drawing was in purple pen, and twice the size of a regular $10 bill, but Boggs examined it, showed Chris how to draw a plate number onto a bill, and then accepted Chris' drawing as worth $10 and gave him the autograph. Chris beamed. But that's only because he's too young to have understood our explanation of how much trouble he could get in if he continues down this path of drawing his own money.

Boggs is in enormous trouble with the Treasury Department. Specifically the Secret Service. For most of this decade they've been confiscating his work, harassing him, claiming they're going to build a big counterfeiting case against him but never doing it.

Of course, they never do it. When these cases against Boggs have gone to trial in other countries, he's always won handily. Juries conclude that he's not counterfeiting. No one could mistake his drawings for real bills: They're blank on one side! (Well, blank except for his signature and fingerprint.) He also sometimes monkeys with the wording on the bills, the portraits, and the color (he makes them orange).

Not long ago, Boggs sued the government, saying they were subjecting him to a campaign of harassment and that either they had to bring him to trial on some sort of charges, or they had to return the hundreds of works of his art they'd confiscated. The case has worked its way up to the Supreme Court. He's waiting to find out if they'll hear the case. If they don't, then it'll mean the government is in fact free to just take his property and never bring a trial, ever. I don't feel like I'm leaving the territory of journalistic objectivity to say that somehow this does not seem fair. Our government is seizing his property without any trial, any chance to argue his case, any due process at all.

He's trying to generate some press about all this, but so far the attention he's got is modest.

What's crazy about the whole thing is that he's convinced he'd have stopped drawing U.S. currency years ago, because he's got tired of it, but now he has to keep doing it to keep his income up for this lawsuit. The money drawings are the only thing he creates that earns him the kind of real cash he needs right now. But he's weary of drawing money. He's tried every variation on it. He's ready to move on to other kinds of artistic creation.

In short: If the Treasury Department weren't harassing him, trying to bully him into quitting his money drawings, he'd have quit years ago.

There's some government policy the Clinton administration can be proud of.

We all went out to dinner together after the event at the Art Institute, and Erin Hogan of the University of Chicago Press (which is publishing Weschler's book about Boggs) informed me that as a former Hawaii resident that the place Hawaiians go on vacation is not Vegas but Northern California. Marin County. Hawaiians go there, she said, because they like the changes in landscape and because they like the "dramatic weather." By this she meant "bad weather." Back home the weather's the same every day, she told me. Eighty degrees, rains twice a day. They didn't even do weather forecasts during the nightly news when she lived there. Which is, as far as I can tell, exactly the way we're all going to have it in the Kingdom of Heaven during the Afterlife.

Then somehow we got onto the subject of everyone's first jobs, and she revealed that her first job was as a foot model for Liberty House of Hawaii—an old department store on the islands. An art director on the beach noticed her high arches, and she got the cushy-if-dull $8-an-hour gig. Now be honest: Who among us hears a story like that and doesn't ask to see the woman's feet? After much urging from many adults at our table, Erin showed us her feet. They were, we all had to admit, very impressive.

Then Boggs' 23-year-old girlfriend, Meghan, told me about the part she recently played on the *Mortal Combat* TV show. She was

Mileena, the evil ugly twin sister of Kitana, the lovely princess. For this job Meghan got to wear a pink pleather lace-up halter-top bustier with matching choker. She pushed her breasts together with her palms as she explained this, and when I asked again later, so I could write it down, she pushed her breasts together with her palms again. She also got knee-high boots for the part. They would not let her wear the outfit home for her boyfriend. Also on the negative side, the job required that they put a lot of makeup on her face to make her ugly, she told me. People treated her differently, she said.

Meanwhile, Boggs circled the table taking pictures with his new digital camera, which he enjoys with the undisguised pleasure of a kid with a new toy.

It was all very fun. I was glad to be back in Chicago, back home in my normal life, in the high-minded world of public broadcasting.

Allegra Goodman

Allegra Goodman's most recent book is Kaaterskill Falls.

POSTED Tuesday, April 15, 1997, at 4:30 P.M. PT

I am working late, burning the midnight oil, as my father used to call it. He would come in and check on me when I was staying up late in high school. I sat at my small dark desk with the big lamp shining down in its big lampshade and I worked. My desk faced the window, but it was dark outside, and all I could see was the lights of an occasional car as it eased its way past our house. We lived on a small street, and no one drove by in a hurry. "Just remember," my father would say, "there is a point of diminishing returns." My father is a morning person.

There is something grand and melancholy about working alone at night. The darkness in the window and the quiet house set the stage for the lone figure at the desk. I always feel diligent and lonely and a little sorry for myself. I almost never work at night anymore. I don't have the burden of homework, or the luxury of waking myself. My children wake me every morning, early. But I am going to New York tomorrow, and I have to give a speech there. I haven't written the speech yet. I have left it to the last minute. Now I am fighting sleep. The house is warm. My children are snoring, looking much smaller in their beds than they do when they are awake. My children's days are all separate. They have no appointments or assignments. It would be good to lie down next to them among their stuffed animals, to curl up with their bears and rabbits and the stuffed dolphin.

This must be the point of diminishing returns. Besides, my husband needs to use the computer. His evening has just begun. My husband really is a night person.

POSTED   Thursday, April 17, 1997, at 4:30 P.M. PT

This afternoon I gave my hastily written talk for the ladies' luncheon in Long Island. I wrote most of it on the plane from Boston. I was supposed to speak about the Jewish family, and so I did. I illustrated my points by reading selections from my fiction in *The Family Markowitz*. Some of the ladies seemed to find this confusing. They were a group of 200 women, ranging in age from 50 to 80, and their chairwoman looked at me with my book in my hands and said to me dourly before I got up to speak, "I hope you're not going to give a book review." Fortunately, as I read, much of the audience laughed heartily and seemed to enjoy the performance. However, I could see during the question-and-answer period that these women did not want to know about my fictional portrait of a Jewish family. They wanted to know about my family, and my parents. How I grew up, and how I raised my children. It was facts they were after, not imagination. Truth, not fiction. But there was one question about a detail in my book.

"What made you think of using Tilden High School as the school Ed and Henry attended in the 1950s?" "Well," I said, "my grandfather taught there a long time ago."

"What was his name?" the ladies asked me.

"Joseph Schwartzbach."

A shriek went up from the back of the room. "I had him! I had your grandfather for French!" There was delighted clapping at this. Almost as much applause as there had been when the raffle winner was announced at lunch.

I smiled from the podium, but somehow I felt like crying. My grandfather has been dead for more than 20 years, and his wife, my grandmother, was gone, and—this was what I felt most keenly— his daughter, my mother, died six months ago. I was standing there before 200 women, and one of them remembered my grandfather. And even his house was gone, and all his things long sold and given away. I just laughed with the audience and went on to the next question, but I wanted to sit down. The woman's shriek of recognition overwhelmed me somehow. Her remembering and my loss.

POSTED   Friday, April 18, 1997, at 4:30 P.M. PT

Late this afternoon I fell asleep because I was so tired from my trip and all the catching up I've had to do since then. The window was open and it was raining, and as I drifted off I heard a bird calling. I began to dream I was in Hawaii again, in the house where I grew up. The warm, damp spring air, the rain, and the bird all reminded me of Hawaii. As a child I always slept with the windows open and felt the warm breeze. The mynah birds calling to each other woke me each morning.

But today, when I opened my eyes, I was not in Hawaii. The rain had stopped, and the bird outside my window was a glossy black crow. I wanted to close my eyes again and bring back the dream, and imagine myself back in the house in Niu Valley with its grapefruit and tangerine trees; the big oversexed mango tree that produced hundreds of mangos three times a year. We could never get rid of them all. And all our neighbors had mango trees too. There wasn't a soul on the island needing mangos. I wanted to be there again. I remembered it all so clearly. Every bit of the house and the lanai where we had our Passover Seders, all the china and silver laid out formally in open air. If I were there again, my father would read me stories each night, and my mother would be alive.

I got up and looked around me and I was grown up, and this was my house. I cleaned up and made phone calls, and worked on clearing my desk. Still, I felt homesick. At last I went out into our tiny city garden. We have one tree, a Japanese maple, and a baby rose bush about a foot high that is meant some day to cascade over the fence, and we have daffodils just starting to open, and a little patch of grass. It is nothing like the garden my parents had. Still, the plants were soaking up the rain; stems and grass blades were turning green.

Lakshmi Gopalkrishnan

Lakshmi Gopalkrishnan, a former copy chief at Slate, *wrote this while visiting her family in Kerala, India. She is now the lead site manager for Microsoft Office.*

POSTED Monday, July 14, 1997, at 4:30 P.M. PT

Beef blood, I discovered this morning, doesn't dissolve in the rain. Not for a while, anyway. Eventually, it is washed off the way almost everything is at this time of year, during Kerala's monsoon. The rain has been relentless these last three weeks—not the leaky-faucet drippings I'm used to in Seattle, but umbrella-annihilating stuff that scoops snakes out of holes and into homes, that smells earth-fresh for the first few minutes, then takes on the fine stench of rotting mangoes, dead cats, and whatnot—good things gone bad.

But the blood tripping over the steps of the beef shop opposite my parents' apartment building smells clean. Ribby bulls are slaughtered there early each morning and, going for a walk today, I saw the fluid flow fresh for a second, then become crusty, corded, protuberant. The vadose rush thinned the red edges, chipped at the ceramic slickness, and the steps were suddenly clean. Tomorrow's beef is tethered opposite the shop—that is to say, in an unused courtyard adjacent to this building, tied to a tree stump, its field of vision dominated by the meat hooks opposite. I see the hooks, too —my room looks right onto the courtyard.

Rain has taken over more than the landscape. The papers are abuzz, as are such phone lines as are still working. Each visitor has his or her own crisis to report, and each is more than mildly competitive in the telling. "Woke up and found 10 inches of water in my room," said one. "My mother-in-law spent 24 hours on a treetop," said another, grateful for it. "Stepped on a dead puppy that had floated into the room," said a third. (She was so freaked out that she didn't go to teach today—unbelievably, colleges and schools are still open.) Snake stories abound. The dead-puppy woman made it to her doorway, then found a clutch of kraits (a particularly venomous class of snake) looking in, contemplating a move to higher, drier ground. (She claims they are kraits, anyway, but the rains have made a krait, or two or three or four, of every grass snake and centipede.)

However, the visits, the hordes of people "dropping by" to chat, haven't stopped, much to my chagrin. If cars can't ply—and they can't in several areas—boats do. Catamarans and paddleboats are doing brisk business on low-lying streets, and buses, their drivers thrilling in the opportunity to splash one and all, will not be deterred. So the visitors come, and tea must be made and stories told. I have no rain tales of my own, being tucked away on the sixth floor, far from the froth and flume. I could tell them about my housefly-swatting technique, which I've perfected over the last few days, but I don't think they'd be interested. Flies are a poor match for kraits, and it's too hot to embellish anyway.

POSTED Wednesday, July 16, 1997, at 4:30 P.M. PT

They say South Pier will collapse any day now. It's a few centuries old, one of two moldering black structures that mark the beach close to my parents' home. My mother grew up in this town, Calicut, and can remember catching crabs under that pier with my grandfather. Too small to be cooked, the crabs would be fed to her chickens. The chickens didn't make it to the table either—they were raised as pets. So the crabs got the short end of that stick, but their dead weren't talking. The translucent hordes kept coming, and the chickens eventually died of old age. Those were the pier's glory days, days when dhows laced winter horizons, their holds full of dates and attar and the like. Today's Arab traders prefer air travel, though, and the pier lies abandoned. The sea seems determined to reclaim that part of the beach, and there's little doubt that it will succeed. No one seems to care, though people talk about it all the time: There is too much putrefying history here, all of it eons old, for South Pier's wheezing black posts to make a strong case for survival.

I'm told you get the best view of the pier from the parapet that runs the length of the beach. I haven't tested that claim myself—the wall, you see, is overrun at all times by "Eve teasers," idlers intent on harassing female strollers. The precise nature of these men's attentions varies: My neighbor claims that one Lothario grabbed at her breast, and I keep hearing stories about exposed penises. I have no nipple pinchings or penis sightings to report, but am careful to stay with my friends if I'm in the area. One remains vulnerable to comments, however, and of these there are several. The wallfolk are vocal, as are fishermen returning from market, their catch sold, bikes loaded with empty boxes tracking slime. I barely understand their patois, and incomprehension inures me somewhat. What I do understand I sometimes find incredibly funny, actually (the humor is lost in the translation, so you'll have to take my word for it)—but to laugh is to invite trouble.

Had no option this morning, though. Walking with my friends on an overpass close to the beach, I stopped to look at an abutting wall thick with movie posters. South India's film establishments, while no match for Hollywood's, are prolific, and they are known for three kinds of films: artsy-fartsy parallel cinema, hugely successful commercial soap, and softcore sleaze. I'm not sure where

Miss Madras, one of the movies being advertised on the wall, would fall—but the poster would suggest the last category. It showed an improbably buxom woman supine, her lips pursed, legs spread, knees bent, feet crossed at the ankles, the words "Miss Madras" strung between her thighs in a pungent pink. Picture it. There was a man somewhere in the shot, I believe—but I wasn't looking. Nor were these two fishermen who roared up on a motorbike, then stopped abruptly by the wall. They stared at the woman for a few minutes, saying nothing, oblivious of the three of us watching them from above. Then one of them gathered up the free end of his lungi (the saronglike garment favored by men here), spat into it, and rubbed fiercely at the woman's crotch. The entire crotch promptly disappeared. No less good-humored for her loss, she continued to smile wetly. The men left as abruptly as they had arrived. No words exchanged but enough said.

Karenna Gore

Karenna Gore wrote this while working as an editorial assistant at Slate. She is a recent graduate of Columbia Law School and chair of GoreNet, a network of young Al Gore supporters.

POSTED Monday, Jan. 20, 1997, at 4:30 P.M. PT

I am hiding from my eighth-grade English teacher—she's downstairs, along with hundreds of other celebrants, to kick off the inaugural weekend. Having just emerged from my post-red-eye stupor (Seattle to "the other Washington"), I innocently slumped downstairs for some coffee, right into an episode of *This Is Your Life*—my old next-door neighbors, long-lost cousins, the veterinarian who revived my dog Coconut after her brush with death. The surreal quality is enhanced by the characters who step out of my television world and into my living room. I just discussed withdrawal from Seattle lattes with the actress who played the mother in *National Lampoon's Vacation*.

My house, the Naval Observatory—"the compound" or "Twin Anchors" as we like to call it—is completely decked out for the occasion. The tents in the yard are attached to the house by plastic tubes, the deck is encased in clear insulation, volunteers march around purposefully. Times like this remind me of the scene at the end of *E.T.* when the government takes over Elliot's home and he and E.T. lie side by side on cold metal tables, exposed and shivering.

Not that I'm complaining. Any disadvantage of being the daughter of the vice president pales next to the experiences and opportunities that come my way. The itinerary for this weekend is a chock-full reminder of that and, as I was driven home from the airport at 5 A.M., I admonished myself to appreciate and take advantage of this interesting period of my life.

The least I could do is come up with a better Secret Service code name. Ever since four years ago, when I was put on the spot and told "two syllables" and "It has to start with an s," I have been cringing in the back seat when identified as "Smurfette." I have to act on this now. Snowball? Skycap?

Inaugural plans have been haunting me for weeks, and I lurch between micro-management mode and lead-me-around-I'm-a-smiling-vegetable mode. The latter is definitely best for any event I go to with my parents. Like a lot of things in politics, my behavior can't be a strong positive, but could be an overwhelming negative. There actually isn't much I could accidentally do to mess up the ceremonies this year. I used to fear falling off the stage, but that has become pretty commonplace.

It's odd to put on spangly eveningwear at 3:30 P.M., but the Presidential Gala begins at 5 P.M. so they can edit the tape in time for prime time. I went to the rehearsal gala last night with a vanload of my friends, and we watched Stevie Wonder test the sound and some random woman in big glasses have her moment in the sun as a Gloria Estefan stand-in. The gala four years ago was a key moment in the tidal wave of change. First I heard my father was running for vice president (while I was in a hotel in Costa Rica); next I watched the election returns in Little Rock; and then I was arm in arm with Michael Jackson and Barbra Streisand on a big stage. Chuck Berry stepped on my foot. Tonight will be different—I have some idea of what to expect. Anyway, I have to hurry; the motorcade leaves in 10 minutes.

Orianda Guilfoyle

Orianda Guilfoyle filed this from the classifieds department at an alternative weekly in the Pacific Northwest. She's now a technical writer for a start-up.

POSTED Monday, Oct. 25, 1999, at 10:00 A.M. PT

Edna Tilley is reading me her ad for nude haircutting. "Do you like the proximity of a beautiful woman?" she dictates. "Next line: As she nurtures and shapes you. Bold: NUDE HAIRCUTTING." I never find out who is nude, Edna or the haircuttee—clients, as she prefers to call them. Edna charges the ad ($43.50) to her credit card and hangs up. By then I have two messages waiting in my inbox.

Today is deadline day in the Classifieds Department. The calls begin at 8 and do not cease all day. Many people have changes to make. They want to add a hyphen or change their phone number. I take hundreds of ads: We provide a unique form of physical therapy, using horses. You may be an experienced horse person or just have seen horses grazing on the side of the road.... 2BR condo for rent NS/NP [No smoking, no pets].... Local Lusty Ladies Seek Sex in the Next 5 Minutes.... At 4 P.M. our last ads will be entered in our rickety, DOS-based ad-taking program, and the Production Department will begin to lay out the ads. Until then, I'll stay by my phone and do my best to keep up with the constant flow of calls.

A hallway separates Classifieds (Classy) from Editorial, where I always thought I'd be. When I took this job, the publisher made no bones about what kind of work it entailed. "This is not a writing job," he warned, pointing to the publishing internships listed on my résumé. And then: "How do you feel about working with sexually explicit material?" I told him, fine, no problem, I was so not offended by that. In college, when I interned for a New York publishing house, I believed that I was "paying my dues" and that a bright editorial career was beckoning, full of expensed lunches at Michael's, book parties, and those blissful "early Fridays" of summer. Then, after graduation, I drove out here on a whim and my job prospects, both real and imagined, changed. Suddenly I found myself applying to be an "Account Executive" on the grounds it would spare me from the injustices and silent humiliations of administrative-assistantship—the puncture wounds of paperclips, the hovering of tyrannical office managers.

At 10:24, I'm behind on my voice mail, a frightening thought. Once you're behind on deadline day, it's extremely difficult to catch up. Not only do I have to return all calls, I have to re-solicit from a list of advertisers whose ads are expiring this week. It's rare to fall behind; I've pretty much mastered the art of controlling the conversation and gently getting people off the phone once I have those credit-card numbers. In my first week, I spent 45 minutes helping a self-described shaman decide if he should describe his business as "a place of healing" or a "counseling forum." I didn't have the heart to tell him that I'm working on commission and that the entire call would yield me 45 cents. Later, I was advised on ways to increase my turnaround. "Don't chat with them," a sassy middle-aged ad rep named TJ told me. I like TJ; I'm not sure if I trust her. I think she just stole one of my accounts, a display ad promising "Big, SQUEEZABLE women tonite!" When I figure out the commission at stake ($10), I decide to let the issue slide. Tensions get high when you point fingers, especially surrounding new accounts. We're a territorial bunch, here in Classy.

POSTED   Tuesday, Oct. 26, 1999, at 10:00 A.M. PT

The Internet was *made* for workers like me—on the phone all day —and no time is better than Tuesday morning, in the calm after yesterday's deadline storm. I spend 20 minutes e-touring a research station in Antarctica, peering into the tiny domiciles, personalized, like cubicles, with postcards and knickknacks. I imagine myself on the lonely continent, conducting vital scientific research, venturing out in the sub-zero temperatures to gather data. Then the phone rings: It's Bill Bicks calling to change the font size on his ad "Make Big $$$ From Home—Up to $2K/Week!" (I'm wondering if the folks in Antarctica have considered this for those long winter months.) Bill works for a company that goes by the misnomer GoodWork Management. They rotate their ads weekly: from phone sex to employment ads for collection agents to get-rich-quick schemes. When I tell him his four-line ad will run him about $12—and that's at the cheapest frequency rate the paper has to offer—he cries out, "Whoa! That's pretty pricey!" Bill's niggardliness and expressions of shock and outrage over sums under $20 earn him entry into my Golden Circle of Pain-in-the-Ass Advertisers—they're all so fun to hate. Last week, when I missed a space between two words, Bill called to report the error. "It's really the principle of it that bothers me, and I'm a principled person," he explained, demanding that I comp the ad for the next three weeks.

The calls trickle in all morning. Inevitably, someone has missed yesterday's deadline and believes he can beg, plead, or bully his way into the upcoming edition. Some people I feel genuinely bad for, and I regret informing them that their employment ad for a desperately needed nurse at an elderly care facility will have to wait for more than a week, as the seniors go without health services. For obvious reasons, I'm not allowed to tell these latecomers to put the ad in a daily paper, and it always surprises me how many people fail to recognize this option. As for the latter class of callers —expletive-spewing, I'm-going-to-talk-to-your-manager-threatening, and otherwise obnoxious — well, there's something quite delightful about mustering up my most saccharine voice and chirping: Sorry, the paper is already at the printers (lie). For the future our deadline is Monday, 4 P.M. sharp. Well, we're sorry you feel that way, as we consider you a most valued customer.

After lunch I begin "prospecting": making cold calls to businesses based on leads, other advertisements in our rival paper, or just a plain old hunch. My beat is health and real estate (although I do have my share of the "adult entertainers" such as Edna Tilley — more about them later). A lot of my advertisers in the health category straddle the lines between psychotherapist/New Age healer/psychic/mentor/yoga instructor. Some provide a deluxe package: therapy, incense, and a demonstration of the full lotus position. Today, I make calls out of the phone book. This week, I target New Age healers and throw in one cosmetic surgeon for good measure (ambitious, yes, but stranger things have happened). A lot of these "holistic professionals," as they like to be called, do business from home, and they all must be in session, because I hit voice mail every time. Voice mail must be the enemy of telemarketers everywhere. Just hit pound, and *poof!* We're erased.

At 3:15 I get a bite. The plastic surgeon who does hair-removal returns my call. She's interested in a display ad with a photo of a woman's long, shiny (hairless) legs. My department, Classifieds, sells line advertising (like the help-wanted section) and all the display advertising (larger ads that includes graphics) that appear in the back of the paper. The Display Department sells ads only into the main body of the paper, next to editorial content. Because we're a free publication, ads are our lifeblood — and they're everywhere. Once I explain the difference, damn, she opts for the front of the paper. Which means I'll have to transfer her to Display.

The separation between Classifieds and Display is emphasized by a physical separation — they are located on the other side of the building. After three months here, I still can't name one Display-ad rep, but I've heard they distinguish themselves by dressing better.

Display's clients are bigger, richer, and more respectable—a standard full-page announcement of a movie release being a classified-ad rep's pipe dream. There is secret resentment, talk of "switching over." We have Wet, Wild & Barely Legal. They have Cleaner, Brighter Teeth with Cosmetic Dentistry.

When I hit the street at 5:50 P.M., it's just started to rain. The unending rain in this city, I've found, is conducive to introspection. Self-criticism, to be exact. (Studies claim that this region produces an inordinate number of serial killers, suicides, and general laziness at work. I think it's due to the rain.) Tonight, I wonder about where this job will lead. Friends from college are in med school, joining the Peace Corps. New friends in this city are making millions at Internet start-ups. Lately, I've been feeling that I missed the bus and there's not another scheduled for a long, long time. I tell myself I'm learning valuable skills in salesmanship that will be with me in whatever career I ultimately choose to pursue. But then again, maybe this is a line I'm just selling myself.

POSTED Wednesday, Oct. 27, 1999, at 10:00 A.M. PT

Morning staff meeting at 10 A.M. Meet the four other Classy reps in my manager's office. He discusses how to pitch upcoming articles in the paper to our advertisers. Personally, I'm not good at coming up with the right angles. Like, *Hey, we're doing a story on militias in the Northwest, are you interested in buying space in our real estate section?* Maybe this just proves how much more I have to learn.

Everyone in the room is holding notepads and pens, including me. I've never actually written anything down in any of these meetings, and no one is taking notes today. As a group, we realize the importance of adhering to certain rituals of professionalism: arriving at meetings prepared with writing instruments, peppering conversation with talk of "the team" and "team goals," and never once uttering the word "prostitution"—favoring instead the sanitized term "adult entertainment." Some formality is necessary; it reminds us that despite whom we're selling to, we still have one foot (some days, more like a toe) planted firmly in the corporate world. We who traffic in magic love elixirs, hypnosis, and low-fee bankruptcy.

At 11:30, I get a call from "Ladies of Lust." They'd like to change the headline of their ad from "Ashleigh: 19 Years Old" to "Babs: Voluptuous 18-Year-Old." The adult entertainers, as a rule, are extremely demanding, requiring last-minute word changes and tinkering with their graphics, as in *I'm thinking I want the fleur-de-lis border this week, not the little hearts.* I've divided them into three categories: the pimps, the independents, and the corporations that masquerade as independents. "Veronica," for example, who says that she is a "Bored and Horny Housewife," is actually a corporation based in Tucson, which places ads for phone sex in thousands of classified venues throughout the United States (and beyond?). Tara, my account representative, is my only contact with this "housewife." Tara is courteous and conversational, her e-mails fluid and always spell-checked. Change "Barely Legal!!!" to "Barely Legal—JailBait!!" And please make that "Jail" with a capital J, and "Bait" with a capital B, no space, thank you.

Among the independents, there is Talya, who's been a "college freshman" for two years and counting, and Debbie, a bleach-blonde "model" about 25 pounds overweight. Neither looks remotely like a model/student, but one imagines that their patrons accept some degree of hyperbole. Generally, this group is the easiest to deal with, aside from breaks in advertising due to short jail terms, or recuperation following surgical enhancements. Or the occasions when Debbie appears in the office 20 minutes past deadline to pay in cash, a thick wad of 10- and 20-dollar bills. Or when she calls in and I can hear a baby wailing in the background.

The pimps, the least likable of the lot, are mostly men and most likely to bounce checks or give phony credit-card numbers. Processing credit cards actually can be fairly time consuming, espe-cially when you have to alert the customer that her card has been denied. One guy who calls himself Pacific, with no irony, has actu-ally slammed down the phone, only to call back another rep and try the same card number. Another guy wigs out when I inform him that, no, photographs may not include exposed nipples or gen-italia. I ask my boss how much revenue actually comes from adult ads. His answer: "A lot."

I return from an afternoon coffee run to three messages from massage therapists. There's a controversy brewing in the massage-therapy community over the definition of "sensual massage." By law, anyone advertising massage services must have a license and provide the license number in the ad. We require this of all mas-sage advertisers—but the problem is, in addition to massage, some provide other services (headlines like "Massage Man & Master" should offer some clue). Legitimate massage therapists are sick of getting calls from johns, and the state doesn't enforce the regula-tion. We don't have the resources to check the authenticity of every license number, find out exactly what they're selling, and so forth. So the "sensual" masseuse types charging $250 per hour run next to the actual massage therapists, charging $60 per hour. I spend 10 minutes trying to console one recent massage-school graduate. Her training at an accredited massage school cost her thousands of dollars, and now, after two years of school, and state certification, she gets calls from men who angrily hang up on her when she informs them that she does not offer *special services*.

Then I feel like a traitor when I have to call "Massage Man & Master" back to renew his ad.

Daniel Handler

Daniel Handler is the author of two novels, The Basic Eight *and* Watch Your Mouth, *and writes the children's books "A Series of Unfortunate Events" under the name Lemony Snicket.*

POSTED   Monday, April 24, 2000, at 10:00 A.M. PT

Sometimes Sundays feel like a lifestyle commercial, and this is one of them: pajamas, coffee, a smoothie in a wedding-gift glass, my wife at one end of the couch with the crossword, and me giggling at something she said. The couch, maybe, or the coffee, or something invisible like investments or a dot-com: They could sell anything with this. We're both white and happy. We haven't had a lifestyle commercial morning in several weekends due to a heap of dead-lines: Lisa is an art director and had some free-lance layouts some-body needed right away, and I had a book overdue. Our past few weekends, we were scurrying around the apartment making each other look at things: Is this done? Laundry piled up; we left takeout cartons open on the counter so we could sneak back for a few bites. Now our first drafts are done and we are relaxed enough to feel as languid as catalog snapshots. I have a pile of CDs I've been waiting to play when it got a little calmer around our apartment.

The overdue book is called *The Ersatz Elevator*. In it, the Baudelaire children—Violet, Klaus, and Sunny—are adopted by a loathsome nouveau-riche couple who organize an auction. The auctioneer calls himself Gunther, but he is really Count Olaf in disguise and has two of the kidnapped Quagmire Triplets locked in a cage at the bottom of a secret passageway. If you can't follow this, you probably haven't read the five books that precede it in "A Series of Unfortunate Events," a collection of children's books I write under the name Lemony Snicket. In each book, the three Baudelaires encounter a number of unpleasantries that I can't believe a large corporation like HarperCollins believes are suitable for young people. I first pitched the idea to my pal and now editor, Susan Rich, over sidecars at a small dark bar. The idea was something of a joke; after writing my first novel, *The Basic Eight*, under my own name, I had an urge to write a mock-gothic novel—you know, a mysterious stranger, an innocent damsel, a bog, somebody locked in the attic, the whole bit. I had just tossed this idea out when Susan called and told me about her new job. She owed me some sidecars after I helped her drown her sorrows when she got sacked from her old job. Sidecars taste like candy: brandy, Cointreau, and lime juice, and the small dark bar liked to add a dusting of sugar around the rim of the glass. All that candy in the dark made the gothic novel turn into something for children: dark, dark books, as dark as the books I wanted to read, but could never find, when I was 11 and finally turned to Agatha Christie and V.C. Andrews rather than the fluff the librarians suggested. The small dark bar is now closed and the mock-gothic novel is now a projected 13-book series, the sixth installment of which was absolutely, I mean absolutely, Daniel, please please please give it to us, or else the illustrator won't possibly have enough time, please please please won't you please finish it by Friday. And I did, Seders and all. Now it's Sunday and Susan is reading it over the weekend. Truman Capote said that finishing a book is like taking a child out to the backyard and shooting it in the head, but I like kids. There's a little postpartum, but mostly I want to hear all about his first day at school. A nagging feeling about something in Chapter 5 makes me think that little Johnny might get his ass kicked, or maybe the queasiness in my stomach is only what comes from having too much matzo.

In the afternoon, the queasiness returns when I'm checking the galley proofs for the British publication of *The Basic Eight*. They've assured me that all the typos have been weeded out, but on the first page my mother's name in the acknowledgments is spelled "324" instead of "Sandra."

POSTED Tuesday, April 25, 2000, at 11:00 A.M. PT

Mondays I take a groggy, ill-lit train out of New York and teach a writing class at Wesleyan University, my alma mater, a weekly reminder that I am not a college student, by any stretch of the imagination, not by a long shot, no. I just turned 30 and still feel like I'm pretty much straight out of college, that my days slacking glumly around San Francisco and lollygagging around New York, while years in duration, only amount to a couple of new articles of clothing and a small jaded glaze around the eyes, maturity-wise. It ain't so. My students are skinny little things and wear Guatemalan pants. They write things down on their hands. When they drive me to the train station they're listening to music that, um, sounds like noise. My friends told me that I'd develop crushes on them, but something has happened to me, and I cannot have a crush on anyone who might not, 100 percent of the time, wear shoes when walking out of one building and down three tree-lined blocks to another building, no matter what the weather, no matter how difficult it is to find the shoes underneath the futon that my wife and I gave away — we gave it away — and, instead of giving our money to Amnesty International, bought a big bed, on a bed frame and everything, like grown-ups sleep in, and we did this without hesitation. I do not have crushes on these people. They say "good morning" when they arrive for class, because they have just woken up. The class begins at 1 P.M.

And the thing is this: I attended Wesleyan. I graduated during the decade that I still think of as happening now, although it isn't. I watch one of my students walk in wearing a T-shirt so ripped that I wouldn't use it to put furniture polish, which I own, on my table, which I did not take from a pile on a street corner, or even buy at a yard sale and throw in the back of a truck I borrowed from a guy in my ethnomusicology class, but simply purchased, at a store. I ask him what's written on his T-shirt. He doesn't know, and I remember, suddenly, a party I attended in college that got too hot. I was wearing, probably, a black turtleneck, and, if memory serves—and memory always serves when mortifying moments are on the menu—a pair of wire-rim glasses with clear glass in the frames. The party was held by a dance major, as all the best parties were. We were all dancing to music that would have sounded like noise to hopelessly square people in their 30s, had any been in attendance. It got too hot. I asked the dance major for something to wear instead of my turtleneck and he gave me a hopelessly ripped T-shirt with a poem painted on it. I wore the T-shirt home and kept it, because it was comfortable, ventilated, and cool. I remember how it looked, the hole in the armpit so gaping that I sometimes put my head through it when I overslept and had to run to my 1 P.M. class, throwing on my most comfortable T-shirt and a pair of shoes if I could find them; but get this, I never read the poem that was printed on the shirt I used to wear all the time, my cool shirt from the dance major's party. It is astonishing to me, that I dared to do these things and scarcely thought of them as things at all, let alone dares. My students give me this nostalgia freely; they don't need it. His shirt reads "PIKEY," I think; the felt-tip ink has smudged a little.

It's a nonfiction class, which is a blessing, because I have to read the stuff and sometimes it's bad. Bad undergraduate fiction is derivative and pretentious; bad nonfiction is a gossip, and who doesn't want to read that on the train back to New York? They write about everything, everything, with such wide-eyed joy that it's an

insult to call them unflinching—they don't think to flinch, they
don't know that flinching will be desired of them, along with
shoes. They come out. They hate their parents. They throw open
each other's dorm rooms and break up, down six beers, stay up all
night talking about vegetarianism and masturbating, never thinking of the vivid mental images they might conjure up when they
turn this all in. They've worked in sugar plantations and strip
clubs. They've read Jack Kerouac nine times and never heard of
Virginia Woolf. They're in a glam-rock band and never heard of
Roxy Music. They're wealthy, but they've been thrown out of the
house. Their friends are in prison, in the hospital, in magazines, 6
feet under, they don't have any friends. They show up at my office
and bring me paragraphs they wrote in the middle of the night.
They bring me five versions of a 10-page paper and ask me which
is the best one. They want to know how William Maxwell did that
thing, how Joan Didion did that other thing, how they can write
like David Foster Wallace but about love instead of a Caribbean
cruise, like Elizabeth Gilbert but about a divorce instead of working
in a bar. Over and over they say, "I want it to be good."

Me too.

Beck Hansen

Beck Hansen is an award-winning musician whose work includes Mellow Gold, Odelay, Mutations, *and* Midnite Vultures. *He filed this while on tour.*

POSTED Monday, May 26, 1997, at 4:30 P.M. PT

We woke up in Chicago after a long overnight from Minneapolis. I climbed out of my bunk on our tour bus and got my bag and stepped out into the icy morning. Foul weather has followed us for six months now. Where it's supposed to be spring, it suddenly turns to rain and cold when we arrive. We are hungry for any sign of sun or warmth.

I got into the hotel as quick as possible. The lobby was full of commotion. The holiday weekend was in evidence. Families were crammed into elevators. Out-of-towners were gathered for farm conventions.

I was trying to adjust to the hustle and activity all around. We were all groggy and slow, collecting ourselves in the lobby. Though we'd slept all night, it wasn't restful. Sleep on a bus is never restful. The continual jostling of the road and hum of the engine keeps one in a state of half-sleep and weary semiconsciousness. It's a very specific kind of sleep. If you look into the eyes of a touring musician, you can see that look, which only comes from having slept on buses for months on end. There is a tacit sympathy between those who recognize that look in each other's eyes. It is a look of imminent maniacal laughter and abject resignation.

Actually, it isn't as bad as all that, but for the 20 minutes or so after one wakes up on a bus and stumbles into a new town, it feels MUCH WORSE. But we have developed rituals to soothe ourselves while out on the road. In Chicago, we repair to a certain diner on Halsted and order ourselves an apple pancake of epic proportions, which we feast mightily upon and afterward feel satisfied that it was a job well done.

In the afternoon we rode out to the New World Music Amphitheater to play at a festival put on by a local radio station, Q101. We are currently on a tour of "radio shows." Several times a year modern rock stations all across the country put on such festivals, where bands who fall under the format of their playlists (and have a current song) are brought together for all-day extravaganzas. The audience that attends usually comes to hear their favorite song and experience the sounds of bands they might not get a chance to see otherwise. Today's bill featured bands ranging from Veruca Salt to Bush.

We pulled into the massive backstage complex of buses and semis. It was the same venue we played during the Lollapalooza tour, summer '95. That was during the week of the big heat wave. Temperatures were 115 degrees. The death toll was around 300. The humidity was unbearable. We moved slowly, our souls nearly cooked. Our show was a test of endurance. Staying conscious was the objective. The audience was a distant gaseous cloud. The great structure of the amphitheater seemed oppressive. Today, two years hence, it is bitterly cold and overcast. Everyone is bundled and shivering.

We headed backstage and waited to play. Jamiroquai was across the hall. They circled round with smoke and whiskey, engulfing anyone in their repartee. We went on at 7 P.M. The audience was ready to go. We got them moving, if only to keep them from freezing to their seats. We walked to the car while thousands sang along with the singer of Bush, who was playing electrified sans band.

We drove back to town and headed over to the Soul Kitchen as recommended by our in-town companion, Chris Holmes. Cibo Matto had said it was the best food in North America. A tide of large plates with nuggets of delicious food came and affirmed Cibo's proclamations.

POSTED Tuesday, May 27, 1997, at 4:30 P.M. PT

We received sad, sad news today. Our friend Tim Taylor, the singer of Brainiac, was killed in a car accident over the weekend. We were just on tour with Tim and Brainiac in England last week. We all got along great and we're huge fans of each other's music. Tim was an inspired performer. He exploded onstage with alien voices, violently bashing a synthesizer. Between songs he would exclaim to a befuddled English audience, "We're BRAINIAC from Dayton, Ohio, U.S.A.!!! LAND OF MILK AND HONEY!!!" We will miss him.

We sat shocked by the news while riding from Chicago to Milwaukee. Today, the Milwaukee station and The Point in St. Louis both had radio shows going. Somehow we ended up on the bill for both. The stations agreed to charter a jet to fly us from Milwaukee to St. Louis. It was the only way it would work logistically.

We arrived in Milwaukee at 2 P.M. It was another cold and overcast day. Dennis, from the Frogs, showed up with his wife and two little children. We hung out till it was time to play. There was trouble with the PA, so we ended up going on late and only played for 30 minutes. At the end of the set I jumped off the drum riser and twisted my foot.

We all piled into the bus and left straightaway for the airport. The promoter got some police cars to escort us. We all laughed mightily as cops raced ahead of us clearing out empty Memorial Day streets. We pulled up on the runway and loaded our equipment into the plane. The cops wanted me to take a Polaroid with them in front of the jet. As five of them stood posing behind me, one of them leaned in and said, "Hey, we could snap one where we're pretending to beat you up. You could use it for a record cover or something." I declined and got on the plane. All 16 of us crammed inside and fastened our seat belts. The little jet took off with great force. Soon we were up 45,000 feet. We ate sandwiches and looked down from outer space.

We got to St. Louis in an hour. As we descended out of the clouds, the runway was right there, and BAM!—we landed. It was even colder in St. Louis. We drove straight to the Riverport Amphitheatre. We were onstage in less than an hour. The audience was very receptive and the mood was relaxed. My foot was starting to ache badly. I hobbled offstage and set it on ice. A girl presented us with a cowboy-boot cake.

At the hotel, we holed up in the lobby for drinks and chicken sandwiches. As midnight came, we raised a toast to David, our sax player, who was departing for Bali in the morning to get married on a deserted beach by a disciple of Rumi. We raised a toast to G– 2 jets and two shows in two cities in one day. We raised a toast to sprained ankles. We raised a toast to Tim, our departed comrade.

POSTED Wednesday, May 28, 1997, at 4:30 P.M. PT

Days off on the road are filler days. They never really start, and you never notice them ending. They are in between everything else. They are for sleeping in a few extra hours. They are for taking a nap after you've slept in a few extra hours. To commit to any great endeavor on a day off will be paid for in the days afterwards. Therefore, inactivity seems to be the appropriate conduct.

My day of inactivity was preempted by a trip to the hospital where I got X-rayed and poked at. The outcome—a sprained foot and a nice dark-stained bamboo cane. I also got wheeled all over the place by a pregnant nurse.

Back at the hotel I limped up and down the halls breaking in the new cane. I believe canes are very hip-hop at the moment. If this is true, then it will truly save me during these next few shows. As I am currently limited in my range of motion, I will not be able to perform in my usual fashion. So, in the meantime, until recovery is complete, I expect the cane will have to speak for me when I'm onstage. The stance that a good cane affords will take the place of peripatetic showmanship any day. It is a saber of funkiness, a baton with which to lead audiences into ecstasy.

I suppose at this point I should introduce the personages with whom I am traveling. Let me start with our tour manager, Ben Cooley. To some he is known as the rock and roll rabbi. To others he is the youngest older brother they never had. And still to others he is the oldest younger brother they could never get rid of. To most of us, we might as well be married now. We depend on him to guide us, most importantly to the bathroom when we are caught up in unfathomable sports facilities and mega-structures where we seem to find ourselves from time to time.

Next, I will introduce the band. Joey, a k a Stagecoach, is our faithful Slagwerker (German for drummer). He is the longest-standing member of our group. He is a sensual percussionist, and more importantly, a percussive sensualist. His tastes are refined and his skills are generous. We look to him for thundering delicacies and the warmest of eyes.

Justin, a k a Showboat, is our bassist. He gets shit started like no other. He hits it hard and never drops it. His madness is meticulous. His patrons are gassed. He knows how and when to drop bombs. Taking care of business is his hobby.

Smokey, a k a Smokestack, is our guitar player. He is the veteran. He has played his way across this land through honky-tonks and convention centers. He makes the familiar exotic. His lonesome slide can become swallowed by the hissing squall of appended machinery at any time. While nobody's looking, his experienced hand tosses off miracles with ease.

Theo, a k a Hound Dog, is our keyboard maestro and tabla player. Born in Bangladesh, he worked his way from Moog player on '60s Indian film soundtracks to L.A. sound engineer extraordinaire. Like some gas station Miles Davis he rips a B–3 line, then wails on tablas. Offstage, he smokes a Sherlock Holmes pipe and tells tales of Ravi Shankar's girdle.

The newest member of our ensemble is the enigmatic D.J. Swamp. With a bandana on his face, incognito, he steps to the turntables and wastes the room. He rocks beats in a way nobody else can. Some call them tricks, we call them eruptions. After smashing his records, he walks away like a Southern gentleman. The freaks bow down because they have no choice.

Our bus driver is called Em. White hair and beard, his eyes always on the road, he suffers no fools. Ex-bodyguard for Kenny Rogers (and a fair resemblance to), he protected him from rabid elderly women. He had an album on Capitol in the early '70s called "Time of Man." If you have a copy, let us know.

Michael Harrison

Michael Harrison is a pseudonym for the dean of students at a private school in the Midwest.

POSTED Tuesday, Nov. 2, 1999, at 10:30 A.M. PT

I'm making announcements during break with my bullhorn: "Students may drop off cans for the Thanksgiving Food Drive in MacArthur Hall; freshmen — be sure to turn in permission slips for your class trip; will the following students please see Mrs. Donovan in the Development Office this afternoon. . . . " The bell rings, signaling that break is over.

I use my bullhorn to herd the students back to class. (Is this why it's called a "bullhorn"?) The seniors are the most difficult — they've become inured to the bullhorn and, as they have the admonitions of their parents and teachers, learned to tune it out. I need to call each senior by name to get them to move.

Senior Stan Robinson stops me as I'm trying to motivate a pack of juniors who look comfortable on a picnic table. "Mr. Harrison," he asks, "can I use the bullhorn to make a quick announcement?"

Normally this question is a slam-dunk. "No" is the reflexive answer, followed by "Go to class." And yet today, on a whim, I hand the bullhorn to Stan. Stan hurries away from me and leaps on top of a nearby table. He turns on the bullhorn and begins making the percussive sounds of a boom box while waving one hand in the air. The students, en route to class, stop to watch. He begins to rap:

"Ki-yi-yi, yippee yo, yippee-yay. My name is Stan, and I'm here to say, that I'm in the groove, that I'm feelin' good, that I'm sayin' it loud like ya knew I would."

The boom box sounds again.

Students look nervous; Stan has hijacked break, hijacked the bullhorn, hijacked school.

"Stan!" I call out. "Give me the bullhorn!"

Stan looks worried as he hands the bullhorn back. I'm scowling. "Uh-oh," he says. "Am I busted?"

I leap onto the same table Stan had been standing on. "Ladies and gentlemen!" I say. "Senior Stan Robinson! Let's give it up for Stan!" The students clap and laugh.

"Now go to class!" I yell into the bullhorn, aiming for Stan.

Just got back from lunch, where I blew it.

At the beginning of lunch, I'm sitting down in an empty cafeteria, doing some work. Students begin to file into the cafeteria, and the table next to me quickly fills up with sophomore girls, each of whom has a glass of milk and two pieces of cake. I notice the cake and ask them, "What, no lunch?"

"No, it's cake day," Jenny replies. "We want to see if we can break our record—30 pieces for the table."

"Doesn't sound too healthy to me."

"Feel this muscle!" Alissa, the star of our girls' soccer team, demands, flexing her biceps. "I'm plenty healthy! Besides, cake tastes good!"

I laugh and go back to my lunch.

Later I'm in conversation with a student at my table when Mrs. Green, our music teacher, grabs me by the shoulder and points at the table of sophomores. In the middle of the table is a stack of approximately 30 cake plates.

"Mr. Harrison!" she says, glaring at the girls. "What do you have to say about all this?" The girls look up from their cake and await my reply.

"About what?" I wonder, but don't say out loud. "About poor dietary choices? About selfish cake consumption? About whether they broke their record?" I don't want to challenge a teacher in front of students, and yet I'm not particularly concerned about the cake. I'm stuck.

So I jump down the girls' throats.

"I think there's a real problem with all the cake you're eating," I tell them. "There are a number of other students here who may want cake and won't be able to get any because you've monopolized it. It's selfish — why don't you take a piece at the beginning of lunch and then if there's more left at the end of lunch, you can have another piece?"

The students make an attempt at lighthearted banter with me — the same sort in which we had engaged only a few minutes before. "Maybe they could make more cake since it's cake day!.... What about cutting the cake up into smaller pieces so we can break our record?" But I'll have none of it — not with Mrs. Green standing next to me, scowling at the students and watching my every word. I shake my head sternly at the students, say some things about "community" and "broadening your perspective," and walk out of the dining hall.

It isn't until I get halfway to my office that I start to feel like an asshole. If teen-agers are sensitive to one thing, it's hypocrisy. And I have just defined the word for them — I went from being their buddy to being a cop within the course of one lunch period.

Should I find the students? Talk to Mrs. Green? I guess I'll just chalk it up to rocks and hard places.

POSTED Wednesday, Nov. 3, 1999, at 11:30 A.M. PT

I received the following e-mail this morning from one of our house masters:

> Wynn Lee ordered a textbook from Chesterton Publishers posing as a faculty member. When the book came, Jeff [one of the house masters] thought that something seemed funny, so he brought it to me. I opened the package and then contacted the publisher to ask if they send out sample books to students. They said no. The book was an advanced-placement organic chemistry text. Wynn receives a fair amount of mail addressed to both "Professor Lee" and "Doctor Lee." Seems to me this should be addressed with him.

Wynn Lee is a shy, brilliant Indonesian boy. It is his fifth year at our school, and aside from winning last year's chess tournament and playing in the orchestra, he has kept a fairly low profile. This will be his first trip to my office.

Sometimes being a disciplinarian is like being a math teacher. When students fail to understand a problem, my job is to walk them through the steps. Consequences are like grades—they simply help to reinforce learning. I tracked down Wynn during lunch and asked him to come to my office.

"Wynn, I understand that you've been receiving textbooks from publishers by telling them that you're a faculty member. Is this true?"

"No. Well.... Yeah, I guess."

"Why did you do this?"

"I wanted to get the books."

"So you just called up the publishers?"

"No. I was looking at books on the Internet and I saw you could get free books if you were a teacher."

"So you lied and said you were a teacher?"

"I guess."

"Do you think that was wrong?"

"I guess so...it seems like they have so many books that it doesn't matter."

"If you walked into a bookstore that had hundreds of copies of a book you wanted, would it be OK to take it?"

"No. That would be stealing."

"And you weren't stealing?"

"No. These companies give their books away."

"Who do they give them away to, Wynn?"

"Teachers."

"Why do you think they give them away?"

"So teachers will read them.... maybe they'll like them."

"Why do they want teachers to like them?"

"Maybe they think it's good if teachers talk about them?"

"Why else?"

Pause. No answer.

"If a teacher likes a textbook, what do they do with it?"

"Use it for their class."

"And if they use it for their class, perhaps a hundred students will need to buy the book."

A light bulb goes on—he understands. Or maybe this has all been an act—I can't tell. For my purposes, it doesn't matter.

"So they give away one book and sell a hundred," Wynn says.

"Exactly."

Wynn thinks about this for a moment, and then says, "I feel guilty."

"Good. That's what you should be feeling. Even though it seems like these are big companies, it's still wrong to lie about who you are. And it still hurts them to have to spend money sending you free books.... You didn't think you'd get caught, did you?"

"No, I guess not."

"One of the hardest things to learn in life is to do the right thing even if you think you won't get caught—even if you think nobody is looking."

"That's called integrity."

"Exactly. How did you know that, Wynn?"

"We're learning about it in morality class."

"Good. It's an important thing to learn about. Do you know what reparations are?"

"No."

"Reparations are something you do to try to make things whole, to repair or fix things when you've done something wrong. I want you to think about making reparations for lying to these publishing companies."

"OK. How?"

"First, I want you to perform service. Service to the publishing companies would be best, but this may be impossible. So you can do community service here at school. Fair?"

"OK."

"What else do you think would be good?

"Well, I guess I could pay for the books, but that would be too easy."

"Why?"

"Because it's my parents' money. I wouldn't be doing anything."

"That's honest. I want you to pay for the books anyway. I also want you to write me a morality paper. I want you to discuss the morality of what you did. Why was it wrong? What did you learn?"

"How long?"

"Three pages typed, double-spaced. On my desk Monday morning."

Wynn looks upset.

"What's the problem?"

"I will be very busy this weekend. But I guess this is OK. It needs to be hard for me to make—how do you say it? "

"Reparations?"

"Yes. Reparations."

Michael Hirschorn

Michael Hirschorn filed this shortly after leaving his job as editor-in-chief of Spin *magazine. He is currently co-chairman and editor-in-chief of* Inside.com.

POSTED Thursday, Jan. 23, 1997, at 4:30 P.M. PT

Paris Review parties have always had a satyric quality to them—jowly novelists well into their third marriages and fifth drinks, the latest batch of overripe lit chicks off the bus from Oberlin, George Plimpton glissading through the throng, urging everyone on to greater gin-and-tonic consumption. One half expects a Brueghel painting to break out. (For complete verisimilitude, one would have to paint James Atlas in the corner not having fun.) When I had just arrived on the New York literary/media scene—which, as are all such scenes, is made up of about 1 percent literati and 99 percent pseudos—I began going to these parties with some regularity and learned the essential art of talking to novelists whose books one hadn't read. I also met my wife there, and so will always have fond feelings toward the place.

I went back tonight and found virtually the entire late-'80s crowd gone. No Jay. No Bret. No Tama. And as if to confirm that times had really changed, the young novelist being honored bounded up to me and said, "Hey, you're the only person left here

I haven't met." Plimpton was still there, of course, and he continues to be an object of wonder. No younger person could ever pull
off his brand of élan, his ability to greet someone whose name he
can't remember, or possibly never knew, with a magisterial, "Ah,
there you are." People just don't live life grand cru anymore,
though there are a surprising number in the younger generation
who play at being baby Plimptons. It doesn't quite work. For one,
Plimpton actually wrote a lot of books and continues to produce on
a regular basis. The new literati have more or less ditched the
achievement part—a few bylines for branding purposes—and focused entirely on the lifestyle part. As the *Times Magazine* put it
in a fashion spread awhile back that spotlit some of the hot, young
littérateurs, "Today's New Beats Favor Prada and the Gap" (or
something like that). I decided things had become completely silly
when I received a mailing for one of those "spoken word" evenings
in the East Village. It was for a reading by a sporadically published
young freelance writer. He would be sharing with the crowd his
"selected works."

I am sad to say that our generation's main gift to the culture
may turn out to be self-promotion. We have precious little to pro-
mote, but we do it with ferocious ingenuity. I blame Prozac. And
Freud. Atlas may have been on to something with his end-of-fun
piece in *The New Yorker*. People were just less over-therapized and
-drugged 20 and 30 years ago. (I know the golden age of psy-
chotherapy was after the war, but just as more people had cheap
sex in the '70s, even though the golden age of cheap sex was the
'60s, I maintain that seeing the shrink only became something
everybody did as a matter of course in the last 10 or 15 years.)
Deeply fucked-up people are, by definition, more interesting people. And most young people I know are way, way too in touch with
their feelings, and as a result go through life affecting a kind of
world-weary resignation or a bland, narcotized contentment. No
fun, I say.

POSTED Friday, Jan. 24, 1997, at 4:30 P.M. PT

Now that I have some free time, I'm becoming reacquainted with my neighborhood. It is, I'm discovering, a strange, perhaps even sinister place. I live in Chelsea, on one of those nondescript, mix 'n' match side streets that exists only in New York: movie stars in lofts, a mysterious convent, tenement-style walk-ups, quasi-government agencies, strange old guys who sit around listening to transistor radios, a drunk who free falls on his face like clockwork every three months (I've called the medics twice myself). And drug dealers.

There used to be a high-volume drug operation further west on my block, but the cops blocked off the street to cars and the Jersey-plated Camaros eventually went elsewhere. Or so I thought. Really, the transaction just became more subterranean. Walking west last week, I saw a complicated transaction in which a car with the obligatory Jersey plates pulled up in front of a parked car. A man from the Jersey car jumped into the parked car, which sped up 15th Street. Parked-car guy got out and went into a building. Meanwhile, the other guy in the Jersey car moved up to block the second car. Parked-car guy left the building and got back in his car. Then Jersey guy got out of the car, back into his own ride, and headed for the West Side Highway. Now, you tell me.

Walking my dog this afternoon, I saw one crusty old guy pass another crusty old guy in the street and hand over a baseball-sized wad of what appeared to be $100 bills (I was literally two feet away). They exchanged very Jim Jarmuschian "my man"s and sauntered off. Looking on the bright side, there are always people standing around on the street waiting to be helpful. This evening, seeing that I was in imminent danger of dropping a rickety tower of birthday presents and cake I was trying to shove into a waiting car, a young guy came to my rescue. Moments later, someone else wandered by, and the two of them snuck off into a dark driveway to transact who knows what.

The birthday was my father's and, picking up on a series of hints over the previous year, I bought him a computer—his first. He has done an extraordinary amount in his life—he's basically the guy who pioneered the idea of noise control—but he has managed to become a prototypically American success story while remaining blissfully untutored in the American cultural and consumer culture that is most everyone else's lingua franca. In a recent effort to, like, clue him in, I had mentioned the magazine *Rolling Stone.*

"Mort Kondracke writes for that," he said. "I saw it on that *McLaughlin* show."

"No, dad," I said testily, "I promise you that's not the case."

My father was adamant: "He writes for Rolling Stones."

"*Rolling Stone*, dad. That's a music magazine. The Rolling Stones are a rock band. And Mort Kondracke writes for *Roll Call.*"

In any case, he seemed to like the computer—a Compaq laptop —but became flummoxed by the tabs you press to open the thing. When I opened it for him, he grabbed the Compaq by its scruff end, jabbing his thumb into the screen, and began poking repeatedly at the on/off key as if at a typewriter. I am hedging my bets. If he ever reads these words, we'll move on to Step Two: that big Keith Richards/Jack Germond reunion tour.

Jim Holt

Jim Holt wrote this when he was editor of the New Leader, *a political biweekly. He currently writes about science and philosophy for* Lingua Franca *and the* Wall Street Journal.

POSTED Monday, Feb. 24, 1997, at 4:30 P.M. PT

There are two marine creatures that I have always identified with. One of them is the juvenile sea squirt. This is a little thing that wanders through the sea looking for a nice rock or hunk of coral to make its home for life. When it finds the right spot and takes root, it no longer has any use for its brain. So it eats it. In much the same way, I have been wandering through Manhattan these 20 years in search of a suitable hunk of coral to attach myself to. A month ago I found it. It is a magazine called the *New Leader*. Finally, I can eat my brain.

I have happy news for all those welfare moms whom Clinton and the Republicans are throwing off the rolls: After decades of idleness, it is good to have a job. I am by way of being work-shy, not exactly a man of ginger and push. Since college I have had only two real jobs, for a total of 37 months' employment. Being unoccupied is fine if you are under the age of 40. Until you pass that milestone, you are "young and brilliant," by definition. At 40 you are suddenly "veteran," a status you retain until 60, whereupon you become "distinguished." In my young-and-brilliant phase I had one good idea, a metaphysical discovery, actually: I figured out why there is Something rather than Nothing—why, in other words, some kind of universe has to exist. (I'll save the explanation for later in the week, as a hedge against uneventfulness.) That gratified whatever intellectual ambition I had. It seemed like enough for a lifetime. After all, when Epimenides thought up the Liar's Paradox, a similar breakthrough, he called it a day's work and proceeded to sleep soundly for 57 years, right through his "veteran" and "distinguished" phases. He would have been even better off declining into the editorship of a small political biweekly, as I have.

Monday morning, I get up, dress negligently but with unimpeachable taste, and head for the subway. As I cross Broadway at 86th Street, a cab almost a block uptown honks at me. Foolish Hindoo! I am not even in his light-cone (thus he cannot casually interact with me by running me over—see Einstein). A few minutes later, as I try to board a crowded No. 1 subway, the conductor announces, "Please enter the train through all available doors." What does he think I am, a quantum particle?

By the way, the other marine creature I identify with is the hagfish. It is a jawless thing that, when attacked, secretes enough slime to cover itself and repel the predator.

POSTED Tuesday, Feb. 25, 1997, at 4:30 P.M. PT

Editing a magazine is really the perfect job for one who is lazy and spottily educated yet wishes to make a decent living. Editors are like PR people and investment bankers, in that it is somewhat mysterious just what they do. But whereas an investment banker can at least say, "I float new issues," there is no such pat but obscure self-justification available to the editor.

I had always imagined that the task of the magazine editor was to choose between Trilling and Fiedler to do the new Roth, say, or between Kissinger and Brzezinski on the meaning of détente. Great thinkers would propose, I would dispose, and the rest was up to the printer. Occasionally there would be a jolly party. The reality is very different, though scarcely less agreeable. Most of my time is spent at a desk with a mechanical pencil and an eraser. Using these implements, I effortlessly trim manuscripts of their rococo excrescences, so they are not embarrassing to publish. Sometimes an author's prose simply needs a good rinsing, so I go into the bathroom and do that. On rare occasions a truly execrable submission shows up on my desk. Then I generally spend two hours trying to wish it into the world of Unbeing, and another hour or so butchering it. When I am finished, it fits the designated page perfectly. It has become a "good piece."

In the interstices I do a bit of woolgathering. I think of the problem of theodicy. We live in a world that is supposedly the handiwork of a God who is all-powerful and all-good, yet is filled with evil and suffering. Either God is willing but unable to prevent this, or he is able but unwilling. How to resolve this dilemma, other than by plumping for Leibniz's lame inference that ours is the best of all possible worlds?

The answer, I decide, is simple. The world is not presided over by a deity who is all-good and all-powerful, but rather by one who is 100 percent malevolent but only 80 percent effective. That explains everything.

Now that I am an editor, I must acquire gravitas (even though I am at a magazine whose most famous past editor was Levitas). This must be done by gradation. From now on, I resolve, when I would ordinarily blurt out, "No way!!" I will compose myself and instead say, "I think, perhaps, not."

Taking the subway home in the evening, I am suddenly seized by *alfear*, uncontrollable anxiety caused by elves. But it passes in a moment and I am content again.

Mary Jordan
and Kevin Sullivan

Mary Jordan and Kevin Sullivan filed this while serving as the co-bureau chiefs for the Washington Post *in Tokyo. They now serve in the same role in Mexico City.*

POSTED Monday, Sept. 8, 1997, at 4:30 P.M. PT

Nothing unusual this morning: A big earthquake shook us awake, and our 2-year-old had a bowl of olives for breakfast.

Our house in Tokyo rocks and rolls every few days. Books fall off shelves, and the windows rattle; we try to be cool about it. Living in this city is like having something alive and angry under your feet: It's huge, and it wants out. And when it moves, everything shakes. Like everybody else here, we keep an earthquake kit by the front door, although ours is a little unorthodox. Most people have things like prescription medicines, a flashlight, a radio, and a lightweight blanket. We have six bottles of mineral water and a mammoth package of cheese crackers that we bought at the Price Costco in Washington. We bought a Price Costco first-aid kit, too. It is very big and orange, but we can't remember where we put it. We could go buy another one, and have an award-winning kit that we could brag about, as some of our neighbors do. Partly, we're too disorganized to do that. But mainly, we hate the pessimism that an earthquake kit represents.

Historically, Tokyo is whacked by a massive earthquake every 60 or 70 years, and by that reckoning, we're already years overdue for the Big One. Today's tremor was a 5.2 on the Richter scale. Scary, but not bad enough to dive for the cheese crackers.

Of course, we can't be cavalier about earthquakes because we have two kids counting on us not to be bozos. But you can't let it run your lives like some jittery Americans here do. We refuse to move from one house to another each time a new apartment building goes up and claims to be "the most earthquake-proof," as someone we know did. Another friend talks about how she has one earthquake kit in her car, one at the front door, and one at the back. She'd probably love to make her kids wear a helmet in the bathtub, too.

We think we've been reasonable: We fasten furniture to the wall in the rooms where our kids sleep. We don't hang pictures with glass on the walls, because they could fall. We know where the emergency gathering spots are in our neighborhood. Beyond that, we prefer to spend our time thinking about more interesting things, like why our little Kate prefers olives to oatmeal for breakfast.

This is harder for us to get used to than the rumbling walls. How many preschoolers wake up from a sound sleep, toddle into their parents' room, and say, "Mommy, olives?" Ours does, and we must say, she has a fine olive-eating technique. She gnaws away the green flesh and announces, with an admonishing wag of her index finger, "Don't eat the middle, OK?" Then she pops the pit out onto her plate. Maybe we were sheltered as children, but neither of us can remember eating an olive until we were in college. But Kate, not even two-and-a-half, gobbled a dozen of them this morning and washed them down with a big slug of milk in a bottle shaped like a teddy bear. We have the vague sense that this probably makes us lousy parents. But hey, it's not like we're giving her Hershey bars for breakfast. Maybe this way she'll grow up with an appreciation for Italian food and culture, which will lead to a

successful career as an opera star at La Scala, followed by the overwhelming urge to buy her parents a beautiful retirement home in
Tuscany. Or maybe she'll just like martinis too much. Tomorrow
we should probably start pushing the oatmeal again.

POSTED   Tuesday, Sept. 9, 1997, at 4:30 P.M. PT

We walked into the Doutor coffee shop in our building this morning, drenched and dripping from Tokyo's second straight day of
apocalyptic rain. Like every other coffee shop in this city—every
other public place, really—our Doutor is filled with cigarette
smoke thick enough to hang our umbrellas on. It is nearly impossible to get into a taxi or to eat in a restaurant here without stink-
ing of smoke. This coffee shop is like a blue-gray curtain we pass
through every morning to get from the sidewalk to our desks.

The tables are filled with people drinking watery coffee and eating pastries that look good but taste like pulp. Japan is home to
some of the world's most delicious food—nobody does it better
with rice and fish—but morning food is maddening. Tokyo's coffee shops and bakeries sometimes don't open until 10 o'clock. Finally, a bagel store opened in our neighborhood and, sure enough,
it opens at 10 and is closed on Sundays. One day we delayed going
to work and waited for it to open. As we walked in, a huge tray of
sesame bagels was waltzing out of the oven. Delirious, we asked for
half a dozen. "Oh, no, sorry," said the clerk. All these were for a
special order. Right at this moment, there were NONE available.
So it was out the door and back to those Japanese muffins and
croissants that toy with you. They look all fluffy and inviting. But
it's an illusion, like virtual food. The pastries rip sickly in your
teeth like a gas station cheese sandwich. It's like they were made by
somebody working from a photograph, not a recipe. Maybe that's
why so many people eat hot dogs instead. Japanese coffee shops do
a big morning business in wieners. Our Doutor has three kinds:

the lettuce dog, the spicy dog, and the German dog. Nothing like a cup of Joe and a sauerkraut dog to get the pistons pumping in the morning.

As bad as the pastries are, the coffee is worse, which makes no sense at all because the Japanese consume tons of it. Chains like Doutor and Pronto are always packed with customers: businessmen in their blue suits bingeing on cigarettes and espresso; schoolgirls in their blue skirts and saggy white socks giggling over tall glasses of milky iced coffee; "office ladies" in their blue uniforms sipping cups of weak "blend" coffee. Although tea is Japan's traditional drink, the caffeine buzz that keeps Tokyo humming comes from coffee. But most of it is nasty. The espresso drinks are bitter and harsh, and the "American"-style coffee is weak and thin. If you're a caffeine addict, it takes at least two cups to even get your sleepy brain's attention.

Thankfully, Starbucks has arrived. We never thought that grass-green Starbucks logo would look so good. When we left Washington two years ago, there were at least six cafes within a mile of our house. We joked about being glad to be away from all that silly coffee lingo, glad to never again hear anybody order a tall skinny mocha latte. But when the first Starbucks opened here last year, nobody got there faster than we did. There are now nine or 10 Starbucks shops in Tokyo, but none of them is close to our house or office. On weekends, we have been known to take a $10 taxi ride to the closest one, where there is coffee with actual taste and real cranberry muffins. Oddly, the prices are about the same as they are in Washington, even though everything else here is priced as if every person in Japan owned a Saudi Arabian oil well.

This is not to say we think American stuff is better than Japanese stuff. (But the United States really does win when it comes to breakfast: These Japanese squash muffins and potato pastries are disgusting.) Maybe this is why Japanese people are so skinny: They don't eat breakfast, aren't tempted by a waffle with strawberries and whipped cream or a Spanish omelet or an all-you-can-eat

IHOP run. Still, this country is on a diet craze: Young women who would have to shop in the petite department of any American department store are taping their index fingers because it is supposed to control the appetite. They are swearing off sweets and, at lunchtime, they eat rice balls and hit up the vending machines for one of the many no-calorie Japanese diet drinks. Of course, when we use the vending machines we are not going for the Zero Calorie High Vitamin Drink. We buy the $5 Asahi beer (one very large can, ice cold). We have never actually plopped in $16 for the really bad Chilean chardonnay that one of our neighborhood machines offers, but we have often wondered what stops 10-year-olds from getting smashed on all the booze, even whiskey, that is dispensed in outdoor machines. Now, there are many, many things available in vending machines here: $100 stuffed bears, cameras, gift-wrapped ties, $20 bags of rice. The country is mad about automation. But why, we wonder, can't they make breakfast? At this point we would take a cab ride for a good box of Hostess doughnuts.

POSTED Wednesday, Sept. 10, 1997, at 4:30 P.M. PT

We had dinner last night at a restaurant near our office, in the Omotesando section of Tokyo. Some people call this tree-lined boulevard the Paris of Tokyo, but that's a bit of a stretch, much like calling Central Park the Montana of New York. It would take more than a few open-air cafes to make this city French. Still, Omotesando is a lovely area, where young couples wander happily along the wide sidewalks past art galleries, the sleek showroom of Japanese clothes designer Hanae Mori, and a slew of interesting boutiques. Omotesando and its younger, trendier neighbor, Harajuku, are Tokyo's prime sites for watching new fashion fads. Platform shoes have been big here lately: Last night, we saw a woman with 4-inch-high red velvet ones. Lime green is the hot color nowadays, and we saw one guy dressed head to toe in it: He looked like a Popsicle. One of our friends at dinner even showed up in a lime green polo shirt. The cool kids cruise Omotesando nonstop, hitting landmarks like Condomania, which—you guessed it—sells nothing but condoms, every kind from strawberry-flavored ones to those specially designed for men based on their blood type (honest). Interesting tidbit: Japan has the world's highest rate of condom use, largely because birth-control pills are illegal here.

Our friends Jesper Koll and Kathy Matsui had found a new restaurant they wanted to try out, so seven of us headed that way. Tucked away on a side street, the place is very hip, and an indication of what's going on in the Japanese economy these days. Ten years ago, this piece of property was probably worth more than the assessed value of Capitol Hill. But Japan's "bubble economy" has burst like an overpumped water balloon, and land prices have plummeted. Some prime real estate in Tokyo is now worth just 20 percent of its value a few years ago. That's good news for young entrepreneurial chefs, who can now afford to start up their own places. Many of them have begun new ventures like this one, which is to standard Japanese restaurants what lime green bellbottoms are to navy blue business suits.

First we took off our shoes, because some things never change. (By the way, is it just us, or does anyone else think that if American restaurants made customers leave their shoes by the door, an awful lot of people would have their shoes stolen?) We were led to a private room in the back, which was a little worrisome. Often, private rooms are the least interesting spaces in Japanese restaurants. They are considered formal and elegant, but we usually find that they distance you from whatever buzz and atmosphere has been created in the restaurant's main room. But this turned out to be different. We walked past the diners sitting on mats at the sushi counter and others sitting on the floor around low square tables. Way in the back, we turned into a tiny passageway, where we stepped on slates set in a bed of gravel. At the end, we ducked through a small entryway, like a cave entrance, into a dimly lit room. In traditional Japanese style, there was a long, narrow table for about eight people. The space beneath the table was sunken, so we had plenty of room for our legs, even while sitting on the floor. One of the two small lamps that gave the room its warm glow was a simple bulb inside a straw basket. Already waiting for us were a dozen small dishes: eggplant stuffed with raw tuna, a salad of avocado and caviar, raw beef sashimi, short ribs, a casserole of potatoes and squid, and various raw fish and seaweed dishes. The food kept coming, delivered by a chef who came and went through a tiny sliding door in the wall. The bill was a shocker: With beer, the total tab came to $40 per person. In a city where one cup of coffee can cost $10, that's practically a free meal.

Economists and pundits are making lots of gloomy noises these days about the state of the Japanese economy. We're sure they have their reasons, but this cozy restaurant in Omotesando is certainly one little economic indicator to cheer about.

Japanese taxis are also a reason to love this place. Some of them have tiny electronic screens that display the latest news, ticker-tape style. Others have tiny vending machines that sell soft drinks. Some have a little recorded voice reminding you not to forget your valuables. Taxi drivers here are almost always polite, and they wear white gloves. One of them once drove all the way to our house to return a briefcase left in his taxi. All cabs here have a lever on the dashboard that the driver uses to open and close the rear door for passengers. It is very bad form for a customer to touch the door. Friends of ours who have lived in Tokyo for years tell hysterical stories of visiting New York and walking away from taxis without closing the door, or tipping, which is also a no-no here. New York cabbies do not appreciate the humor in this. They just scream. At times like that, you remember: It's more than just the Pacific Ocean that separates Japan and America.

POSTED Thursday, Sept. 11, 1997, at 4:30 P.M. PT

We've been interviewing a rare breed of Japanese this week: people who are actually dangerous. We're writing a story about an organization in Japan that has, in the past, demonstrated a proficiency for killing people. Since we're still working on the story, we wouldn't even tell our mothers whom we are talking about. But that's beside the point. The bottom line is that while these people aren't Uzi-packing Colombian drug lords, they are a potential threat to us and to our kids. So we did something we've never done in two years of living in Tokyo. We started locking our front door.

About 30 million people live in the Tokyo metropolitan area. This is one of the world's most crowded cities, but it has managed to avoid most of the crime and violence that plague other big urban areas. It is remarkably safe to live here. Murders are rare, and robberies are almost nonexistent. However, in the past couple of years, teen-agers have been mugging each other to steal their Nike Air Max sneakers, which, in Japan's faddish economy, sell for about $300, with rarer models running to $2,000 or more. Handguns are illegal, and only Japan's "yakuza" mobsters carry them. Gun crime is so rare that when robbers shot three people to death in a grocery store stickup two years ago, the flabbergasted police announced that the crime was probably committed by foreigners.

We live in a fairly nice section of town, which in many cities would make us an even greater target for break-ins. But we leave two expensive mountain bikes unlocked in our driveway, along with a couple of baby strollers that are worth a few hundred bucks each, a couple of kiddie bikes, and a little red wagon. In the Washington neighborhood where we lived before moving over here, we would be little-red-wagonless in a heartbeat if we left that stuff outside unattended. We have never locked our front door here, because it seems pointless. We routinely tell delivery people that if we're not home, just open the front door and leave the package inside. We walk a shortcut route home from the subway station, which includes a long, secluded, unlighted road. In the States, we would never take such a path late at night. But here, it's almost laughable to worry about it.

There is institutional honesty here. We know one woman who has lost her wallet three different times, and each time it has been returned to her with nothing missing—not even cash. Nobody counts change in Japan. We found a watch on the street the other day, so we did what everyone does here. We took it to the local *koban*, the little police kiosks located in practically every neighborhood in Japan. It's ours in six months if nobody claims it. And if anyone wants to claim it, they are required to come to us first to formally thank us. It's a nice system, one that demands honesty and gratitude. Although, to be frank, we're secretly hoping nobody comes forward. We saw the same watch in a store selling for over $1,000.

All this doesn't make the Japanese saints. Japan's politicians wrote the book on graft and corruption—one big shot used to collect bribes so big he needed a shopping cart to take the cash home. But in daily life, it just doesn't seem to occur to the Japanese to be dishonest. Some say it's because of Confucian traditions; some say it's because the Japanese are so afraid of shame and of losing face that they wouldn't dare commit a crime. Who knows, but we're grateful to a place where we never have to worry about our kids being abducted or abused, where it's generally OK to talk to strangers, and where we don't have to worry that the guy driving next to us is going to pull out a gun and start shooting. Having those keys made for the front door yesterday was probably the saddest thing we've done here.

Ben Katchor

Ben Katchor is a cartoonist and author of The Jew of New York *and*
The Beauty Supply District. *His comic strip appears in the* Forward
and several other weekly publications.

POSTED Wednesday, July 9, 1997, at 4:30 P.M. PT

11:00 A.M. Crossing the street to the hardware store for light bulbs,
I am struck by a familiar smell. As a frequent visitor to the Upper

West Side, during the months spent
looking for an apartment, I began to
associate this particular fragrance
with Broadway. I thought it was
some popular brand of perfume
mixed with the scent of the fruit and
cut flowers sold on the street. It took
me several months to isolate the
smell, and now I know that it's the
smell of dry cleaning. On almost
every block, from 72nd Street to
116th Street, there's a dry cleaner
and all boast that their work is done
on the premises. Learning of the
deadly nature of the fumes released

by this chemical process has made the fragrance all the more titil-
lating; I think of expensive wine stains on impossibly delicate fabric and of the fragility of life. In the rest of the country, it's illegal
to operate a dry-cleaning machine in a residential building—on
the Upper West Side, it's a necessity. The machines in many of
these stores are new Italian models, with names like Razzioni and
Feodora—I haven't seen a French dry cleaner for fifteen years. The
motorized racks which hold the cleaned garments cover the ceilings of these stores and are always filled to capacity. The dry
cleaner closest to me has a computerized retrieval system.

11:15 A.M. To avoid returning to work, I walk to the post office.
Having moved uptown, I changed my P.O. box from Church Street
Station to Cathedral Station. Will I ever again run into the elderly
black man whose job it is to collect the mail returned from SROs to
the post office? He approaches the pick-up window and presents
the clerk with a document, laminated in plastic, which attests to his
authority. When the clerk refuses to release a certain party's mail,
the elderly man reprimands him in an elegant, almost 19th-cen-
tury form of speech. "My fine young man, you may not understand who I am and what I am doing here today...."

8:30 P.M. Shopping at the Associated supermarket. I do not understand how it is arranged that only certain brands of milk are
sold in each neighborhood, but the milk most commonly available
around here comes in a package I find so painful to look at that I
cannot bring myself to buy it. On the front is a large, insensitive
drawing of a cow's head, surrounded by a noose of brown rope. The
background of the entire carton is covered with a close to life-sized,
black-and-white representation of cow hide. On 2 percent milk the
lettering is in purple.

Chris Kelly

Chris Kelly filed this when he was head writer for the TV program Politically Incorrect with Bill Maher. He now writes sitcoms.

POSTED Monday, May 4, 1998, at 4:30 P.M. PT

Jay Leno does about 25 monologue jokes a day. Letterman does about six, sometimes more, but of those six, three are throwaways: Times Square contains hookers, foreigners have odd names, a cab driver sold a squirrel crack. Conan O'Brien does three, I think. At *Politically Incorrect* we do five. I mean, Bill Maher performs five. We write about 250.

Writing a daily monologue is easy when bad things happen. Right now it's 12:15 A.M., Monday, May 4, and nothing is happening. The lead stories in the *New York Times* are about Dan Burton, affirmative action, and cocoa beans. *Newsweek's* cover story is "Building a Better Boy." No one knows who Dan Burton is, so we're screwed there. Affirmative action isn't funny. The cocoa bean story is useless. That leaves us, and Letterman, and Leno, and Conan with the guy who killed himself on television on the freeway last Thursday, Al Gore overseas, and NATO expansion. Luckily it's only midnight. There's still plenty of time for something horrible to occur.

Sometimes, just when things are at their bleakest, Bob Dole will fall through a railing, or a mansion full of Star Trek fans will kill themselves to rendezvous with a comet, or a Scotsman will clone a sheep, or the president will turn out to be a flasher. Sure, then it's easy. Then anyone can do it. The man who's worthwhile is the man who can smile when the lead stories are about Dan Burton, affirmative action, cocoa beans, and better boy building.

As the Fox TV network points out so gleefully, there are only so many magic tricks. There are also only so many monologue jokes. The job is dressing them up differently. I'm not making an elephant disappear, I'm making a hovercraft disappear. It's not a Pee Wee Herman joke, it's a George Michael joke. The art—well, the art should be making a truly beautiful and searing observation about current events. But the craft is making the same old jokes about new subjects.

Lenny Bruce used to talk about replacing Mort Sahl's newspaper. (Sahl would work off that day's paper, carry it up onstage with him, flip through it, and riff off the stories.) Bruce's idea was to get to all the newsstands anywhere near where Sahl was playing and replace that day's papers with really old copies. Sahl buys the paper, gets onstage, says, "Let's see what's happening today. . . . Well, it looks like the Hindenburg exploded."

Challenger jokes were Hindenburg jokes. Flight 800 jokes were ValuJet jokes were Challenger jokes were Hindenburg jokes. Dead Chris Farley jokes were Dead John Belushi jokes were Dead Lenny Bruce jokes.

Even on a new, fresh subject, Leno can do the same joke for a week. Or maybe it just feels like a week. (Premise: Someone, anywhere on earth, does anything that has anything to do with marijuana. Punch lines: Monday—they get the munchies for Doritos; Tuesday—munchies for pizza; Wednesday—munchies for doughnuts; Thursday—munchies for the release that death will bring.)

At *Politically Incorrect* we're not allowed to hit the same news story twice. And that's a pain, because we have to put all that extra effort into tricking Maher into thinking the story has advanced so far in 24 hours that it's new again — "Terry Nichols' lawyers say they're closer than ever to a plea bargain"...etc., etc.

Maher also makes our job difficult by the jokes he won't do:

No Teddy Kennedy drinking jokes. (Teddy Kennedy drowns people jokes — considered on a case-by-case basis.)

No Boris Yeltsin drinking jokes. (Making Russia, as a subject, almost impossible — the fall of the Berlin Wall was also the fall of the great Russia Premises: You wait for a long time in line for a potato, the Yugo is a piece of crap, and the KGB watches everybody at all times.)

No matter how cleverly it's phrased, Al Gore is neither a tree nor a robot. (Al Gore visited flood victims and got his hard drive wet. Or: Al Gore visited flood victims and, when a local levee broke, allowed some to take refuge in his upper branches.)

Sports are off-limits, as a rule, and in particular, jokes where a team on a losing streak is used as an all-purpose punch line. (Newt Gingrich is never going to be president — know whom he just hired for his campaign strategists? The Nets!)

Maher has a deep antipathy toward jokes involving the deaths of obscure celebrities and funerals that mirror their lives. (The inventor of the refrigerator light bulb died, and mourners spent three days opening and closing his casket to see if he stayed that way.)

Of course, like a Ted Kennedy temperance pledge, these rules were made to be broken.

A Letterman writer explained to me once that his boss's comedy "advanced glacially." For example, right now, and for the next six months, half of all monologue jokes will end with the word "intern." Sooner or later another subject will emerge, some advertising phrase like "Godzilla: Size Does Matter." This will, slowly, drive "intern" out. Leno's monologue is more timeless than that. Leno knows that politicians are a bunch of blowhards; that O.J. Simpson was accused of murder, John Bobbitt had his penis cut off, and laxatives make people go to the bathroom. He has that to fall back on, the way, in *Islands in the Stream*, Thomas Hudson can rely on the sea. It's what he has instead of God.

I'm not going to say what we fall back on; that would be giving it away. But if we do a Dan Burton joke this week, it will somehow play off on the idea that Ken Starr is insane. If we do affirmative action, it will hinge on there being very few black Republicans. *Newsweek*'s "Building a Better Boy" = Michael Jackson. And it always will.

No monologue writer alive is better at what he does than Gerard Mulligan, who writes for David Letterman. One day some other writers were working on a "Chyron Quiz"—a piece that requires writing printed jokes over videotape footage of average people. Mulligan walked through the meeting and, without pausing, gave the right answer, the exact winning punch line to the footage that was frozen on the monitor. It doesn't matter what. It was a great joke, and an old joke, and everyone knew it would be the joke performed on the show that night. Jeff Stilson, who's also a terrific monologue writer, said, "Gerry, don't you ever feel like you're in a rut?" And Mulligan told Stilson, "It's not a rut, my friend, it's a groove."

David Kemper

David Kemper is chairman, president, and CEO of Commerce Banc-shares, Inc., in St. Louis.

POSTED Sunday, April 12, 1998, at 4:30 P.M. PT

Easter dawned blue and brilliant, so I went for a jog through my leafy suburban neighborhood. The most interesting site on my running course is a 30,000 square foot, faux French château rising from the dust of a tear-down on a street of '60s brick colonial ranch houses. A 9,000 Dow and the realities of urban sprawl have unleashed the "tear-down and build big" phenomenon in St. Louis; a couple of other houses on the château street are already fated for the same untimely demise. I suppose as a banker I should encourage such overconsuming behavior, but it does lead to some—er—uneven architectural results. Some latter-day Schliemann will no doubt carefully excavate Chateau Nouveau a century hence, sifting debris in a vain attempt to try to explain Richard Gephardt's childhood.

I returned for a quick and competitive Easter egg hunt—the youngest of our four children is 9 and, strange as it may seem, may possibly still believe in the Easter bunny. We then set out for church with the specific strategy of getting there early enough to get seats—a problem last year—and also a good parking place, so we could then zoom out for brunch afterward. Billy, the 9-year-old, had a little trouble finding his Easter finest shoes and then complained about foot pain as he hobbled up the steps to the church. Once we settled into the pew, we discovered his shoes were indeed from two years ago, and thus two and a half sizes too small. To give up our parking place would not be heads-up play — and we figured he would only have to make it down the aisle to receive Communion — a round trip of no more than 200 feet. He made it to the altar and back, no problem. Our very thoughtful priest, Father Krawinkel, delivered an appropriate sermon, ending by quoting Malcolm Muggeridge in his *Chronicles of Wasted Time*, lamenting the loss of the years he'd wasted before finding faith. This closing was particularly stinging to me because not only was I unsure I had yet found any faith, but also I have had *Chronicles of Wasted Time* sitting on my bedroom bookshelf for about five years, waiting to be read.

The rest of the day was classic peaceful Sunday afternoon in the 'burbs — a little gardening here, a little baseball there with Billy, and the occasional unheeded lecture on the sun and skin cancer to my two teen-age daughters. The highlight of the day, however, may have been trying to retrieve my car from Easter brunch at the — yes — country club. Against my better instincts, I had to use valet parking because of the hordes of upper-middle-class merrymakers. Naturally, I didn't have a bill less than a 10 to tip the crack team of car retrievers, but I figured they must have some change, since they'd been shagging cars for a couple of hours. As one parker sprinted to find my car, I approached the remaining two to see if they could break a 10. The more mentally challenged asked, "How much change do you want?" While I was thinking about my reply, the cannier of the two pointed out to his partner the fairly straightforward arithmetic; after all, he observed, I wasn't tipping them. Seeking to join in the parking banter, and drawing on my professional training, I then alluded to the old *Saturday Night Live* fake commercials for the bank that just made change ("We make change"). As my audience of two actually seemed to show some interest, I closed with the punch line: "And you know what they said when asked how they make a profit: 'Simple, we make it up on volume.' " No response from half my audience, but luckily my car appeared; 10 seconds and two dollars later, we escaped.

POSTED Monday, April 13, 1998, at 4:30 P.M. PT

I woke up early today, as I was scheduled to take a day trip to the wilds of Arkansas — Paragould and Marmaduke, to be specific — to tour some plastic-packaging plants with one of my customers. I opened the paper to the rather startling news that NationsBank and BankAmerica as well as Banc One and First Chicago/NBD were merging. Deregulation and a sky-high stock market have indeed provoked human nature — a number of 50- and 60-something bankers are making some big, empire-building moves, while others are counting their options and golden parachutes and heading for the door.

When I was but a cub banker on Wall Street in 1977, I wrote an article for the *New Republic* about life at Morgan Guaranty. I titled my piece "Lush Places" in honor of William Boot's nature column in Evelyn Waugh's *Scoop* and, in fact, life was pretty lush around Morgan. Now bankerly antebellum gentility has vanished into right-sizing, top-line growth, and demanding mutual fund investors. Mighty Morgan's stock went up 7 points today — on the hope, no doubt, that some unknown financial angel will emerge to buy it. Morgan even stopped serving free lunch to its officers last month. Well, you know what they say....

We took our Citation 2 (your basic corporate jet) down to Jonesboro (yes, *the* Jonesboro), Arkansas, which, our pilots said, had the longest landing strip in northeast Arkansas. Hooey! Arkansas has been a favorite refuge for many St. Louis industrialists fleeing unions; last year, I toured Yellville, the biggest town near that wonderful resort of Whitewater. This is not glamorous business travel—we jogged around 400,000 square feet of warehouse, avoiding large bubbling machines extruding plastic in a Dickensian landscape that would have pleased William Blake. The surrounding neighborhood, however, is booming—orderly new subdivisions of brick and frame houses, most of which are equipped with satellite dishes. Despite the fact that we're in the middle of nowhere, there don't seem to be any available new workers. Most of the nonbusiness talk is about the start of the turkey season, which, I have to admit, will probably start without me.

We arrive back in St. Louis by midafternoon, landing in a strong crosswind right before a fierce spring thunderstorm. Having been incommunicado all morning, I check in with my trading desk and find our stock is up 1 3/4—the market likes these morning deals, for reasons that are beyond me. Returning to my office, I find several messages from investment bankers and the *Post-Dispatch*—Missouri banks over the last couple of years have been falling like flies. In fact, I had just had a shrink session last Friday with our investment adviser, the aforementioned Morgan, about current mergers and the Travelers/Citicorp deal. (That was the deal of last week.) The fact that Morgan is rumored to be on the block adds that nice ironic twist, as if you had just discovered your own psychiatrist is in therapy. The most salient point of the Travelers deal is that Sandy Weill's net worth went up $300 million the day of the announcement. There is no question who the alpha male is in that merger, but the phrase *enrichez-vous* does come to mind. In the words of Marcel Proust's financial adviser, *"Où sont les banques d'hier?"*

POSTED Tuesday, April 14, 1998, at 4:30 P.M. PT

I arrived at my office at 7:45 this morning to find messages from three different investment bankers saying they'd like to chat, as well as another voice mail from a consultant claiming the tornado that went through north St. Louis last night had led to the cancellation of her flight. Investment bankers and consultants are remarkably resourceful people; I just sensed I'd get another call from those bankers and that the consultant would show up somehow for her appointment this morning. I was certainly right about the bankers—by 9 I'd received thorough postmortems on the NationsBank and Banc One deals. The analyses were remarkably similar to those in the *Times* and the *Wall Street Journal* but, of course, the whole point of the calls was to see what I was thinking. There was the underlying implication from my informants that commercial bankers (e.g., me) who were not in the middle of a deal were like the Grande Armée waiting behind the Maginot line while the panzer divisions blitzkrieged across Poland. I decided the best course of action was to get out of my office and away from the phone.

The consultant's office called; she'd found a non-TWA flight from Newark and actually showed up close to our appointed time. She was a little glazed over, since TWA had called her at 3:30 A.M. to let her know she wouldn't be flying with them today. I spent most of the morning with her and my retail people, talking about databases, phone routing, and whether or not customers would pay for extra service. Luckily, we concluded they would. My favorite course in college (I was a history major) was Anthropology 103 (Primate Behavior), which, among other things, pointed out that most aboriginal tribes had about 500 members. (I can't remember if they ate the extras.) My professor claimed that was the ideal size for a society where everybody could know each other. It turns out most of our bank branches have about 500 really profitable customers and a lot of, shall we say, marginal contributors. Perhaps our defense against the mighty Citigroup and BancNations would be the TribalBanc, a confederation of friends using their local bank branch in defiance of 800 numbers and in support of myth-telling while waiting in teller lines.

By midafternoon, people seemed to be having some second thoughts about all these big deals. America Online had set up an e-mail center for people's opinions on bank mergers, while a few members of Congress were beginning to rattle their swords. One of the more perceptive e-mail messages (perhaps in the wrong chat room) claimed credit unions were communists (something I had long suspected) because, among other things, they didn't pay taxes. The politicians were talking about the dangers of concentration of power and the cost for deposit insurance if a really big bank failed. Jacksonian democracy was raising its righteous arm to slay this hydra — well, it would certainly pep up our company's annual meeting tomorrow.

I ended the day with an open house at my third grader's school. Four children and countless similar evenings have made us wise in school logistics. Despite being late, we crept past cars being ticketed on the road and in adjacent subdivisions to squeeze the minivan under a crab apple by the back door. Didn't even need an SUV. We spent a good part of the evening looking at the computer with Billy's best friend, Andrew Chang (yes, the smartest kid in the class). Billy's journal on growing his bean plant was pure *Into Thin Air*. The final entry? "Plant is dead."

Alex Kozinski

Alex Kozinski is a federal judge in California. He sits on the
9th U.S. Circuit Court of Appeals.

POSTED Wednesday, July 24, 1996, at 2:26 P.M. PT

I look back with nostalgia on the days when I had writer's block. Faced with a memorandum or term paper, I'd brood for hours — sometimes days — as the deadline approached. Finally, I would approach my typewriter the way one greets an enemy, and begin pecking out a tentative first sentence. Unhappy with the flawed effort, I'd noisily remove the offending sheet of paper, crumple it into a ball, and toss it in the trash like so much hazardous waste. So too with the next dozen attempts. Eventually, with the deadline closing in, the need to write something would become pressing, so I'd rescue some discarded scrap from the basket and push on. Much of my professional life now consists of writing — court opinions and orders, memoranda to colleagues, letters, e-mail, articles, book reviews. There is so much to do that I can no longer afford the luxury of writer's block. Time is so tightly budgeted that the subtle pleasure of procrastination is no longer available to me.

Nor has writing gotten much easier over the years. I've always found it painful — sort of like extracting something from deep inside and putting it on paper. But I know I must do it, and I also know that when I'm done I will likely delight in it. But the words seldom flow easily and of their own force — usually more a cricket pump than a gusher. In fact, I revise habitually, sometimes going through 50 drafts or more, but wait until I have a complete first draft before allowing myself the pleasure of revising, reorganizing, cutting.

Today's tough drafting job is a dissent. Two of my colleagues have signed on to an opinion that, in my view, is just plain wrong. They've misstated the facts and distorted the authorities. In a dozen or more ways, their view of the case differs from mine. How best to explain these differences so maybe, just maybe, one of them will change his mind? Or if not, perhaps another judge at another time will find my view persuasive. A dispute about a legal principle is never conclusively resolved in a single case; it can take years or decades, and dissenters are sometimes vindicated. Justice Harlan's dissent in *Plessy vs. Ferguson*, resoundingly rejected in 1896, be-came the law 58 years later in *Brown vs. Board of Education*. This is the exemplar we all secretly strive to emulate.

But first I must get past that first sentence. Let's see:

"My colleagues miss the boat because they're on a wild goose chase after having swallowed a red herring."

Hmm, a bit much. How about something more conciliatory: "Well-intentioned jurists can have honest differences of opinion in difficult cases."

Nah, too namby-pamby. I really want to say that my colleagues are out to lunch, but in a way that won't tick them off. How about: "Were we writing on a clean slate, this would be a difficult case. But we're not. Our cases, and those of the Supreme Court, blaze a clear path; my colleagues have strayed from it. I cannot join them in their misguided journey."

What I'm really thinking is, "Why couldn't THEY have writer's block?"

POSTED   Friday, July 26, 1996, at 2:26 P.M. PT

It's the week before oral argument and the office—known some-what pretentiously as "chambers"—is bustling. One week a month, eight months out of the year, I am assigned to an oral argument calendar with two of my colleagues on the U.S. Court of Appeals for the 9th Circuit. Arguments are heard throughout our far-flung territory; next week's calendar is in Anchorage. About five weeks ago the briefs and records for the Anchorage cases arrived in the office, thousands of pages filling a dozen or more boxes. My three law clerks divided the cases between them and recruited six externs, law students who are spending the summer with us, to help us digest the masses of documentation.

When they first come in, the cases—some 35 of them—are only names: *United States vs. Doe; Smith vs. Jones Corp.; In re Insolvent Q. Debtor*. As the law clerks and externs start reading and talking about the briefs, the cases come into focus—each a story of someone's usually unfortunate entanglement with the law. Memoranda from the three judges' offices start flowing over the court's e-mail system; we begin to make decisions, sometimes dispositive ones, long before the cases are even supposed to be heard.

"*Smith vs. Jones Corp.* is a simple contract dispute controlled by the law of Alaska. There is Alaska Supreme Court authority directly on point," one of my colleagues writes. "I believe the case can be submitted on the briefs." Submitting a case on the briefs means that there will be no oral argument, as it would be a waste of the court's time and the clients' money to have the lawyers come and argue a case where the result is preordained.

"Appellant in *United States vs. Jones* has filed a motion to move the argument from Thursday to Tuesday, as his lawyer is tied up in trial. I vote to grant the motion," another colleague writes. My law clerks offer their recommendations and we send consent by e-mail in both cases. Slowly, the argument calendar is pared and shaped, leaving us plenty of time to focus our attention on the cases raising the most difficult issues.

As argument week approaches, the law clerks and externs carefully review each of the cases and present them to me in memos and conversation. They analyze the issues, pull out key portions of the records, and gather the relevant authorities. All the materials are then put in briefing books that I consult, in conjunction with the parties' own submissions, as I prepare for the sitting. Careful preparation for argument is important, not only because it helps me to engage in meaningful colloquy with the lawyers about their cases, but also because it enables me to vote at post-argument conferences with my colleagues.

Meanwhile, work on other cases continues. I am making progress on a dozen or so opinions or dissents from prior calendars; reviewing opinions circulated by my colleagues; writing memos to my colleagues about their opinions; responding to memos they have sent me. The flow never abates. During the course of a year, each of our judges decides some 300 cases.

After more than 10 years as a judge of this court, I find that the flow of cases begins to resemble a moving train, with each window revealing a still life of an individual human drama. The sheer volume of cases and the fact that we rarely see the faces of the participants—just written words on paper and, sometimes, the arguments of lawyers—make it difficult to remember that there are human beings somewhere looking to us with hope and yearning for a decision in their favor.

The law, too, is quite complex. Cases often turn on legal technicalities that bear only a tangential relationship to concepts such as fairness and equity. Justice, we tell ourselves—and I do believe this —is done if the law is applied without regard to the outcome in a particular case. One of my law clerks walks in to talk about an opinion he has been drafting. The plaintiff has a strong case on the merits, and presents a heartbreaking human tragedy. But there is a difficult statute of limitations question; the case may have to be dismissed. We've been discussing the case for several days, looking for a credible way to vault the limitations hurdle. We find none. We try another approach, but to no avail. Could I write an opinion that steps around the issue? That would fudge the facts just a little bit to make it come out right? Who would really care, except, of course, the defendant? I'm tempted but can't see my way to doing it. Is it a matter of principle or a subtle form of hubris?

There is a story, no doubt apocryphal, about the lawyer who fights ferociously for his client in a criminal case. He is brilliant in his cross-examination, moving in his summation. The jury, nevertheless, comes back with a conviction. "Where do we go from here?" the frightened and bewildered client asks the lawyer.

"Well," the lawyer answers, "I'm going home and you're going to jail."

Lawyers and judges, the professionals of the legal system, do their best to untangle the painful knots created by human interactions, but ultimately they must disengage lest they be sucked into the vortex. My law clerk and I go over the case one more time but find no solution. I take a deep breath and turn back to preparing for next week's calendar.

The train moves on.

John Lanchester

John Lanchester is the author of The Debt to Pleasure *and* Mr. Phillips.

POSTED Wednesday, April 19, 2000, at 10:00 A.M. PT

I often ponder a remark of Tom Wolfe's, to the effect that the reason Balzac managed to write 60 books was because he had no labor-saving devices to "help" him. Yesterday I had to go into town—that's central London—to do a variety of labor-saving-device-related chores. For instance, my shiny new printer, which prints in lavish Technicolor, but eats through cartridges like a sumo wrestler with a tapeworm, needed yet another fix of its favorite supplies.

Anyway, the silver lining was the chance to go to the greengrocer. Our part of town has an excellent fishmonger and butcher, but it doesn't have a place to buy half-decent vegetables. We don't have farmers' markets in England; or rather, we're only just beginning to have them: The single one in South London is open only on the third Saturday of the month.

On my way home, I therefore parked illegally outside a shop called Villandry and ran inside to see what looked good. This is a snooty French-run deli with high-grade, distinctly uncheap imported produce. Unfortunately, they didn't seem to have all that much stuff in. The new-season Italian asparagus looked fine, fat, and white, but it cost £10.80 (about $17) for a small bunch. I did a double take when I saw the price. £10.80 for about eight asparagus? To be worth that much it would have to leap into the pan on its own and then wash up the plates after you'd eaten.

Then I saw something looking green and healthy and fresh at the same time as, through the window, I saw an approaching traffic warden. Broccoli tops. I'd never heard of broccoli tops, indeed I would have been hard pressed to tell you whether broccoli had a top, but on the other hand they were £1.20 a kilo—the cheapest thing in the store by far. I grabbed a bunch and headed for the tills. On my left, a well-groomed-seeming woman, looking a little like Anne Bancroft, was buying caviar. On my right, a man who looked like a 60-year-old Danny DeVito having a bad hair day was brandishing two different brands of matzo meal while trying to hit on the counter assistant, who looked like Sarah Michelle Gellar. "So you've never tried the French one?" he was saying. "*Meme que vous êtes Français?*" —even though you're French? She didn't blink. "I'm from Romania," she said.

I arrived at the middle till. The woman there looked at my bunch of greenery. "I have no idea what that is," she said. "Broccoli tops," I said, more confidently than I felt. "One twenty a kilo." Anne Bancroft, Danny DeVito, Sarah Michelle Gellar, and I all looked at each other, and then at her. Everybody shrugged. I bought the broccoli tops and beat the warden to my car. In the evening, while my son was running around the kitchen, I tried to work out what to do with the greenery. I had thought there might be something in a wonderful 19th-century Italian book called *The Art of Eating Well* by Pellegrino Artusi (a huge hero in Italy, hardly known elsewhere), but no. I tried Alan Davidson's amazing new *Oxford Companion to Food*. You never look in this book without finding something remarkable. On this occasion, I learned that broccoli "is one of the most puzzling members of the cabbage family," for the surprising reason that "although shopkeepers and shoppers can easily distinguish it from the cauliflower, botanists cannot"—in fact, they are both the same species, *Brassica oler-acea*. Weird. This seems to me worthy of an episode of *The X-Files*, one of the jokey ones that wins an Emmy. But no hint about how to cook the tops.

In the end I went for a stir-fry. It isn't even clear whether you eat the leafy bit at the top or the thick stalky part at the bottom, so I decided to chop them and cook both. "Dangerous," I said to my son, as I picked up the kitchen knife and started chopping. He said, "Dan'gus." As he did so I slipped and cut myself deeply in the middle pad of my right index finger. I can't quite figure out how I managed to do that, since I'm right-handed and was holding the knife in that hand—but anyway I did.

The received wisdom in kitchens is that sharp knives are safer since you don't have to press as hard and are thus less likely to slip. True—but when you do slip and cut yourself, you really cut yourself. As a result, although I usually touch-type, I'm writing this by the hunt-and-peck method, making great use of my right middle finger. My index finger is still throbbing under its plaster. As for the broccoli tops, the leaves had almost no taste and the stalks were inedibly chewy, and I recommend never trying them.

POSTED Thursday, April 20, 2000, at 10:00 A.M. PT

It's a melancholy truth that most writers lead pretty boring lives. It's this that underlies the often-desperate attempts, in profiles and interviews and blurbs, to make us sound much more interesting than we are. The most hackneyed of these tactics is the long list of summer jobs, tarted up to make some keyboard-bound, teaching-job-cosseted scribbler sound like a cross between Jack London and Mata Hari. X worked as a stevedore (i.e., in the back office of his uncle's shipping firm), bartender (i.e., once poured a drink at the students' union bar), farmhand (i.e., once picked his own strawberries at a pick-your-own-strawberry farm), etc.

The truth, which every writer and most readers know, is that the only real interest in any writer's work lies in the words on the page, and the best part of their lives lies in sitting alone in a room putting those words down. How interesting is that? On the other hand, it might make a refreshing change to read the truth. If I were to read an interview or blurb about how someone never went anywhere and never did anything and had absolutely no non-literary claims on our attention, I for one would hurtle out to buy the book.

As for myself, my own life is so externally eventless that what to do about coffee in the morning counts as a significant choice. I usually drink one cup a day—I like to think of this as being a little like James Bond. "I only like one drink before dinner, but I like that drink to be very large and very cold and very strong and very well made."

The choice used to be simple, since there was for a brief period a very good cafe about a 15-minute walk away (in our infrequent good weather) or a five-minute drive (most of the time). The coffee shop was part of a chain started by two investment bankers who had spent time in the United States and calculated that the vogue for designer coffees would, like every other American trend, arrive in the U.K. about three years later. They went to Starbucks and proposed to start a franchise in the U.K. Starbucks turned them down, so they began their own chain, wittily called the Seattle Coffee Company. This was in every respect a slavish imitation of the U.S. original. The coffee, however, was very good, and that's where I used to go.

Anyway, Starbucks eventually wised up and bought the chain from the investment bankers for, if I remember correctly, £52 million ($82 million)—a million pounds per branch. Then they gradually abandoned the Seattle Coffee Company logo and rebadged them as Starbucks. And now the coffee sucks: weak, thin, and frighteningly variable as to the all-important milk-vs.-foam balance in a cappuccino or latte. There's always a different person at the espresso machine, usually a trainee, and you can tell it's all random because the cup literally weighs a different amount each time you go there. I have tried coming down with HMS syndrome—that's *Harry Met Sally* syndrome, where you come on all hyper-specific about what you want, in this case asking for a strong very dry latte that isn't quite a cappuccino—but it doesn't work. So that's that.

There's a rumor that there's a very good Italian-run cafe in Northcote Road, about a 10-minute drive away, in a part of town that—because so many young families move there, owing to the relative cheapness of South London—is known as Nappy Valley. I seriously contemplated checking this out yesterday, but then added up the time: 10 minutes there, possibly five minutes to find somewhere to park, 10 minutes to order and drink the coffee in situ, 10 minutes home. That makes it into a proper excursion rather than a businesslike pre-work small treat.

No, it was a school day, so I stuck to my new routine. A while ago a friend gave me one of those small home-scale cappuccino machines. Proper coffee aficionados disapprove of these, on the grounds that they don't generate enough pressure to make serious espresso, but this one seems to work fine. Or at least it did until the measuring jug broke. Now you have to guess the correct amount of water by eye—which adds a nerve-jangling note of excitement and unpredictability. Too much water and it doesn't get hot or pressurized enough. Too little and there's nothing to drink and no foam. Yesterday, and indeed this morning, I got it just right. Who da man? You da man! As a leisure activity this might be less attention-worthy than machine-gunning my initials into a shark's head—one of Hemingway's pastimes—but I'll bet it made me just as happy.

Jim Leff

Jim Leff is the Alpha Hound at Chowhound.com and the author of
The Eclectic Gourmet Guide to Greater New York City: The Undiscovered World of Hyperdelicious Offbeat Eating in All Five Boroughs.

POSTED Monday, March 27, 2000, at 10:00 A.M. PT

It wasn't until mid-chew of Maria's luxuriously tender, mega-
toothsome galbi-jim that a lump formed in my throat. I'm not referring to an errant shred of relentlessly marinated Korean beef
rib. This was a lump Heimlich himself couldn't maneuver; an emotional node of sheer despair. Bo, one of the greatest New York City
restaurants, would, as of Sunday, be no mo'.

I'd arrived for this Last Supper with a heavy heart, but attacked
my meal with vigor, impelled by a solemn determination to commit to memory every magical bite. The fried mung bean pancakes
were profoundly crisp and so golden they actually shimmered. The
kimchi hid infinite layers of complexity beneath its perfectly balanced flavor façade of sour heat and fresh vegetable snap. Sliced
eggplant was unbelievably pure and expressive, and spring chicken
with ginseng and sticky rice in soup was almost entirely unsalted,
allowing the nectarous broth to sing its delicate bel canto without
distraction.

It wasn't just the food that was singing; Maria had been playing
Carmen over and over throughout this, her final week of opera-

tion. While I raptly ate my dinner, growing ever more ecstatic yet ever more doleful, the opera built toward its climax. Then, precisely as I bit into the aforementioned sacramental morsel of galbi-jim — re-entering the rarified blissful realms those marinated beef ribs had so often revealed to me — the soprano screeched a high undulating wail of misery and despair. I found myself so worked up by it all that, in spite of my disdain for opera, I couldn't help but get choked up.

Maria (a k a Hoon Mee Cho) had worked as pastry chef at the ritzy Sign of the Dove but quit to establish a place of her own where she could return to her Korean roots. Her fare at this elegant but modest Queens storefront was so personal and so deep that it completely transcended any notion of Korean restaurant food. This feat was accomplished without the use of clever fusion-y elements or fancified ingredients (nor were there pastries; an exquisitely selected few bites of sliced fruit was the only dessert ever offered). No dishes were served that couldn't be found in hundreds of other Korean eateries, but Maria's versions tasted like a completely different cuisine. Bo wasn't a Korean restaurant. Or, perhaps, it was the *only* Korean restaurant.

Nonetheless, the place never caught on, though it wasn't for lack of effort by Maria, her intensely loyal cadre of fans, and New York's food writers, whose rave reviews plastered Bo's walls and windows. Sometimes when I'd drop by, Maria would tell me I was her first customer in days. It was heartbreaking, but, amazingly, she never slackened. On the contrary: As the situation grew more and more desperate (the waitress, unable to live on 15 percent of nothing, went back to Korea months ago, leaving Maria no choice but to wait and bus tables herself), she responded by determinedly making everything *even better*. Nearly every meal I'd eaten at Bo was superior to the preceding one. She was daring the world to eat elsewhere; creating food that might, via the sheer magnetic pull of its almost diabolical goodness, lure customers off the streets. Yet only a trickle of business was ever conjured up.

A year ago, Maria spoke about closing shop, so drastic measures were called for. I mobilized the New York chowhound community via my Web site, and local hounds took up the rallying cry, renting cars for pilgrimages to Bo and posting rapturous post-meal paeans on our message boards. But while this brought some relief, once-per-month regulars cannot sustain a restaurant.

Everyone tried to drum into Maria the recognition that Bo—with its impossibly obscure address—never had a fighting chance but that fame and fortune awaited her across the river, in Manhattan, if only she could find investors. The truism used to be that hard work brought sure success in America, and perhaps that's still true today—but only if you also have a good location. And polished marketing skills. And a few million bucks of seed money. In the meantime, Maria's heading back to Korea, though she says she hopes to return

After dinner, Maria walked me to the door—as she did with all her dejected customers this weekend. She seemed relieved that her Sisyphean struggle was finally over. I, however, was pretty bummed out. Heading back to the chowmobile, I felt like Charlie Brown, grimacing over his lost kite. And then I remembered that Charlie Brown's gone forever, too.

POSTED Wednesday, March 29, 2000, at 10:00 A.M. PT

Still haunted by the recent closure of one of my favorite restaurants, I went for a slice of white pizza, and the ricotta reminded me of the tofu at Bo; Mrs. Schneiderman at the bagel shop looked, to my grief-addled perceptions, exactly like Maria. The wind whispers "mung bean pancakes." I've really got to get out of here.

I was thinking of pulling a Marlon Brando and running to Paris to rent a flat and have impersonal sex with a total stranger in order to shake all this off, but I decided that city isn't like the best possible place for a chowhound to decompress. So I fired up the chowmobile and set course for Chappaqua, a one-hour drive upstate. I've heard that Bill Clinton's favorite dish is a Big Mac, and, given such anti-chowhound propensities, I think he and Hill made a superb choice with their home purchase there. There's nothing to eat for miles around; this part of Westchester County is a near chow vacuum. Perfect.

I only got about three miles before the chowhound decompression plan fell apart. One cannot pass the Belmont section of the Bronx without stopping for a bourek at Tony and Tina's, and the road to Chappaqua runs right by that nabe. Well...one of the roads to Chappaqua does. Actually, it's a pretty out-of-the-way road.

OK, so I made a special trip. But man, was it worth it. Tony and Tina's, an erstwhile pizzeria, is a legendary bourek bastion. The pizza is standard, but insiders flock here for their three flavors of Albanian zillion-layered pastry pies: soft, coarsely chopped lamb, tangy cheese, or tender spinach. The insides are moist and noodly, the outsides crispy/chewy. God.

The bourek had restored some of my *joie de manger*, so I arrived in Chappaqua all stirred up and eager to find something great, against all hope, for dinner...decompression be damned. I'd hoped to hit a Chilean bakery in Sleepy Hollow I'd read about in a Chilean newspaper (I read all the ethnic press), but it closes early. Then I remembered a previous project, still uncompleted: Ossining, home of Sing Sing prison and, potentially, some terrific undiscovered eats.

Many northern Westchester communities keep their minority populations underground, but Ossining has an almost mainstream Portuguese community. There are two Portuguese sit-downs and one lesser-known Portuguese barbecue joint, but I've long suspected there might be treasure hidden in the cracks.

So a friend and I zigzagged through Ossining's hilly streets in search of something undiscovered, something awesome. We passed the better known — more obvious and Zagatesque — of the two local Portuguese restaurants, and saw that they'd adopted a new, distinctly un-Portuguese name: La Puerta. A sign promises "Portuguese/Mexican Cuisine." The two couldn't be more dissimilar; think Japanese/Italian or Swiss/Jamaican. But I had a hunch it was worth trying, and I always follow my hunches (after years of this stuff, I find I'm seldom wrong; my friends never object when I make squealing U-turns when we pass places I deem to "look good").

The crowd at the bar was indeed a Porto-Mex hybrid, but no one was eating. A blackboard behind the bar promised, "Buy four drinks, get one free!" Not an auspicious sign. We were presented with terrible chips, weak salsa, and a schizo menu of middle-of-the-road Portuguese dishes and the most touristy Tex-Mex items (chimichangas, etc., etc.) imaginable. The temptation to bolt was strong. We ordered glasses of wine (clearly, I hadn't yet fully regained my chowhound instincts) and found ourselves drinking what tasted like Château Pine-Sol. But then the food arrived and all our angst melted away. It was amazing.

We'd ordered a hodgepodge. A couple of Portuguese soups were very nice, but then came chorizo quesadillas from heaven. It dawned on me that peppery chorizo sausage was the common denominator between Portuguese and Mexican cooking. In fact, the Mexican chef was using the Portuguese chef's fancy, custom-smoked rich meaty sausage, which was almost too good to melt cheese over and stuff in a tortilla. It was unbelievable. Alongside: great buttery school-cafeteria rice and refried beans that managed to be both light and lard-redolent. Pork tacos were just as deftly cooked, perked up with a mind-bendingly complex sauce full of lime juice and coriander (which, come to think of it, is the other common-denominator ingredient). We thought we had peaked, and then along came a side dish of mole poblano, a rich chocolaty-spicy sauce, that was pure ambrosia—by far the best I've ever tasted.

The chef—though forced to prepare a Tex-Mex menu straight

out of Chi-Chi's—has a wonderfully fresh touch. Sure enough, he/she turned out to be from Jalisco—and quite possibly the only Jaliscan chef in this part of the country. I'd scored big-time, in a region with a chowhound difficulty rating of 9.5, no less! Tomorrow I'll attend to another unfinished project up here in the hinterlands: a Hudson Valley village that's turned Central American!

POSTED   Thursday, March 30, 2000, at 10:00 A.M. PT

Some people dream of traveling to Hawaii, Rio, or the Côte d'Azur. For me, a destination that has long enticed is West Haverstraw, N.Y., an anonymous little village a few miles south of Bear Mountain. I've never been there, but a reliable source once told me that it's a haven for Central Americans, and there would surely be lots of places serving my favorite Salvadoran, Honduran, and Guatemalan dishes, and perhaps (I quake at the thought!) even Nicaraguan, Panamanian, Costa Rican, and Belizian—cuisines I've been looking for for years.

So, I crossed Bear Mountain Bridge and pointed the chowmobile down Route 9W, paralleling the Hudson River, in high spirits. I was savoring last night's chorizo quesadillas, enjoying the spring day, and glad to be back in the saddle again, doing what I love: driving somewhere new and intriguing for an afternoon of contented chowhounding.

I passed a fast-food joint called Annie's, a kind of old-fashioned roadside drive-in New Yorkers only find upstate, and on impulse I cut the wheel and skidded into their parking lot. What had caught my attention was a handwritten note tacked to a takeout window reading "Onion Rings!" It was essential to conserve appetite, but I knew I had to try those onion rings.

The counter girl fried up a fresh batch, and they were extraordinary. Nothing fancy or revisionist (not that there's anything necessarily wrong with fancy or revisionist), but simply a perfect execution of the classic recipe; these were truly the ur-onion rings. Oil was fresh, onions were sweet and just firm enough, and batter was ultra-crisp yet melted instantly in the mouth.

Though I normally show professional restraint and discipline while working—sampling mere bitefuls and letting The Mouths Along for the Ride clean the plates—I finished the entire order. I didn't feel guilty at all; life is short and great chow is fleeting.

Not as fleeting as West Haverstraw, however. The place didn't seem to actually exist. As far as I could determine, it consists of a stretch of nondescript residential land that weaves its unshapely self around Haverstraw. As I drove along side roads, signs constantly announced my leaving and then re-entering West Haverstraw. There was no town center other than a half-mile of 9W filled with generic sprawl—certainly no Salvadorian pupusarias or anything. So I ventured into the village of non-West Haverstraw.

I'll cut to the chase. In Haverstraw, I spotted a few Latino restaurants, but only Mexicans and Dominicans, and those are cuisines easily found back in the city. I did quick take-outs in two of them, and enjoyed impressive cooking…but no Central American wonderland.

I probably should have felt frustrated and disappointed, but in fact I smiled all the way back to Chappaqua. I might yet one day find West Haverstraw, and in the meantime those superb onion rings were an accomplishment sufficient to satisfy me both personally and professionally.

Which got me to brooding about my job; whether it's a self-indulgent waste of time and energy to drive around and write about onion rings.

Here's the thing: People will go to Annie's, they'll try the onion rings, and something may spark in their eyes as they begin to realize that things can be better; life can be better. They'll see that if only they try a little harder, drive a little farther, any occasion can be a special occasion, and life can be a rich and satisfying adventure. That there's no reason to settle for the charmless junk that's constantly marketed at us in *all* realms, not just food. That it's incredibly liberating and rewarding to jump off the treadmill.

I also recalled how much it meant to Maria (the miraculous chef-owner of Bo) that at least a small group understood and appreciated what she was doing. If I can tip discerning eaters to the Marias of the world—many of whom toil outside the media/marketing spotlight—they'll eat and live better, and deserving chefs will have more of a shot at cultivating the following they need (unlike a painter or musician, a chef, working in an inherently participatory art form, is nothing without an audience).

It's the passion of chowhounds (the 10 percent who live to eat, but who—unlike "foodies"—refuse to eat where they're told) to seek and revere such unappreciated treasure, and I happen to be a professional chowhound...and host of a cyberhaven in which we hounds can compare notes. This strikes me as legitimate work.

We needn't settle for the bland, the uniform, and the highly processed. It's a matter of training one's attention on the treasure in the cracks and choosing to patronize those heroic few who take pride and care in what they do rather than the vast majority who coldly seek maximal profit from minimal effort. Most of us, sadly, live our lives oblivious to all this.

An onion ring can change the world.

Michael Lewis

Michael Lewis is the author, most recently, of The New New Thing.

Posted Monday, Jan. 10, 2000, at 10:30 A.M. PT

We landed at Charles de Gaulle Airport a couple of days before Christmas. One dog, one infant, nine books on how to get along with the French, and 11 pieces of luggage, three of which had already gone missing. We drove for 90 minutes in heavy traffic, the baby howling, the wife attempting to hide her exposed nursing bosom from the driver, and the dog scratching her bottom across the floor of the minivan. At length we arrived at our new home on the Left Bank, which we'd never actually seen, except in photographs. It was a small cluster of room-size houses in a tiny garden tucked away at the back of a courtyard of an old apartment building. We piled out of the car and rushed to the front door, a small teeming peristaltic bundle of needs and hopes and anticipations. The door failed to open. The key mailed to us by the landlord did not fit the lock.

For the next 30 minutes, we sat in the cold, dark Paris courtyard and waited, mainly because we couldn't think what else to do. We were being punished for our sins; we had wanted to dance, now we were paying the fiddler. It had been fun, when people asked us where we lived, to say, "Well, that's hard to say, since at the end of the year we're moving to Paris." They were all envious, or pretended to be, which was just as gratifying. For the past six months we had been playing our new role: People Who Are About To Live in Paris. Now here we were, in Paris itself. We knew no one. We spoke so little French that it was better to claim we spoke none. We had no purpose. And that, I should have reminded myself, was the point.

About 18 months ago, my wife, Tabitha, and I were on an airplane when I began to complain about adulthood. One of the many things I dislike about being a grown-up is the compulsion to have a purpose in life. People are forever asking why you are doing whatever you happen to be doing and before long you succumb to the need to supply an answer. The least naturally ambitious people can have ambition thrust upon them in this way. Once you've established yourself as a more or less properly functioning adult, it is nearly impossible to just go somewhere and screw off.

Five months pregnant with our first child, Tabitha pointed out that the feeling of being weighed down by adulthood wasn't likely to improve anytime soon. Parenthood loomed. There was a time when I suspected this wouldn't have much effect on me. I figured that the chemical rush that attended new motherhood might get me off the hook—that Tabitha would happily embrace all the new unpleasant chores and I'd stop in from time to time to offer advice. She'd do the play by play; I'd do the color commentary. Five months into the pregnancy that illusion had been pretty well shattered by the anecdotal evidence. One friend with a truly amazing gift for getting out of things he did not want to do wrote to describe his own experience of fatherhood. "Remember that life you thought you had?" he wrote. "Guess what. It's not yours anymore."

At any rate, since a door in our lives seemed to be closing, we went looking for a window. As we sat on the plane, one thing led to another, and before long we had spread out on our laps the map of the world at the back of the in-flight magazine. We had no idea where we would wind up; we just knew we were going someplace foreign. My vague desire to live in Africa got swapped, unfairly I felt, for my wife's even vaguer one to live in Asia. Whole continents vanished from our future in an instant. After 40 minutes we had shrunk the world to two cities: Barcelona and Paris. A few days later we were at a dinner party. The man across the table, an old friend, mentioned that his sister had this old, charming place in Paris occupied by tenants she couldn't stand. There it was: Our bluff was being called. We agreed to rent the place, sight unseen.

Now we are in Paris, in the cold and the dark, homeless and friendless and tongue-tied. Unbelievably, I hear myself asking: Why on earth did we come? Just then an elderly woman hobbles into the cobblestone courtyard and makes for the door nearest ours. Our new French neighbor! A distant memory lifts my spirits.

Fifteen years ago, when I arrived in London to live outside the United States for the first time in my life, I was fitting the key into my new front door when an elderly woman called to me from the neighboring garden. "My name is Amanda Martin," she said in an ancient voice, "and I'll be your friend if you'll have me." Just like that, Amanda Martin had taken me into her life; I had a friend. She'd turned 100 that year. The queen had sent her a telegram to congratulate her. When you know someone with that kind of standing in society, you somehow feel you belong, too. Assimilation is just another word for acquiring a bit of the local status.

I eye our new old French neighbor with longing. And even though I know that the moment history looks as if it is repeating itself is exactly the moment it is not, I feel a little leap in my spirits. I walk over, open a door for her, and say bonjour. She doesn't even look up, just keeps tap-tapping on by with her head down and right into her apartment. As she closes her door, the odor of stove gas wafts into the courtyard. A voice behind me says, "She so old she forgets to turn off her gas burners when she goes out." I turn around. There stands a young man wearing a black stocking cap, a navy pea coat, and a grim expression. He looks like something dreamed up by Dostoevsky, yet he sounds perfectly American. He motions to the door closing behind the elderly French woman: "One day she'll come back here, light a match, and this whole building will be a crater."

He puts his hand in the pocket of his pea coat. "I have your key," he says.

Sarah Lyall

Sarah Lyall reports for the New York Times *from London.*

POSTED   Monday, Jan. 13, 1997, at 4:30 P.M. PT

Studies have shown, the papers reported last week, that people's brains actually shrink when they're pregnant. (This is apparently why pregnant women are so spaced out and inept, and why no one trusts their testimony in court.) Leaving aside the fact that these were the British papers and you can't believe anything they say, unless they are reporting that Prince Charles communes with aliens, this is not news to me. My brain is so small now that if I were killed by cannibals, they would put it back. Why haven't I mailed my Christmas cards yet? My brain is too small! (It's not too late, is it?)

Even without the benefit of reason, these last few weeks of pregnancy are supposed to be a wonderful time of joyous anticipation, and I'm sorry to have to say that this weekend all I wanted to do was yell at my husband because the house is such a mess. Apparently that was because of the "nesting instinct," in which, as the pregnant person, you supposedly spend all your time putting charming little touches on your home, like installing floral borders in the baby's room, gluing ruffled pieces of fabric next to the windows, I don't know—needlepointing cunning animal cushions or stripping down the paint and stenciling in scenes of sweet wee fairies living under toadstools. But at our house, it's all we can do to pick the mail up off the floor. My husband—who has, in a miraculous feat of one-upmanship, turned out to be a bigger slob than I—leaves trails of papers behind him wherever he goes, like a snail with its path of slime. He glowers if you touch anything. It's not pleasant. Until now, I have always held that people should do what they want. But not any more. Now I believe that people should do what I want.

We are both so scared that after the baby comes we won't have time to do anything ever again (this has something to do with the knowing look people with children give you, when they say, ominously, "Your life will never be the same"), that we both spent the weekend in a frenzy of work. Since we're journalists, that involved dropping even more pieces of paper on the floor, to add to the ones that are already there. If our house were in America, it would be a Superfund site (they don't have them here). All this working makes me sad, because I had dreamed of spending these last baby-less days in a valedictory fit of self-absorption, trying new hair products and having lovely creams slathered on my face and attending daily body-awareness classes (I'm too fat for actual exercise). Alternatively, I hoped to go to a lot of movies and to spend time holding hands with my husband (too fat for anything else) while discussing the philosophical implications of parenthood. Sorry. I have so much left to do that, the way things are going, if the child (due in about two weeks) is early, I'm screwed—brain shrinkage is even worse postpartum. This means that every time I feel something funny in my stomach, I start to panic. Not yet! Get back in there!

Of course, all this means that I am in major denial. At this point, women are supposed to be dreaming of the baby—pleasant anticipatory scenes of hugs and cuddles, or else frightening narratives in which you leave the child somewhere, like down a well, and can't find it again. Me? I either dream about doing the tedious things I do anyway (I spent hours the other night paying my American Express bill, for instance — that was meaningful), or I dream about dogs. I did, in fact, lose two dogs in a dream last week. Given that the dogs were clearly supposed to represent the baby — in a Freudian, metaphorical sense — what did the dream mean? I think I'm going to give birth to a dog? I like dogs better than children? Both choices are frightening, given that it's too late to send the child back — even people with no brains can see that.

POSTED Tuesday, Jan. 14, 1997, at 4:30 P.M. PT

"Hey, he's almost as fat as you!" one of my office mates said cheerfully this morning, showing me a photograph of an extremely large man poised over an extremely large side of beef in a gourmet-and-lifestyle magazine. What could I say? When you're pregnant, you become an enormous blank slate upon which people freely impose their own fears, aggressions, and worldviews, in an apparent form of transference that does not involve an actual therapist. "I spent yesterday with a friend who has a child," confided my co-worker Sarah Jo at the coffee machine yesterday, "and it's enough to put you off having babies forever." Pam, another colleague, can't pass me without making some dire remark about her own children ("I never had such a bad backache," or "I was really depressed afterwards," or "They get worse as they get older"), while everyone else leaves me exaggerated amounts of room in the hall while eyeing my stomach and making jolly remarks like, "Getting bigger!" I know they don't mean to be mean, but hey — is there something going on here? Or am I just too sensitive?

I went to the doctor yesterday — an ordeal, getting across town — and I'm happy to report that nothing's happened! Maybe nothing will ever happen. Maybe I'll be pregnant for the next 50 years, getting bigger and bigger and evolving from my current status (youngish, smallish water buffalo) through the really mammoth parts of the animal kingdom (aged, enormous whale). These last few weeks are so strange, as you stand on the edge of a precipice but can't tell when you will finally go over the edge. You don't know what you'll get, either. It's like waiting for a guest who will be staying with you for the rest of your life, only YOU DON'T KNOW ANYTHING ABOUT HIM (or her). And, of course, you have to read *Goodnight Moon* aloud at least 6,000 times before the child finally gets a place of its own.

Lumbering around with all this extra weight makes you tired, and last night I had to stay up until 2 A.M. writing a story for the paper. That was fine, except that when you're that exhausted, you're much more prone to error. I don't think I made any mistakes last night, but you never can tell. I've made a lot in the 10 years I've been a reporter, and they always end up in the space of shame: the corrections column. When I started out, I thought you could trust your instincts, which was incredibly stupid.

Among the things I've done wrong, along with the requisite misspellings and garbled quotes, were to misdefine a megawatt (I said it was 1,000 watts), to underestimate the speed at which radio transmissions travel (I said that it took three days for the first trans-Atlantic radio message to get from Europe to Newfoundland), and to say that the New York State government was short by $789 (actual shortfall: $789 million). But what may have been the best correction of all time was not my fault. It came nearly two years ago, when the paper ran a transcript of Sen. Al D'Amato's unflattering remarks about Judge Lance Ito on the *Imus in the Morning* radio show. (Moral: Don't go on the radio.) Anyway, the next day, the paper announced that part of the D'Amato quote had been rendered inaccurately. "He said, 'I mean, this is a disgrace. Judge Ito will be well known,'" the correction said. "He did not say, 'Judge Ito with the wet nose.'"

POSTED Thursday, Jan. 16, 1997, at 4:30 P.M. PT

The handout they gave my husband at our childbirth class last night included a survey of fathers' attitudes toward labor. Most of the men surveyed said they were thrilled to be there, looked forward to delivering the next one single-handedly at home, wished they could have a baby themselves, etc. But it was the response farther down the page that caught the attention of my particular husband. "Three percent of respondents," he announced, "said that they got sick."

It cheered him up, knowing there were others like him. His attitude toward prenatal classes has been that of a political prisoner forced at bayonet-point to watch videos of other prisoners being tortured by means of electrodes attached to their genitals. At the first class, he arrived spectacularly late and — surveying the room of pregnant women slumped against beanbags, upon which their husbands were sitting so that they could rub the women's necks in a supportive and loving manner — came down and sat on the floor beside me, taking up half the beanbag space. Then he fell asleep. The instructor, meanwhile, was using her props (plastic uterus with plastic fetus; sculpture of a human spine on a wire; fake baby with the top of its head sticking out of a large sock) to make various labor-related points. She had a big board, too, filled with informational sheets. It was when she flipped from the page labeled "Pain Relief During Labor" to the page labeled "Parking Near the Hospital" that my husband finally woke up.

Last night was particularly awful, because they showed us videos of several actual women going through childbirth. Stephanie, the first one, decided to take only nitrous oxide, so she spent a jolly 12 hours moaning and whimpering and occasionally laughing at nothing, the way we did when we got high in college. "She looks like she's gone insane," my husband said. All around the room, the men were riveted to the video, their jaws dropping as they watched scenes of heaving and panting, unbearable pain and carnage. The placenta — truly unspeakable, bigger and meatier than any piece of liver you will ever see — seemed particularly to engross them. "I found this kind of upsetting," I said to our nuts-and-berries-ish instructor afterward, "particularly the woman without the painkillers." She looked at me with narrowed eyes, as if I had a can of pesticides and was proposing to spray it throughout the room. "That," she said, "was the most real. THAT IS THE WAY IT IS." (My husband, meanwhile, had discovered the plate of sandwiches laid out to allay the hunger of the pregnant women. He ate five.)

So touchy-feely was the whole thing that when we went across the street to look at the hospital, I fully expected to see labor rooms planted with little mini-fields, complete with crops that you could harvest right after you gave birth. I wondered why we had to spend so much time learning about a process that takes, at most, 48 hours, when what we really need is instruction on the next 48 years. How about a class on what to do when the kid comes home with pierced nipples, a collection of hubcaps culled from neighborhood vehicles, and a baggie filled with what he describes as "talcum powder"?

My husband? He's trying. And he is comforted by the fact that, as lame as he is, he isn't as lame as another man I heard about, who arrived at his childbirth class and proceeded to sit stiffly in the only chair in the room (his wife was slouching helplessly against her beanbag somewhere else). He looked increasingly unhappy. The instructor noticed this and thought she could help him confront his repressed, but obviously intense, emotions. "What are you thinking?" she asked him gently. "I was just thinking," he said, "that I'd like to go skiing."

Mary Manhein

Mary Manhein is a forensic anthropologist, a coroner,
and the author of The Bone Lady, *a memoir of her work.*

POSTED Monday, March 20, 2000, at 10:00 A.M. PT

This morning I woke up a little earlier than usual, around 4, due in part to my one-eyed Siamese cat, Maggie, who was nipping at my toes, and the baying of my beagle, Bogey, who wanted to get to the raccoon that nests in the tall tree just beyond my back fence line. I got up and made coffee (I can never eat before 8). Early mornings are the only times I have to myself.

My job includes examining decaying and skeletonized bodies to try to figure out the person's identity. We are the bone people. We establish a profile of age, sex, and race by looking at different bones. We use the skull for race and the hipbones for sex and age. We also look at trauma and describe what happened to the person. Finally, we make a statement about time since death. Climate, coverings over the body, weight, and other factors influence the rate of decay. I have seen a body become completely skeletonized in Louisiana after lying on the surface for just two weeks in the summer. In contrast, I had a case where the man was buried in a bag for five years and was so well preserved that we identified him with his fingerprints. Every case is different. I guess that's one of the things I like about my job. I never know what's going to happen next.

This morning around 9, I received a phone call from a coroner's investigator in a south Louisiana parish. We're the only state in the Union that has parishes instead of counties. The investigator wanted me to look at two bones and tell him whether they were human. The bones had been discovered between the walls of a man's house when he was doing a little remodeling. He thought they might be human. The coroner's office was unsure. That's when they called me. The bones arrived at my office around noon. I took one look at them and told the investigator that he had two ham bones from a pig (probably a joke played by a worker when the house was originally constructed). The man could continue working on his house without fear that a human was walled up inside. But it could just have easily been human; it wouldn't be the first time we had human remains associated with a house.

In one case, a woman kept noticing that her dog would disappear under the house and return to the front driveway with a different bone each time. When the dog brought out a leg bone, the woman became suspicious and called the sheriff's office. They called me. Sure enough, someone had buried a body in a shallow grave underneath the raised house. The renter moved out.

I get between 35 and 40 cases a year, but follow-ups on old cases can continue for years. We have worked more than 500 forensic cases in the last 15 or so years here at the FACES Laboratory. The acronym "FACES" stands for Forensic Anthropology and Computer Enhancement Services. We also do age progressions on missing children and adults by using computer software, and we complete clay facial reconstructions on unidentified persons to try to help get them identified.

I received a case today from Nevada. The skeletonized remains are supposed to be a male who has not been identified. Nevada has requested that we complete a facial reconstruction on the person. First, we start by doing an analysis of the case to determine its age, sex, and race. Our conclusions will help us decide which tissue depth markers to glue to the skull to guide us in making a clay face over the bone. We will place these tissue depth markers across the skull at about 50 locations. The markers are cut to very precise lengths, for example, 4.5 millimeters in length for the area just above and right between the eyes. The length of the markers tells us how thick to place the clay in those areas. Glass eyes, a clay nose (whose length and width are determined by measurements on the skull), and a clay mouth (lips are usually the height of gum line to gum line and stretch across the face from canine tooth to canine tooth) will help to finish the reconstruction. Once we finish, we photograph it and send it to the agency that requested our help. Hopefully, someone will recognize the person when the photograph is publicized in newspapers and on television. We have helped to identify several people with this technique.

During the day, my phone rings constantly. People call requesting my assistance on forensic cases, asking me to give a public presentation about my work, or maybe wanting information on our graduate program in anthropology. I also get calls that I designate as "referral phone calls." These calls are asking for assistance with things outside my area of expertise, such as DNA analysis, or help with problems where other agencies should be called, such as blood analysis on samples associated with animal cruelty. I redirect these calls to other agencies if I can. I received a phone call recently asking for my help in a civil case. The lawyer wanted me to examine "something like a bone" that had allegedly passed through someone's digestive system. I respectfully declined, for a number of reasons... not the least of which was the fact that I don't do civil cases.

I ate a late lunch of a prepackaged sandwich and a bottle of water. I ended my workday with a two-hour workshop I taught from 6 to 8 P.M. to local health-care providers. We covered everything from skeletal anatomy to trauma and provided the group of 20 with continuing education hours they need to help maintain

their accreditation. I'm tired. I'm going to bed. I hope the raccoon
has gone on vacation.

POSTED Tuesday, March 21, 2000, at 10:00 A.M. PT

When I arrived at the lab this morning, I began work on a historical burial that we retrieved recently from the banks of a bayou (we
call it "by you" in south Louisiana; in north Louisiana, they call it
"by oh"). These small, meandering freshwater streams are all over
Louisiana, especially in the southern parts. They provide a wonderful natural environment for many kinds of waterfowl, other animals such as nutria (looks sort of like beaver) and, of course,
alligators. Because we had such a dry winter and were way below
normal on our rainfall, the old burial became exposed in the side-
wall of the small channel. Such cases are generally considered to be
historic in nature, and forensic anthropologists across the country
often help law enforcement analyze them and determine their age
and origin. The jurisdiction for them falls under the purview of the
local sheriff and the U.S. Army Corps of Engineers if they are associated with waterways. They asked for my help in retrieving the
remains and analyzing them.

I grabbed my rubber boots and drove the 40 or so miles that day
to meet them. We then went by boat up the bayou and came to the
small fishing camp where the owner had found the burial while
walking along the banks the day before.

The top of the old coffin was missing, but when I looked inside
I saw quite a few bones, all human. Some of them were floating in
water that nearly filled the coffin from the wake of our small boat.
We decided to take out the entire coffin, which was made of cy-
press and could remain intact for hundreds of years in such a moist
environment. As I reached down to feel around the edges of the
bottom of the coffin to see whether the suction would affect our
picking it up, I raked my hand across something sharp and felt a

pain shoot up my arm. I withdrew my hand, pulled off my glove, and watched the blood flow freely from two of my fingers. I quickly wrapped my hand and finished loading the coffin into the boat. Back at the university, I hurried to the health center, had the cuts examined, and received a tetanus booster shot after my records were checked. I had had my last booster eight years ago. The doctor scolded me, saying that even though the shot is good for 10 years these days, anyone in my field should have a booster every five years. A lesson learned.

My analysis of the bones from the coffin indicated that the person was a young teen-ager—the bones had not finished growing, and the wisdom teeth were not fully developed (they are usually developed by age 18). The hipbone indicated it was a male. Many of his facial bones were missing, probably having floated out of the coffin the day or so before it was found. Therefore, we could not determine his race. The bones were all dark brown because bone is porous and will take on the color of the soil around it. The soil along the bayou is rich in organic material like rotten wood and leaves.

Wear on the biting surface of the teeth was fairly heavy and suggested that this was a person who probably lived in the 1800s or early 1900s when grit in the diet produced wear on their teeth. Today, our refined diet does not result in heavy wear. The coffin itself helped to confirm the general age of the burial. Its shape was a "toe pincher," which is a coffin that broadens at the shoulder region and narrows down as it moves toward the feet. Also, the nails in the coffin had square heads rather than the round-headed, machine-cut nails of modern times. By looking at historic records we hope to be able to find out who lived in that region more than 100 years ago and determine who the young teen-ager was. That is our ultimate goal, whether the case is a modern forensic case or a historical case. The remains will be reburied along the bayou very shortly, much farther away from the edge than they were before. Perhaps we will also be able to add his name to a plaque.

POSTED Wednesday, March 22, 2000, at 10:00 A.M. PT

I had to leave home at 6:30 this morning to participate in an exhumation (and I thought it was going to be a quiet week). Forensic anthropologists occasionally assist with such cases where a body has to be re-examined, but more often we deal with the recovery of persons from clandestine graves. I have worked on many cases where someone disposed of a body by burying it secretly.

In one such case several years ago, a man's wife disappeared one day. He claimed that she had run away with another man. Her parents thought differently because she had left behind two beloved little girls. The wife was never heard from again. After several years, the man sold the little house where he and his wife and children had lived. The elderly lady who purchased the house paid cash for it. She lived there a short while and decided to sell the house to a young couple. The young couple's lending agency required that a new septic tank be installed in the backyard and a drainage trench (often referred to as a filter bed) be dug along the side of the house. The drainage trench went through a rose garden — and through the grave of the man's wife. He had killed her and buried her at the side of the house eight years before and had planted a rose garden over her grave, a garden he tended regularly until he sold the house. We recovered her skeletal remains and analyzed them for trauma. He was found guilty of second-degree murder and now resides in prison.

In a similar case, a man killed a friend after a heated argument and buried him in a pecan orchard. Many years later, he sought forgiveness for his crime and confessed to law enforcement. We looked for two days for the grave and could not find it, even with heavy equipment. The man appeared to be sincere in his confession, but we were close to giving up on the search when one of the members of the recovery team decided to take a walk through the orchard. He just happened to see a sock sticking up from the ground. We found the burial—the orchard had not changed. The perpetrator had simply miscalculated where he had buried the body.

When I returned from a late lunch today around 3:30, my answering machine was blinking, showing five messages since I had been gone. One message was from a coroner's assistant in another parish asking if we could visit him tomorrow. He had information on someone who had most likely just drowned in the Mississippi River. All of the local and regional law-enforcement agencies know that we are working on a computer model to try to predict where someone might be found if that person goes into the Mississippi at a particular place at a certain time of year. When they have a case, they call us. Thus far, we have gathered data on approximately 300 river victims. We will meet the investigator early in the morning.

Two calls from other coroner's investigators on two other cases, a promise to teach a police workshop this summer, and one blessed wrong number cleared the machine again. A hot bath, soft music, and a tall glass of red wine helped to clear my mind. Good night.

Andrés Martinez

Andrés Martinez filed this while researching 24/7: Living It Up and Doubling Down in the New Las Vegas. *He is now a member of the editorial board of the* New York Times.

POSTED Sunday, Oct. 18, 1998, at 4:30 P.M. PT

I went from craps to Cézanne in three minutes, 12 seconds and probably could have made it in two minutes flat, if the art gallery attendant hadn't detained me to show me how the audio guide worked. Such is the "new" Las Vegas.

I had intended in good conscience to share with you a whole laundry list of other stats on Steve Wynn's stunning new $1.6 billion Bellagio Hotel in Las Vegas. Alas, my promised media kit hasn't been delivered.

Did you know France exports mud? It's true. The purveyor of all things fine to snobs everywhere exports mud.

Having gone 32 years, somehow, without ever having got a mud wrap, I wasn't sure what the etiquette was when Mireille Alfa, the resort's head aesthetician, allegedly from Paris, was covering my body with mud. Should I strive for reverential silence or friendly chitchat? No longer able to take the pressure, I cracked. "I suppose you saved this dirt from the construction site," I teased.

Mireille was not amused. "All good mud for Moor wraps comes from the coast of Brittany," she said sternly. Once I'd got over the disappointment of not having my eyes covered with cucumbers — one of the motivations behind this indulgence, I must confess — I fell into that soothing purgatory between wakefulness and sleep.

When Mireille and I parted, she suggested I also take a Vichy shower in the spa, a suggestion that, needless to say, I found rather offensive, not to mention unpatriotic. I almost told her to go get a Pétain facial but then thought better of it. I did stay on for a very proper posh-spa workout. That is, I spent 12 minutes on a treadmill and two hours consuming a variety of juices, watching college football games, sitting in a hot tub, and sweating in the steam room, all the while doing my best to go through as many towels as some small nations do in a month. This all in an attempt to get physically geared up for a night of the most stressful form of relaxation invented by man: casino gambling.

Casinos have always known that a little disorientation goes a long way toward loosening a patron's grip on his wallet. You've heard of all the tired old tricks employed by casino moguls. Hide the clocks, the sunlight, and the cash, and ply your gamblers with free drinks, provided by mesmerizing waitresses prancing about in what Tom Wolfe once described as "buttocks décolletage." Better yet, have them gamble in a pyramid, a pirates' den, or a fake Manhattan in the middle of the desert. Self-parodying kitsch, stressing the absurdity of life, makes people laugh, shake their heads, and take cash advances on their credit cards. Kitsch is good.

Now Wynn, Las Vegas' most visionary hotelier, has taken this disorientation to new heights with his Bellagio Hotel. Instead of adding to the city's collection of ever more theatrical, excessively themed hotels, Wynn has done something truly shocking. He has blown an unfathomable sum building a hotel dripping with taste in the very heart of the Strip. He has wooed New York's Le Cirque 2000, San Francisco's Aqua, and a dozen other renowned eateries to his beloved Bellagio, along with such retailers as Tiffany's, Armani, Chanel, and a place whose name I cannot recall that sells sparkling $2,789 shoes. But most crazily, as you've probably heard by now, Wynn has amassed a world-class art collection valued at more than $300 million to display at the resort.

No amount of free drinks or sleepless nights could ever match the disorienting power of finding a sublime art gallery, the intimacy and selectivity of which bring to mind Washington's Phillips Collection, under the same roof as a casino—just around the corner, past the conservatory. One minute you are walking down the Strip with what seems like half of America hunting for those $4.99 dinner buffets, and the next you are admiring such gems as van Gogh's *Peasant Woman Against a Background of Wheat*, for which Wynn reportedly paid $47.5 million, and Edgar Degas' *Dancer Taking a Bow*.

But disoriented or not, I am off to the baccarat tables to play the role of False Pretender among the millionaire players in town to help Wynn and his celebrity buddies open the joint. That's because I am writing *Doubling Down*, a book on the Las Vegas phenomenon, and its clever gimmick has me gambling away my advance. My pitch to publishers was as simple as the game of baccarat itself: Give me a decent bankroll to go gambling for a month in Vegas, and I'll write about it. Amazingly, somebody bought it. My weekend at the Bellagio is to be my book's epilogue and my final, mano a mano showdown with Mr. Wynn.

POSTED Wednesday, Oct. 21, 1998, at 4:30 P.M. PT

I am an aspirational packer. I'm not sure when I started viewing travel as the ultimate self-improvement opportunity, but I do. My running shoes have seen the world, mostly from the inside of a suitcase. Some of the world's literary treasures on my bookshelves have also gone on tour. *The Brothers Karamazov* might winter in Bali next year on the frequent-flyer miles they've accumulated while waiting for me to read about them. They're still waiting, racking up those miles. Every time they go back to the bookshelf, they brag about the places they've seen to *Anna Karenina*, who stands next to them. She's only brought along on longer trips. You know, for me to read when I'm done with the *Brothers*.

I would never presume to sit down and read Dostoevsky's classics in my living room (When? During *Monday Night Football* or *Friends?*), but in the fantastical world of travel, I fancy myself a true Renaissance man. So somewhere in the depressingly imposing mound of luggage in my Sunset Station room, I wouldn't be surprised to find a guitar, a Latin primer, a physics textbook, or a knitting kit. You never know what that nutty packer back in New York will throw in.

If Bellagio is a stunning departure from the older Strip hotels that cater to tourists, the Sunset Station Hotel & Casino, in the thriving suburb of Henderson, is an equally revolutionary move away from the classic seedy "grind joints" that once serviced local gamblers. Like the mall across the street, Sunset Station is a pleasant public space striving to become suburbia's answer to the lost town square. And it is a cheery, well-designed, welcoming environment, with its brewery, surprisingly good restaurants, rows upon rows of video poker machines, multiscreen cinema, and Funquest, a place to check your kids. There's even a Borders bookstore next door.

Most of the people milling about in the middle of a school day, or standing in the Disneyesque lines at the buffet, appeared to be retirees. The woman waiting in line in front of me at the coffee shop said she and some "girl" friends have a "Hump Day Club" that meets at Sunset every week. They eat, play the slots, catch a movie, and then go crazy in the bingo hall. She's 78, a refugee from Chicago's winters.

More insidiously, these casinos also serve as full-fledged financial-services firms. Sunset and its sister Station Casinos properties have perfected the art of paycheck-cashing ploys, in which everyone (but especially the house) is a winner. These should make a juicy target for the National Gambling Impact Study Commission when it comes into town for hearings next month. Cash your pay-check at Sunset and you get a "Paycheck Bonanza" scratch-off ticket. And if you don't win that $25,000, you at least get a meal or a margarita. The point being, relax, stay awhile. Got some cash?

On the edge of the casino there was even a booth where you could apply for a Visa card, on which, instead of accruing frequent flyer miles, you accrue points redeemable for cash at your favorite Station Casino. One bleary-eyed guy wanted a card right then and there but had no form of ID. He was swearing at the poor lady be-hind this booth, he found this requirement for credit so unreason-able.

From Sunset, I went to the command center in Las Vegas' fran-tic battle to cope with its Third World-like growth rate—roughly 5,000 new arrivals a month—the office of Clark County School District Superintendent Dr. Brian Cram. Cram oversees the na-tion's 8th largest school district, which grows at a rate of 12,000 to 17,000 kids a year. He puts up a new school every 28 days, on aver-age, and just hired 1,700 new teachers for this school year. Next month voters will vote on a $3.5 billion bond issue to build 88 more schools.

Kelly Murphy Mason

Kelly Murphy Mason filed this while working as a holiday bookseller at Borders in Washington, D.C. She's currently at work on a collection of stories.

POSTED Sunday, Dec. 21, 1997, at 4:30 P.M. PT

For the first time in my life, I am punching a clock. Figuratively, of course. I have a time card that slides through a machine that calculates my wages for the day. This arrangement unnerves me. I can never remember if I've clocked out for the night. I sit wide-eyed on the bus, wondering whether I should call someone from home and double-check. Then I forget to do that, because by the end of a shift, I am dazed and manic all at once. I keep promising to eliminate my late-afternoon coffee, thinking this will help, but the promise is bankrupt.

The coffee is perhaps the chief perk of the job — strong, plenteous, and free. The other major perk is the seasonal discount. Everyone I know is getting a book as a gift. As soon as I clock out, I start my Christmas shopping. During that twilight time, I am a customer. Unfortunately, I spend a good part of my workday second-guessing the choices I made then. A new release or a sideline item (listed in our database as "non-literature," a tag I love) will catch my divided attention. The whole enterprise defeats me on a number of levels. According to my latest calculations, I've spent more at the store than I've earned. Borders might as well pay me in scrip.

My father thinks my working retail is perverse. In fact, he won't even discuss it, beyond asking—in vague terms—what I am doing with my life. Friends are almost as wary as family; one wanted me to assure him that book-selling was "just for the holidays," as if I could see beyond New Year's. A cool acquaintance got called to my register a few days ago and pretended not to recognize me, blinded, perhaps, by embarrassment. She promptly demanded to know what payment functions her bank card could perform. In the confusion, I neglected to demagnetize her merchandise. She sounded the alarms and was stopped by the security guard, which is embarrassing for anyone. I couldn't have been more gratified if I'd done it on purpose.

That's not an instance of customer service at its finest, which only underscores my original point. I don't believe in service so much as magnanimity. Because I—like many booksellers—have a couple of degrees in literature, I've been assigned largely to "information technology." In effect, I'm a mass-market librarian. It's a pleasure to find a pleasant customer a book, because then we can both be magnanimous and part ways.

POSTED Monday, Dec. 22, 1997, at 4:30 P.M. PT

For breakfast yesterday I had five Rice Krispies treats and a cup of coffee; for lunch, two bags of low-fat pretzels, a Hershey's bar with almonds, and a Diet Pepsi, which I don't even like. Dinner was a slice of cheese pizza and another Diet Pepsi. I cannot recall the last vegetable I ate. Today, however, I will eat like someone with a future. Today I have one, because today is my day off.

The sad part is how quickly it is parceled out, between trips to the bank and grocery store and post office and some last-minute shopping. I had visions of a long bath, which did not materialize.

When I was teen-ager, I swore I'd never live for the weekend. Ah, youth. On the bus I ride to work there is an advertisement for Job Corps. "Life isn't fair," it reads. "Get over it. Get a job." As if nine out of 10 bus passengers hadn't figured that out already.

I hardly see my boyfriend anymore. When I taught classes at the university, we had time for quick bites. Now he comes to the store during the lunch-hour rush and watches me work the register awhile. I've yet to see him there. I imagine him staying close to the best-seller tables, pretend browsing. Unable to interrupt, he leaves without saying hello. I cannot explain this measure of devotion. It's completely unearned.

When I help a customer find a $100 reference book, I realize I've covered my keep for two days. Obviously, there are overhead and administrative costs, but I can't account for those. What Christmas does—more than anything else, in its current incarnation—is separate the haves from the have-nots. It's a rotten business, really, commodifying affection. I've never witnessed so many people buying remaindered books in my life.

My designated section is children's books, and a number of grown-ups ask my gift-giving advice. They generally have a generic child in mind, a nephew or niece. They want to know what sort of book a 12-year-old would like. Clearly, it depends upon the 12-year-old. A 12-year-old could read anything, left to her own devices. When I explain that, customers think I'm being intentionally difficult. One requested recommendations for "a fourth-grader with a sense of humor." That's pretty good, as leads go. I suggested Betty MacDonald and Roald Dahl.

"Dahl's weird," he replied.

"That's all right," I assured him. "Kids like weird."

It's striking how easily adults can regress. Occasionally the section resembles Romper Room on a bad day. Why are they all so helpless? I wonder. Why can't they return a single book or find Dr. Seuss when he stares them in the face? The children are far less needy. They're happy to just browse. Because they're impressionable, I try to keep the animation tie-ins tucked behind something more substantive. I don't want to contribute to the Disney hegemony any more than I have to. Madeline must be better for young minds than a Jessica Rabbit in ethnic dress. *Mens sana in corpore sano* and all that.

POSTED   Tuesday, Dec. 23, 1997, at 4:30 P.M. PT

Why do I invariably expect the worst? There was unprecedented good cheer in the shop today, nothing like the crushing desperation I'd anticipated enduring. Or maybe it was there, and we were all too punch-drunk on adrenalin to notice. During a brief lull at lit info, I drilled J. on the Russian texts he'd put on temporary display. He was a translator when the former Soviet Union was still the Soviet Union. Now he stocks untranslated lit, lit crit, and poetry. (He and C. are wild about language poets.) "What this?" I asked, in a toddler's rapid-fire staccato. "What's this?" I asked, flashing another title in Cyrillic.

"*Iambs*," he said.

"That's it? The title in its entirety?" On closer inspection, the word did resemble "Iambs." Inside were small poems with small lines. "Are they any good?"

"You haven't read iambic poems till you've read these."

"So how's it selling?" I joked.

"We think it'll move with a discount."

I looked at the sticker and laughed. The chapbook cost $2.50 already.

Earlier, one of the managers challenged me to sell Philip Roth's *American Pastoral* "by hand," to a customer, cold. Like everyone else at the main desk, I declined. We've sold about a dozen to date, and his stack hasn't dropped in a week. Regardless of how many awards he wins, Roth's still laughing stock to us. No print meritocracy exists. After a person's sold *Don't Sweat the Small*

Stuff...And It's All Small Stuff in armfuls, she can testify to that.

In my graduate program, I was told not to complain until I'd had my 10 years in hell. I've felt reluctantly bound by that, and I keep wondering whether this will be Year 2 or 4. I have to believe the couple of years in school count. What I tried to teach my own students was that human beings love things that offer them no percentage. I mostly failed. For a variety of reasons, I question whether I'm fit to preach the gospel anymore.

My biggest fear this season has been that one of my students will find me in the store. They would worry for me, as I worry for them. They want to know where I will teach next. Because I don't know, I cannot bear their concern. I can't bear anyone's, these days.

Lately, I've been polling some friends as to exactly how I should sell out. "But it has to be big," I insist. "It has to be worth my while." On public radio this morning, I heard another report on the booming economy. Most Americans think their quality of life has never been better. This perplexes me. Few of my peers juggle jobs. They're at the age where they have careers or spouses or houses. When they talk about their lives, I hear a ringing in my ears. I've noticed myself spending less time in front of mirrors. I can't stand the look of my brave face.

Today I searched and searched for the *Encyclopedia of Letters*. A call-in customer said it was the last gift on her list. I put her on hold more times than I could count. She was exceedingly patient. I guessed after a while that it couldn't be had, but refused to give up the ghost. I just wanted her to have everything wrapped up, everything squared away.

Deirdre McCloskey

Deirdre McCloskey teaches economics, history, and literature at the University of Illinois at Chicago. She is the author of Crossing, *a memoir of her sex change.*

POSTED Monday, Nov. 29, 1999, at 10:00 A.M. PT

Sunday I bicycle to Grace Episcopal down the street in suburban Oak Park. The loft near the Loop I'm buying for a move to the University of Illinois has an Episcopal storefront across the street, so I guess in the spring I'll go there. Or maybe commute back to Grace, with its architecture and music and intellectual priest. I've made a few nice friends this fall at Grace. Nancy and I lament that all the available men at Grace seem to be gay. Though nice: Like other women, I love the style and thoughtfulness of gay men. I think this morning: Church is supposed to be a good place to meet husbands. Rats.

Amid the incense of First Advent a baby boy is baptized, like my grandson Connor. I have no pictures of him. I think as I watch the ancient rite of water: My son is so angry at my gender change. He hasn't spoken to me since 1995, in that meeting at the Palmer House, the day after the night in the madhouse arranged by my sister. I look at the little boy toddling up the aisle to the baptistery and my tears well. All right, all right. Put it away, Deirdre. Wait and pray.

After church, the thought forms of my leftover apple pie, hot, with maybe some ice cream. Well, I deserve it. I had made the pie for Thanksgiving dinner at Joel's house in Evanston, proud of my womanly skill (that is, Pillsbury prefab dough from the dairy case plus the package's almost idiot-proof recipe for the filling). I had waited too long to put the completed pie in the oven and the bottom crust had sogged with the apple juice. Aunt Deirdre's tip among the women: Let the bottom crust bake a little before adding the filling.

While the pie is heating, I take my Yorkie, Jane Austen, along to the ice cream store across the parking lot. (Having a dog, I say to myself, is like having a little family.) Dogs will kill for "creamie," and Janie heels attentively as we hurry home salivating. I eat too much, spoiling my Suzanne Somers diet of the past few weeks by mixing fat (the ice cream) with carbo (the ice cream, and the pie) and fruit (the pie). Oh, well: If it's all I eat today. As a man I didn't worry about weight. Men think they look good no matter how they look.

While noshing at the dining-room table I watch part of a movie with a *Saturday Night Live* star as a mother in childbirth. I am fascinated and weep at the miracle, all joking aside. A week before, I had served as assistant midwife to a friend in Holland giving birth at home, and the movie brings back the amazed pleasure. Birth is so thrilling. (I remember being puzzled as a man at how women get thrilled by stories of birth. Heh, Walter Payton's running is thrilling. But a normal birth?) I cry some more, thinking about not seeing my grandchild at birth or at baptism. A weepy day: I'm very, very happy as a woman, and usually I do not cry as much as this, though I cry as Donald never did.

My mother calls from Fort Lauderdale, and we talk and laugh for a half-hour, mother-daughter style. As a son, I seldom called, and she was diffident; now we speak every Sunday. We've gotten closer, closer even than some born daughters get (a daughter-once-a-son has no aching history with a mother). My father is long dead. I think: How would he have reacted? Certainly I never would be Daddy's Little Girl. But you can't tell how people will react. I read about a choreographer in China whose soldier father, surprisingly, admired his new daughter's courage in changing from man to woman. My mother, who I thought would have great difficulty, loves her child regardless of gender.

Later in the day, I hear three men making women's points. I read an essay in draft by a philosophy colleague named Laden about "reasonableness": He says reasonableness is not just a matter of logic but of human relations. A woman's point, I think, and true. Lying on the bed that afternoon, I read Robert Nozick's essay "Happiness" in his book *The Examined Life*, in which he says that happiness has less to do with games and acquisitions and more to do with the shape of one's life. Another woman's point. And hurrying in the dark down the Eisenhower Expressway to meet Rikki in her townhouse on the Chicago River, I listen to Garrison Keilor mocking the "queen mothers" of Lake Woebegone. They can shame their families into gathering up there for Thanksgiving. Look: My family loves me. The shape of my life is my human relations. What's yours?

What's mine?

POSTED   Tuesday, Nov. 30, 1999, at 10:00 A.M. PT

Talk, talk, talk. I drove up to Beloit College on the Illinois/Wisconsin border, a two-hour drive with Janie, my Yorkie, in her little observation basket in the front seat, and spent the day chatting, discussing, lecturing. Odd that a stutterer earns her living with talk. I start the little talk to the assembled econ majors on "Economics as a Life" with: "When I was 11, I would fall asleep praying for two things. First, that the next day I'd wake up and not stutter. I'd just talk like other people. And that I'd wake up and be a girl. At age 53 I finally got half my prayer! As an Episcopalian, I guess that's a good percentage for the efficacy of prayer!" It's better to get these two Big Facts acknowledged early so the kids don't get diverted into giggling to each other about them.

I say that economic principles work in their lives. You should buy a coat when its cost divided by the number of wearings is lower than what you'd pay for each wearing, that sort of thing. (I confessed, though, that I'd just bought an elegant Irish cape suitable for... the opera; well, there are other "wearings," or the opera wearing is worth $50 a throw; or something: Prudence doesn't explain everything, a theme that day in all my talks.) You should take the trip to Indiana to see your brother when the reasons to do so add up: to give him his Christmas present of that Edward Hopper reproduction from the Art Institute, to see if his room is OK, to use the nice day after Thanksgiving, to see cousin Phil and wife Reva in southwestern Michigan on the way back. Technically, add up demand curves for jointly supplied goods vertically. Uh... OK, if you say so. Common sense, a little refined, which is what economics should always be.

The talk was made up on the spot, as a lot of my talks are. A minute before standing and delivering, I ask my host what to talk about. I stutter less if I'm not reading something, and anyway a certain crazy energy comes from not knowing what's going to come out of your mouth in the next 30 seconds. You sketch the talking points in your head and then read them off and... talk, talk, talk. It seems to go all right.

Afterward, the professors of economics stay, one of them the father of a young friend back in Iowa City, himself married to a grad student in economics, friends from church. We talk in the winter afternoon's sunlight about economics — its future, its liabilities, how we love it and hate it. It's the kind of talk professors need to do frequently and often don't let themselves do with enough discipline and focus to arrive at much. Pure shop talk, like truckers discussing the best routes or accountants the latest IRS ruling.

Then I am taken by my host, Emily, a young economist at Beloit (we joke about being the only two postmodern free-market feminists on the planet) over to Women's Studies and talk about my gender change. The professor in charge gives me the sweetest, most intelligent introduction I've ever gotten—a little long, but nice to listen to, very nice. As a woman I am more embarrassed than I was as a man by fulsome praise. But, heh, I can take it.

The gender talk goes well, I think, I hope. I am afraid in academic situations of attacks from a certain school of second-wave separatist feminists, who, for what I regard as goofy reasons, long ago decided they don't like gender-crossers—men "invading" women's territory. When one woman sitting by the door gets up and goes out, I am alarmed. But she comes back in. It's so hard to judge audiences. How well is it going? Lecturing is like what I hear about theatrical performances, for example from my ex-actress mother, who speaks of holding the audience in one's hand. Yeah. One would wish.

The evening talk on "Bourgeois Virtue" is still harder, because the audience is miscellaneous, from demonstrably bored sophomores who attend only because required to do so by their teachers to bright young college professors to perky senior couples who attend every public speech at the college but are not themselves academically oriented. I sweat, metaphorically (ladies "glow"). But afterwards people praise me in that fulsome way again. Was it that good? I don't think so. One would wish.

I sleep in the guest house, late on a cold, starry night, Janie cuddled in her carry case.

Daniel Menaker

Daniel Menaker is senior literary editor at Random House and the author of a novel, The Treatment, *and two collections of short stories.*

POSTED Monday, Feb. 1, 1999, at 11:00 A.M. PT

Last Friday I had a short story rejected by *The New Yorker*. It was about an editor who lost to another publisher a book he wanted to acquire. This rejection of the story didn't bother me much more than an anvil dropping on my head might have, and it would have bothered me even less, had it not been for the content of the rejection. I came back to work from recording four audio descriptions of the books I'm publishing next fall—novels by Gary Krist, Paul Griner, Vassily Aksyonov, and Jonathan Kellerman, if the schedule holds—and found a message in my voice-mailbox saying that my story had been turned down and I should call if I wanted to talk it over.

It's always good to ask for an assay of the metal alloy of the anvils that drop on your head, I said to myself, so I called. "We don't really go for stories about publishing," I was told. (I knew this, from having edited fiction at *The New Yorker* for twenty years, but unlike my rejecter I knew that this story only seemed to be about publishing and was at its core an unutterably funny yet profound existential statement about the human condition.) "This one is lively and reads right along, but there are too many real people in it. And I hate the narrator's voice." Ooof! A pretty heavy anvil indeed, as it turned out—a lot of lead mixed in with the iron, was my guess—and, when I recovered my senses, it made me doubt the wisdom of my curiosity about its composition. "Now really, Dan," my personal Torquemada said to me at the end of this literary equivalent of a root-canal session, "I don't want you to feel bad about this."

What better way to salve an ego bashed in on Friday than to get on a train on Saturday morning and go on a two-hour trip to Dover Plains, New York, where there sits a tub of rust of an automobile, and start it up for twenty minutes (so that it will start up the following weekend so that I or my wife can drive it another hour north to our house in New Marlborough, Massachusetts, while the one who doesn't do that takes our two kids and the whimperingly auto-phobic dog, Pepper, and drives our seriously dented car that we keep on the street in New York to New Marlborough) and then get back on the train and come back to New York? Just about any way would be better, I think, but that was my way. I edited and read on the way up, got off the train, went to the car, turned the key and got as gratifying a response from it as I had gotten from *The New Yorker*. But not to worry. I picked up the battery-booster device that I had given to my wife for Christmas—the kind of intimate and romantic gift-giving I specialize in—and jammed it into the lighter receiver. Fifteen to thirty minutes, and the car would start up. Then leave the car running for twenty minutes to recharge the battery and then for another twenty or thirty minutes to recharge the battery booster and we'd be in business for the next weekend. And—I realized as I set out to buy some lunch while the battery booster did its work—I'd miss the train back to New York and have to wait two or three hours for another one. I couldn't even run the car long enough to recharge its battery.

It came to me how badly I'd miscalculated this inherently ridiculous mission at the exact moment when I saw that the little

bagel shop at the Dover Plains train station that I had been counting on for sustenance had closed a few minutes before the train I'd
arrived on had pulled in. Not to worry, though—a little farther
along, in the blinding blizzard that had suddenly blown into town,
was another little food place, albeit less upmarket than the bagel
place. So, I said to myself, since the battery booster wouldn't have
accomplished its absolutely futile mission by now anyway, I'll just
walk on, hunched over against the snow and freezing wind, and
when I get there—why, when I get there, I find that it has gone
out of business! Perfect!

Now the train's hour of departure is drawing nigh, and so, increasingly hypoglycemic, I rush back through the whiteout and
with anticipatory triumph based on absolutely nothing, since, as I
believe I may have mentioned, I can't keep the car running long
enough to recharge its battery, to say nothing of recharging the
battery booster. I start up the car. Not!—as we all were saying a
few years back. Now I have a dead car and a dead battery booster
and no lunch and a two-hour trip back to the city on a train that, I
know from years of experience, will as it goes south through
Westchester, if in fact it can go anywhere in this polar meteorol-
ogy, pick up more and more teen-agers bound for the big city and
bent on wreaking any sort of rail-travel havoc possible. I have only
a couple of minutes left to get back on the train, so I run toward it
and fall flat on my face in the snow, and when I finally get to the
train my palms are bleeding and my pants are soaking wet.

Here's what I'm going to do. Today I'm going to call the service
station at the corner of Route 22 in Dover Plains and ask them to
go to the car in the station—a heartbreakingly short half mile
away, like Amundsen or Norkey or Lewis and Clark or whoever it
was having to stop heartbreakingly short of their adventurous goal
—and either recharge or replace the battery. But to do that I'm
going to have to send them the keys by express mail, I guess, since
they can't get the hood open without the keys. And then I'm going
to call the battery-booster people and have a little talk, not that it

would have made a bit of difference if the device had worked. It's the principle of the thing.

On Sunday, to try to regain a little equilibrium, I played squash with an old friend, David McCormick, who was my assistant at *The New Yorker*—when I was there turning down stories that really *were* about publishing—and who discovered the great young American short-story writer George Saunders in the slush pile. I also subscribed to HBO, so I could watch *The Sopranos*, which everyone is talking about—including, incidentally, the teen-agers on the train, as they went hurtling about the car that my stomach was rumbling in.

But I'd better stop there.

P.S.: I forgot to watch *The Sopranos*.

POSTED   Friday, Feb. 5, 1999, at 10:30 A.M. PT

If you had told me when I was a sophomore in Nyack High School listening raptly to the doo-wop crooning of the Platters, the Moon-glows, the Drifters, the Flamingos, the Robins (now that my memory has taken wing), the Jays, the Larks, the Crows, the Sparrows, the Orioles, etc., drinking Schaefer beer, driving a nearly defunct '49 Plymouth with a duotone muffler which made the car sound like "tough short," as we used to say, when actually it had all the acceleration of a sea slug, shoplifting *Playboy* magazines, playing church-league basketball, and trying desperately to get past first base in another sport, that I would ever in my life start a sentence with the three words "My British publisher," I would have choked on the king-sized Chesterfield I'd no doubt have been sneaking at the time. Nevertheless, My British publisher walked into my office about a year ago on a Friday, saw what I was up to, and said, "Aha —Friday—it's rejection day." I said, "You do this on Fridays in England, too?" He said yes—he thought everyone did. Maybe so, I say now, with Friday upon me. Maybe there's some publishers' racial unconscious, some archetypal influence, which drives editors all over town, all over the world, to reserve Fridays for rejections. It seems right, somehow.

So today it will be, perhaps, a chapter and proposal for a book about the ordeals and joys of raising deaf Mexican twins. A memoir by the guy who invented Oreos. A literary apologia for boxing. Another one for bullfighting. A coming-of-age novel set in Bergenfield. A history of hairstyles. The Twelve Most Common Dating Mistakes. The Kidney: Miracle Organ. Felis Felis, a Tribute to the Cat. The Eleven Most Common Dating Mistakes. Friday—the day for undeniably impressive expertise. Authentic detail and deep insight. For obviously an accomplished and original writer. For this is not a worthwhile but a highly worthwhile submission. Assured, professional, and intelligent. Distinctive and energetic. Vivid, riveting, and riveting. Livid and ravenous, avidly venal, raveningly vapid. Unfortunately I'm sorry to say that I'm afraid that I regret to say that I wish I didn't have to say that this may not be the right publisher to give this project the 110 percent enthusiasm it so clearly deserves.

The thing of it is that writers generally do mix in their life's blood with the ink in their printers, they generally are passionate and hopeful about their projects, and many of them that one rejects really do have their strengths. I've been at this long enough to see books I've turned down spring up elsewhere with great success, and more power to them. But the submissions can sometimes seem overwhelming—and so can the fifty or sixty thousand books a year that grow out of them. I still read with the hope, every time, that what I'm looking at will take hold, make me forget I'm reading, take me off cruise control. When that little pilot light of hope is snuffed out inside any editor's head, he or she should quit, probably. Maybe it's the pitching and hyping, the flap copying and the catalogue copying, the Lotus Notes and budgeting meetings, the schmoozmeistering and placating that goes on all week that renders Fridays a good day for rejection.

Late today, I hope to get back on the train to Dover Plains and find when I get there that the guy from the Citgo service station has gotten the car keys I mailed him and has recharged our dead car's battery. When I get to Massachusetts, I'll go cross-country skiing down on Lake Buel, near our house, and try to recharge my own batteries. I thought it was the Getty Station. Under that misunderstanding I kept calling a Getty station and asking the man who answered could he please help me with this dead car. He said his boss wasn't there right then, they didn't do repairs anyway, and he didn't think they could get to Dover Plains even if they did do repairs. This was strange, as the gas station and the train station are almost cheek-by-jowl. Call back in fifteen minutes, the man said, in his subcontinental accent. The boss would be back. He was at the hospital. He had hurt his thumb. I kept calling the place back, getting what I thought was a runaround, until the person who answered finally said, "I am the boss. We are the Getty station in Patterson. The place you want is the Citgo station. We are the Indian fellows eight miles south of there." So then finally things began to go right.

On Monday I'll set up my dentist appointments. Monday is the day for starting over.

Lucas Miller

Lucas Miller is a detective with the New York City Police Department and a regular contributor to Slate.

POSTED Monday, March 22, 1999, at 10:30 A.M. PT

At night I make a little pile of the things I carry around every day. My wallet and keys. My pager. My shield — we call our badges shields here in Fun City, probably because that's the shape of the police officer's badge. Because I am a detective, my shield is different. My FBI buddies tell me that the NYPD detective shield is the most recognized badge in the world. And my gun.

You receive a gun and a shield when you are near graduation at the police academy, on, appropriately, Gun and Shield Day. Eight years ago, I expected the skies to part and the hand of God Himself to present me my police officer's shield and a .38 revolver. If not God, then surely his closest earthbound relative, the Police Commissioner, would be there to convey to me the two coolest objects any kid could have. Instead, we marched down to the basement where some salty old detective was sitting behind a desk. "Miller?" he said, and tossed me a little envelope containing my shield. "Go through that door and see Police Officer Rodriguez. He will give you your gun." Several days later I sat with several thousand of my fellow academy graduates and was exhorted by then-Mayor

David Dinkins not to become "the burned-out bullies with billy clubs of old." The crowd, made up mostly of members of the families of my classmates, many of them veteran cops themselves, was a little chilly to Dinkins' remarks. This seemed the wrong place to insult the legions of police officers that went before us.

After the academy, I was assigned to the Sixth Precinct, which contains Greenwich Village. In addition to walking a beat on Bleecker Street, I got sent to riots in Crown Heights, Washington Heights, and Tompkins Square Park. There was some excitement, but it was bracketed by huge amounts of time waiting for something to happen. I guarded dead bodies awaiting detectives and the medical examiner. I guarded crime scenes waiting for, of course, the Crime Scene Unit. I guarded the voting machines on Election Day and primary day. My fellow cops were not burned-out bullies but a mix of earnest young men and a few women, some concentrating on cleaning up New York and some concentrating on earning enough money to raise a family, every single one of them appalled at the sight of a crime victim and willing to risk his life to catch a bad guy.

After working on patrol for about three years, I requested an undercover assignment to the Narcotics Division. I spent the next two and half years buying heroin, cocaine, and marijuana on the Lower East Side and around 42nd Street. Unlike Patrol, Narcotics has one principal purpose: locking up drug dealers. For this reason, it is much more intense than Patrol. No one feels this stress more than the undercover officers. To be honest, I had it pretty easy. Assigned to Manhattan South Narcotics, I worked neighborhoods that were safer than some in Brooklyn and Northern Manhattan. I am a healthy-looking white guy and therefore to some eyes on some blocks possibly a cop. So I am more suited for buying marijuana or pretending to be a stockbroker looking to turn a $10,000 investment in powder into $80,000 than for less pleasant and more challenging assignments like pretending to be a junkie or a street-level heroin dealer.

A year and a half after my assignment to Narcotics, I was pro-
moted to detective. This time, I was sure that there would be some
supernatural fanfare involved in the promotion. I walked into the
room, a secret room deep in One Police Plaza since we were undercover, and there was that same ancient detective. "Miller? Here
you go." He tossed me my detective shield.

I am not undercover anymore. I "rolled over," as we say when
cops stop being undercover, as soon as I could. I continue to work in
the Narcotics Division, doing a lot of paperwork, trying to pick
good cases, and enjoying the NYPD. I remain in love with the City
of New York. Of late, there is a growing sense around the office
and in the newspapers that she might not love us back, but I don't
believe it.

POSTED Tuesday, March 23, 1999, at 10:30 A.M. PT

I am out in an unmarked car with two fellow detectives. My partners today are Joe, a handsome, wry, dark Irish fellow, and Sean,
also Irish, who shares his coloring and general determination with
his yellow Labrador retriever. I am in the back seat. Joe is driving.
We are enjoying the stereotypical cups of coffee, no doughnuts.
Sean says, "Have you guys ever had that Ben and Jerry's ice
cream? I never tried it before. My wife brought home this Chubby
— "

"Chubby Hubby!" Joe yells and starts waving his hands in the
air. The car starts lurching back and forth. Sean catches his coffee
cup as it slides off the dashboard. "I love that stuff! I go through
like a pint of that a night! You gotta try the Phish Food. The
Cookie Dough doesn't have enough cookie dough, though. Too
much vanilla, not enough dough. But the Chocolate Fudge
Brownie is the best. Oh my God, that stuff is so good. I'm losing
control of the car. I have to go find some ice cream."

I pipe in, "I really like the Coffee Coffee Buzz Buzz Buzz."

The car straightens out. Joe cocks his head toward the back seat and says to Sean, "Ah, Miller's got the sophisticated palate."

We are interrupted by the sight of the guy we are looking for. We've watched him buy marijuana a couple of blocks away. Big case. We follow him over to a railing overlooking the East River, where we identify ourselves and request that he hand over the cheeba and not fuck around. Naturally, his reaction is to attempt to pitch his new acquisition into the river, but I catch his hand mid-throw. At this point he tenses up and brings his other hand up like a fighter. Fortunately, as the gravity of the situation envelops him, he relaxes, hands me the drugs, and puts his other hand down. Now, we aren't really that interested in him beyond making a case against the guy who sold him the stuff. Sean puts a friendly hand on his shoulder and asks him, "You got any more weed?"

"No, sir."

Joe asks, "You got ID?"

"Yes, sir."

I ask, "You got any weapons on you?"

"Uh, I have this knife." He withdraws a folding knife. Sean snatches it.

"Let's see that ID," Joe says.

"And this. And this." He is pulling things out from every pocket of his clothing. Knives, blackjacks, little pointed sticks, odd-shaped things that are only identifiable as weapons from the matte-black metal of which they are made. We are getting nervous, but the guy is being pretty docile. He is caught and he probably figures that the easier he makes this on us, the easier we might make it on him. As he takes each thing out, he tells me what it is—kubaton, pakua star, push-dagger. The last thing he takes out is a metal cylinder attached to his keys with some levers on one end.

"Where is that ID?" Joe is getting impatient.

He hands some cards to Joe. The guy actually seems to be enjoying the attention. "Hey, are those Glocks you guys are carrying?"

"What's this?" I hold up the strange cylinder and keys.

Joe, examining two different cards, barks at him, "This says your first name is James and this one says it's Michael. Which is it? James or Michael? This a real license? Where did you get this?"

"What is this?" I ask, still examining the cylinder.

"My first name is James, but people call me by my middle name, Michael, so I put it down for my Florida license. In New York, they wanted my full name for my license. Are you guys taking me to jail?"

"You know, pal, you're not supposed to have two licenses," Sean offers.

As I casually fumble with the strange key chain, I hear a hissing sound, but don't pay much attention. Of course, what I am doing is spraying Mace on Joe and Sean. Obliviously, as they start yelling and coughing, the guy says, "That shoots Mace," and happily waits for our next question. My partners attempt to wash out their eyes with the only liquid on hand, which is coffee, and begin to plan my imminent demise. Our new friend stands there serenely. I begin to imagine the paperwork and questions arising from Macing my partners. The guy asks, "Do you guys really need to take me in? How about I just promise not to do it again?"

Joe manages to glare at me, coffee running down the front of his jacket: "No, you can't just promise not to do it again."

When we are finished with our big arrest, I buy my partners off with ice cream. Joe holds out for Chocolate Fudge Brownie.

POSTED Wednesday, March 24, 1999, at 10:30 A.M. PT

It is commonly held in the NYPD that life in the department is less like an episode of *NYPD Blue* and more like an episode of *Barney Miller*, and there is truth in this. For every day doing something exciting, there are 10 spent doing paperwork, going to court, conducting surveillance, and doing more paperwork. Where the *Barney Miller* analogy fails is not on that 10th day when a cop does something exciting. It fails on the 100th day, when a cop does something extraordinary. On that day, life is not like *NYPD Blue*, it is like the best movie you ever saw, only you are the hero. Today was not one of those days. Today, my lieutenant discovered that I was a little unclear about the meaning of "daily" as in "daily activity report." I had to spend some time catching up. A chief at headquarters required some statistics immediately, and I was dispatched to deliver them. I am sorry to report that the most exciting part of the workday was a brief meeting with an assistant district attorney about a year-old arrest. At least I got to relive past glory, even if it wasn't a big case. That wasn't one of those 100th days either.

The most exciting part of the day came at the end. After a great workout at karate, I was gratuitously invited out for a late snack by the prettiest girl in the class. I had so much fun that I lost track of the time. Afterward, I eagerly offered to drive her home. I promptly discovered that I had left my car in a spot whose witching hour had come and the car had been towed away by none other than the Traffic Division of the NYPD.

So as the blood pounded at my temples, I withdrew the $150 necessary to free my car and stalked up the street to find a taxi for me and one for my friend. Lo and behold, this lovely girl offered to accompany me to the most miserable spot on the island of Manhattan, the tow pound. I told her I couldn't possibly expect her to go with me. It really wasn't necessary. I would be all right. Then I realized I was being a very considerate moron. I was going to the Valley of the Shadow of Death to get my car back and I was turning down a traveling companion. I accepted her offer.

We arrived at the tow pound to find it filled with drunks, kids from New Jersey, recent immigrants unaware of the finer points of New York City parking regulations, and several transvestites, all trying to get their cars back. It began to dawn on me that despite my delight at having such an enviable companion, showing a girl this little version of hell might make for a bad first date. She asked me, "Can't you just tell them you're a cop and get your car back?"

As I was thinking of an answer, we became aware of the woman ahead of us telling the cashier, "Listen, I am a police officer and I only have $138. Isn't there any way you can help me?" The cashier was shaking her head with what looked to me like satisfaction.

As we were waiting to go get the car, the man behind us turned to his wife and said, "This is un-f−ing-reasonable. Can you believe this? A hundred and fifty dollars! That f−ing Giuliani! I hate him and the cops."

In my most friendly voice, I told him, "Listen, I think this sucks just as much as you do, but it has always been like this. It was like this when Dinkins was mayor and when Koch was mayor and probably before that. I think it always cost one-fifty. And before Rudy, they didn't take credit cards. Also, while NYPD does run the Traffic Division, it is made up mostly of civilians, not cops."

The guy looked at me like I had two heads and he was going to punch me in one of them, then went back to talking to his wife. A man in a fur coat was yelling and pounding at the window, "What do you mean, I need picture ID? Is this some sort of police state where we have to carry ID? Hey, I am talking to you. Hey!" His wife and another man were trying to soothe an increasingly nervous cashier who seemed to be on the verge of calling in the real police.

I stole a look at my companion. She was having a good time! This was a good show and we had great seats. Albeit expensive ones. We retrieved my car and headed down the West Side Highway with the lights of my city sparkling all around us.

POSTED Thursday, March 25, 1999, at 10:30 A.M. PT

One of my partners, Sean, was notified to appear today as the subject of a recent civilian complaint. He is the most soft-spoken of the members of my team, the most popular, and also the senior man, so it came as a surprise to learn that he was "no good."

When I started as a cop, it was commonly held among the police officers I met that if one was an active police officer, one could expect about one civilian complaint a year. Right on schedule, about a year after the academy, I got my first complaint. I was in traffic court. A cop from the neighboring precinct whom I knew from the police academy approached me. He told me he thought the motorist who was contesting one of his tickets was carrying a gun. He asked me to help him stop and frisk the man. We found the man in the waiting room. He did have a bulge on his right side at the waist, under his shirt. We confronted the man and asked him to put his hands on the wall. He complied, and we discovered that he was carrying a very large pager. He was understandably angry at having been waylaid. He vented this anger by calling us every name he could think of. In the barrage of insults, I was unable to apologize for having stopped him mistakenly. Months later I received notice to appear at the Civilian Complaint Review Board. I was informed that he had alleged that we had stopped him for no reason and then smashed his face into a wall. The board ruled that the complaint was unsubstantiated. It could neither be proved nor disproved. That remains my only civilian complaint, but it is on my record and always will be.

It seems as if the belief that one complaint a year is the price of police work has gone out the window. If I had one complaint for each of my eight years, the newspapers would call me a persistent offender.

While working buy and bust, my partner Joe and I, minus the indisposed Sean, witnessed an odd little scene. There was a cluster of men struggling with each other next to a cluster of taxi cabs all facing different directions. We identified ourselves, and the cluster of men unfolded to become three cab drivers holding a very agitated young man. One cabbie had a bloody nose. One was crying his eyes out, and the third and largest one had the young man in a full nelson. All at the same time the drivers tried to tell us what happened. As this was going on, other cabs would pull up and the drivers would leave off shouting at each other, me, and the young man to greet the cabs and presumably tell them everything was under control. What we eventually were able to piece together was that the young man had attempted to stick up the first cab. He had no gun, but when the driver proved reluctant to hand over the cash, the young man sprayed him with Mace. This was witnessed by the second cabbie, who stopped his car in traffic and valiantly tried to apprehend the robber. The young man, quite spry, punched this cabbie in the nose. A third cabbie stopped, and among them they overwhelmed the young man.

The cabbie with the bloody nose kept yelling, "He is killing me!" and pointing to the young man. I believe he was just confusing tense and the severity of his injury. I told the full-nelson cabbie to release his prisoner and pushed the young man over the trunk of one of the cabs. I got my handcuffs on one of his wrists. At this point the man began howling that I was violating his civil rights. As I tried to get the other wrist into the cuffs, he pushed himself off the car and took a swipe at me with his free hand. Joe helped me put him properly in cuffs, and we pushed him back down on the hood of the car to search him. He began screeching that we were doing this only because he was Hispanic. At which point I took a good look at his face. The thing was, he didn't look Hispanic to me.

My second civilian complaint is long overdue.

John Cameron Mitchell

John Cameron Mitchell is a New York–based actor, writer, and director whose credits include Six Degrees of Separation, Big River, *and* The Secret Garden. *He wrote this while starring in* Hedwig and the Angry Inch, *the hit rock musical he wrote with composer Stephen Trask.*

POSTED   Monday, March 16, 1998, at 4:30 P.M. PT

It was a fun weekend for my show. I play a rock 'n' roll songstress named Hedwig who was originally a boy in Communist East Germany and wanted more. He agrees reluctantly to a sex change so he can marry an American GI and get the fuck out. He/she ends up divorced in a Kansas trailer park, watching the Berlin Wall come down on bootleg cable.

The musical takes the form of one of Hedwig's pathetic gigs. The rock band Cheater backs me up, and we perform in the ballroom of an ancient flophouse where the surviving crew of the Titanic once stayed. Nowadays, a bunch of welfare cases and a few German backpackers loiter around the coffee machine in the lobby (the condoms are in the candy machine). Our dressing room is in the Rapunzel-like tower at the top of the hotel. People had better not pull on my hair, though, unless they want the wig to come off in their hands!

Last week, somebody overdosed, and the body was carried out through the incoming audience. Last night, the audience was annoyingly quiet. A few too many uptown, button-down folks. The show was tough going at first—my voice was strained by our Saturday doubleheader—but the audience warmed up to us by the end (even though nobody raised their hands when I asked them to in the bombastic finale).

On our way back up to the dressing room, a very cute Israeli cornered me. He had just seen the show and tried to pull me into his hotel room. I considered this a rave. I heard later he was a callboy. On my way out, two very self-possessed 13-year-old twin girls told me they had heard about us on the Internet and come all the way from Toronto to see the show...and to shop at Saks. "A cross between Bowie and Rocky [Horror, they clarified]." Bob Mould, a punk rock god (who played with Hüsker Dü and Sugar), attended the show tonight for the second time. We dined delightfully afterward. He told me he was even more moved seeing the show again. My cranky dissatisfaction with the audience melted.

I've been around actors for 15 years, and I'm not impressed by any of them anymore (except maybe Gena Rowlands)...but a rock star is another story. I just get all giggly. David Bowie and Lou Reed have already come, and I almost did. It's all very heady for the very mainstream meat 'n' potatoes 'n' theater 'n' TV performer that I've been until recently. Last year I was flush with sitcom cash, and now I'm singing in a Farrah Fawcett wig for pennies. And having the time of my life.

POSTED Tuesday, March 17, 1998, at 4:30 P.M. PT

- A nice note from a *Hedwig* idol, Madeline Kahn, thanking me for inviting her to opening night. Wrote her a thank you note. Will she write back to thank me for it?
- A Screen Actors Guild check for 14 cents compensating me for the fourth Serbian rerun of a *MacGyver* episode.

- A letter from a woman I remember as a sweet 14-year-old who came to see me in *The Secret Garden* many times. She is now recording songs, on her own label, that deal with her recovery from sexual abuse.
- A letter from a Canadian guy I met at a bar a hundred years ago. Colored feathers fell out of the envelope. He congratulates me, in a zany font, on my reviews. I remembered introducing him to my friend Derek (now at Microsoft) and later telling Derek this guy was a model. He was silent for a moment. "A foot model?"
- A letter from someone wanting me to contribute to a book titled *How to Be Successful in America*. Other contributors include Bart Conner and Norm Crosby.

On the lobby floor of my apartment building is a monthly flyer from the New York Hemlock Society addressed to a Mr. and Mrs. Clive Small. Handwritten next to the address: "No longer at this address."

POSTED Thursday, March 19, 1998, at 4:30 P.M. PT

Woke up with a sore throat again but slept and decided I was well enough to do the show. It turned out to be a great one. The audience was cautious at first, but I didn't care. I didn't have the energy. Strange, how sickness can focus. Fatigue makes you sloppy, but illness is an emergency. The tiny energy supply must be economized, channeled into small, achievable tasks.

The task for me as an actor is focusing on what I am seeing or imagine I am seeing at any given moment in my performance. I didn't study much acting and have pretty much created my own visual process. When I prepare a role, I break the text down into units, or "beats." For each beat, I will prepare an image that I can summon on cue. For example, when you tell a story about an old lover, you will see this person in your head, and if you're concentrating on the memory, you will find your voice, body, and emotions reacting automatically and unself-consciously. If I can come up with the perfect visual image — sometimes a memory, sometimes a product of my imagination — at the correct moment in the performance, then I find my body, mind, and heart will react equally unself-consciously and realistically. Sometimes the reaction will be wrong for the character or the piece, and the image will have to be changed. Sometimes the reaction surprises me but is still appropriate. That's when things become interesting. That's what happened at this performance. It was a nice blend of craft and flow. There were a lot of surprises. I improvised more than usual, which I really find nerve-racking. This time it was liberating.

That's why I wrote *Hedwig*. I wanted to get a little rock 'n' roll and do it in my realm of the theater. Not like *Rent* or *Tommy* — Broadway fake rock. We have the band onstage as part of the action. I learned some things about singing last night, too. My throat was raw, so I skipped the fancy effects (fake raspiness, difficult notes) and economized. I think I sang better than I have in weeks. I remembered that my favorite artists are economical — Egon Schiele or Gena Rowlands, Peter Sellers and Robert Altman at their best. They completed their emotional and intellectual tasks with only that which was necessary — no more, no less. Sometimes the task is complex, and a painter will require two dozen colors for the simple figure of a child. But two dozen colors was exactly what was necessary to create that child.

John Moore

John Moore filed this when he sat on the faculty of Rockefeller University and the Aaron Diamond AIDS Research Center in New York. He is currently a professor at Cornell Medical School.

POSTED Monday, Nov. 23, 1998, at 4:30 P.M. PT

A photographer was around last Friday, working on the center's annual report. She wanted me to don the traditional white lab coat for the usual "in lab shot." I declined, partly to avoid looking like a demented ice-cream salesman but more because I always chuckle whenever I see any of my colleagues on television or in the newspaper, resplendent in the "scientist's uniform." In the real world, these guys and gals last saw the working end of a pipette years ago. The only time they wear a white coat nowadays is when the building's heating is on the blink again, or when they've been caught in the rain and need something to hide their red silk thong underwear. And I'm no different (except for the thong, of course). All I do on a daily basis is talk, read, and type. My principal occupational health hazard is wearing the ends of two fingers to a stub sending out e-mails. Why is this?

Well, being a scientist is a bit like being in the military. As one rises up the food chain, other people do one's dirty work. There aren't many generals who get strung out on the barbed wire in front of a machine-gun nest, are there? Rankwise, I am now somewhere around a colonel, judging from the uniforms my friends in the Army's AIDS program sometimes wear (I always give them a vigorous salute, the nature of which is conditional upon the contents of their last research paper). Of course, a military man is only as good as his troops, and I am extremely fortunate to have been blessed with a splendid set of privates. These gallant folks enable me to hold my own among the other colonels and generals, and I am thankful for it.

I wander from my office to the lab outside, principally to gossip, partly for the relatively vigorous exercise, musing on the different ways of running a group. A few researchers climb up the greasy pole by trampling on the piled-up corpses of post-docs, students, and technicians, who are mere instruments of the supreme will. Others set lab members into internal competition, with the winner taking the spoils, the loser the shame. Fortunately, these styles are not the norm, and I don't adopt them. My principle is simple: Recruit smart people, point them in the right direction, facilitate their activities, encourage them to work together, and let them get on with it. They do well, I do well; everybody's happy. My thoughts are interrupted by hysterical peals of laughter from the adjacent office, where Tanya the Serb and Alexandra the Austrian, two ballsy and talented senior post-docs, are giggling like pre-pubescent schoolgirls over an e-mail. The hysteria spreads to the others in the lab, and I go to find out what it's all about. Turns out that I'd sent a message over the center's network this morning asking others to join our lab trip to see *There's Something About Mary* but wrote "Marty" by mistake. Marty Markowitz, our balding clinical director, had replied saying he appreciated the thought but never needs to use hair gel. Everyone's a target for piss-taking, and this time it's my turn.

Our lab resembles the United Nations; at one time, we could have re-fought World War I (we even had an American who joined in projects late and tried to walk off with the credit). The different nationalities all interact well, although as we sit together over lunch and plan the lab Thanksgiving party, I get a little concerned. General Tso's chicken is to mingle with lamb rogan josh, toad-in-the-hole, and whatever the hell that awful goulash is they eat in central Europe; seems a tad idiosyncratic from a culinary perspective. Fortunately, Cindy the Southern Belle knows a turkey when she sees one, so there may be some hope for an element of traditionalism. I order in extra Pepto-Bismol, just in case.

So, like many of my peer group, I am just an overpaid two-fingered typist, with no white coat but with acid-holed sweat shirts.

POSTED Wednesday, Nov. 25, 1998, at 4:30 P.M. PT

The day starts with a meeting on Rockefeller's main campus to discuss an embryonic project on how antibody responses are generated—it's good to have a real immunologist around to explain what all the long words mean. In the taxi on the way back, we mull over the Thanksgiving party. I tell Alex and Deep the story of my early days at the Diamond center. I sent a memo round the lab saying that since I was a Brit, we would not be observing the July 4 and Thanksgiving holidays but would have St. George's Day and the Queen's official birthday off instead. The next day, Tim the American plaintively begged me to reconsider, since he had promised his mom he would be home for Thanksgiving. He looked so pathetically upset, I just had to say yes (against my better judgment). I realized that day that America would be a fertile land for British "humour." Alex has a paroxysm, so we scrape her lungs from the taxi partition before we leave.

The e-mail in-tray is flashing when I arrive in the office. I flick through the messages: routine junk and more unsolicited résumés for rapid deletion; gossip from friends, to which I reply in a similar vein; another sick joke from Mario (has he nothing else to do?)—I circulate it further; a couple of requests for information, which I leave to deal with later. And a press release.

I don't like this aspect of AIDS research. There's too much media coverage of too many "non-stories" driven by press releases from corporate PR firms and university/government press offices. The scientific journals are also increasingly responsible, as if they were engaged in a tabloid-style circulation war and not just in the dissemination of accurate information. I reckon there are fewer than half a dozen AIDS science stories each year that actually merit significant press coverage, but there are far, far more attempts to get scientists' faces or words to the attention of the public.

I phone a mate to chat about the latest press release, since I don't know the background too well — the story turns out to be bullshit, as usual. We speculate about what drives some of our colleagues to advertise their work so vigorously. Often, it's just plain old glory-seeking, although we both know some members of the academic community who are little more than financially supported corporate mouthpieces. These people are few in number but can do a fair bit of damage to AIDS research. The worst media hogs are small biotech companies. The more limited the product line, the more hinges on its success, so the more remarkable become the claims sent to the world in press release form (and often in published papers — who reviews these things?). The aim is usually to con financial analysts or federal officials, as ritual exercises in share-price manipulation or investment seeking. Unless I know personally the people involved (or often because I do), I don't believe anything said by a small company about its product until an independent scientist has verified the claim, which is rarely possible. Most professional AIDS researchers recognize cotton candy science for what it is. But does the public? How much harm is done by the all too common flagrant misrepresentation of the facts? For how long will the public and the politicians pay attention to AIDS if we as a research community continually cry wolf about new AIDS cures and (especially) vaccines? When will payback time come? This troubles me.

In the lunchroom, there's an old copy of the *New York Times Magazine*. It's all about "status" — apparently, we scientists measure our own "personal status" by whose lab we have been trained in or which "big name scientists" we have published with. I think that's far too superficial an analysis, so I chat with Jim the Brit as he swills down his bright orange, disgusting-looking curry and I nibble on my usual lettuce leaf. In the end, we agree that what matters most among professionals is the quality of published work — this determines who we do and don't pay attention to, which is a reasonable measure of "status." Yet there's certainly no absolute correlation between "getting it right" and public prominence — some AIDS researchers who are darlings to the media actually have quite a mixed reputation among their peers, because their papers don't always stand up to careful scrutiny. Both of us know a researcher whose work is invariably shoddy but who's notorious for trying to get the press interested in everything his lab does. Perhaps his mom is pleased to see his picture in the paper, but the rest of us have reservations — you can't fool your professional colleagues for too long.

Another e-mail arrives. For weeks I have been trying to get the press interested in the background to last month's insane decision by the South African government to refuse to provide AZT to HIV-infected, pregnant women. This will condemn thousands of children to HIV infection and death, and it could easily influence similar decisions in neighboring countries. The South Africans' pleas of poverty ring false when contrasted with their recently announced intent to spend billions of dollars on new arms purchases, to counter "regional threats." But what bigger "regional threats" are there in southern Africa than AIDS? Now *Newsday* has published the story and has done a really nice job on it. I circulate the text of the article to other AIDS researchers (e-mail has its uses). Maybe some pressure will build on the South Africans. It's ironic that the next International AIDS Conference is being held in South Africa — will the responsible ministers be seeking the media limelight beside the AIDS research glitterati? It wouldn't surprise me—this is what usually happens.

What's going on in South Africa is an AIDS story that deserves extensive press coverage. Why, then, did the rest of the media miss it for so long? Was it, perhaps, buried under the avalanche of ego- or profit-driven press releases?

Cynthia Ozick

Cynthia Ozick is a novelist and essayist who lives in New Rochelle, N.Y. Her most recent book is Quarrel & Quandry

POSTED Monday, Oct. 28, 1996, at 4:11 P.M. PT

A month ago, in the middle of the night, a hot-water pipe suddenly burst, there was a great flood, and the kitchen ceiling came down with a gargantuan crash, ruining everything in its path. For years there had been little baby-leaks here and there, but now it became clear that the rest of the plumbing world would very soon follow suit. Eric Rodriguez and his assistant, Greg, a pair of charming and able young plumbers, spent weeks removing the arteriosclerotic pipes brought into this 18th-century house in 1898, and replacing them all with copper tubes and black-and-silver "no-hubs." But first there was "demo," which may suggest demography or democracy or even a demonstrative nature, but stands, alas, for demolition. Mr. Nunes, the Portuguese excavator, dug up the yard, the driveway, and the garage to give us a new main. (For 30 years we had been drinking water that ran through antiquated lead.) My book-lined study wall had to be knocked out; so did the linen closet; so did half the cellar; and now there are towers of books in incongruous corners everywhere, and towels and sheets heaped cheek by jowl with ripped-out sinks and toilet bowls. You can write your name in concrete dust on any surface you like. And you can look up through a missing ceiling, or down through a vanished floor, and see the strings of copper jewels that are the new water pipes. They resemble Queen Hatshepsut's necklaces.

The next step is getting a contractor to rebuild, from the gutted upstairs bathrooms to the lost kitchen and all the way down to the torn-up basement. We have placed all our hopes in a man of many acts, who used to be a business executive in an office, but gave it up to live in a houseboat and restore, meticulously and artfully, old houses. He stopped by with a measuring tape (he whipped it round like a dancer with a sash) and promised to return with an estimate. Meanwhile, we continue to live like abandoned mountaineers, avoiding falling through the nearest crevasse and awaiting the rescue party.

POSTED Wednesday, Oct. 30, 1996, at 4:13 P.M. PT

Hooray! The contractor arrived last night at 7 P.M., wearing a yellow pullover and looking very much like Gatsby, or rather like Robert Redford playing Gatsby. Verifying numbers, he swept his tape measure around corners as if it were something alive, or else a lasso, or maybe a yo-yo (the way yo-yos in the hands of clever boys seem to halt in midair before diving or looping). Together we went upstairs to look over what real estate agents like to call the Master Bath. The subject was tile, tile, tile. In the ruined kitchen the subject was window frames and soffits. (Soffits! Did I know what these were before the kitchen ceiling came crashing down?)

All this makes me think of Edith Wharton. The truth is I am not in the least like Edith Wharton—nor is this the blazingly self-evident literary judgment it may appear to be. Edith Wharton liked to build and renovate houses. She liked planning villas and gardens. I presume she was even interested in topiary. (I, as it happens, have a black thumb.) I always envy writers who live in organized spaces and beautiful rooms, writers who have file cabinets, writers who have e-mail, writers who have faxes, writers who hire cleaners to scrub toilets and vacuum, writers who can write in the morning and go out to dinner in the evening, writers who have the courage to throw out their mail unanswered, writers who ignore manuscripts sent by other writers, writers who travel (without getting sick on the plane), writers who drive cars, writers who dress well, writers whose gutters and leaders are cleared, writers without a leak in the roof or an animal in the attic, writers who escape clutter and chaos.

Sometimes I try to picture the writing rooms—they are probably called "studies"—of the Very Famous. I see perfect ceilings without cracks. I see broad desks; perhaps two broad desks. I see cherrywood shelves where the books are classified by subject. I see an assistant who answers the telephone. I see high advances from publishers and extensive sales. After that, a kind of darkening sets in; I cannot imagine those rooms or those lives.

I write in a dim snug cell on a table with a single drawer that I have used since I was eight years old, a child's hand-me-down from my brother. There are heaps of books all over the tiny floor; you have to step over or around them. There is a carton to save letters in. There is a second table on which my old Smith Corona rests (the first electrified generation). Until not long ago I was devoted to a favorite fountain pen, but nowadays nothing is so archaic or so hard-to-find as an ordinary bottle of ink. No matter: There is the splendid polymer-point Expresso. (It streams the words lucently, it never skips or blots; it thinks.) I have no defense against humiliating publisher's advances. Two hours ago a graduate student from the Columbia School of Journalism telephoned to ask to do a writer's profile for a class assignment. He admired my work, he said. Apparently he wasn't referring to anything in print; last summer he'd been to see my play, in a small off-Broadway theater. "If I tried to get someone Big," he explained, "they wouldn't want to squander their time."

The Master Bath, so-called, abuts my little workroom (I write close to the cloaca), where my table is under tarpaulins and the walls have been demolished to accommodate the plumbing. Our contractor, the Robert Redford look-alike, is going to rebuild those walls, and then—who knows? With a flash of his serpentine tape measure the room will widen, the desk will broaden, the books will order themselves by subject-matter, and I'll begin to write and sell like Edith Wharton, with advances to match.

And then will my black thumb turn green, and my white hair brown again?

POSTED Monday, Nov. 4, 1996: 10:00 A.M. PT

Over the weekend, I happened to overhear a pair of executives discussing an inefficient secretary. They worried about how to dismiss her, and whether to do it at all. Would she be able to live on Social Security? How would she manage her rent? How, above all, would she deal with the anger and the hurt? In the end, it turned out, they decided to temporize.

I have been fired twice, in both instances with admirable speed. The first time I was 22, just out of graduate school with a master's degree; this was at a time when the degree counted for something, and you had to spend a year writing a thesis. (Mine was on The Later Novels of Henry James.) It makes no sense to me now that I actually applied for a job with an accounting firm, and that they, in their folly, actually took me on. The firm was called Bennett, Chirlian, and the functionary who hired me was named David Hume. "Oh, like the British philosopher," I made the mistake of saying. I had with me, for lunch-time reading, a book on critical theory by René Wellek and Robert Penn Warren, standard literary fodder in that innocently pre-deconstruction period. Monday, my starting day, I was given a mass of numbers and a set of long printed forms; my job was to type the numbers into the white spaces on the forms. Liquid White-Out hadn't yet been invented— if you hit the wrong key you had to scrub away with a typewriter eraser, which often enough scrubbed a hole in the page. I hit many wrong keys and made many holes.

Tuesday, my second day, I was summoned into the office of the potentate, who was either Mr. Bennett or Mr. Chirlian; I wasn't sure which. My assignment was to go over to Schirmer's, the music store, to buy a score for Mr. B's or Mr. C's gifted daughter, who was, I was told, just my age. This was especially humiliating; it put me in mind of a story by Mary Lamb that I had read in childhood, called "The Changeling," wherein one girl is esteemed and the other humbled.

Wednesday seemed strangely quiet. No one asked me to type anything, and Mr. Hume, still unaware that he was a philosopher's namesake, passed me by with cold indifference. Thursday, he handed me a small check and told me I needn't bother to come back Friday. Carrying the talisman of my Wellek-and-Warren, I left that afternoon weeping with the shame of failure. My job had lasted four days.

The second time I was fired, the job also lasted four days, though spread over four months. The late Anatole Broyard was writing a monthly column for the *New York Times Book Review*, and Michael Levitas, who was editor then, had the idea of adding three other columns, one a week, by three different hands. The three new columnists were Denis Donoghue, the eminent critic, the novelist Marilynne Robinson, and myself. Broyard's column was dependably witty, erudite, and always accessible. The newcomers, it soon developed, were found to be too cerebral, too dense, too —in short—highbrow. Shortly after I submitted my fourth (and final) column, the phone call from Levitas came; I knew the message before he spoke. I was in good company; all three of us were fired simultaneously, while Broyard went on as before, the unique master of his difficult monthly art.

This, by the way, is the sixth day of the 10 days I was hired to write this "Diary." It seems to be more reminiscence than diary. Will I be fired before the rest of the week is out?

Jan Reid

Jan Reid is a founding writer at Texas Monthly, *and author of the forthcoming books* Close Calls: Jan Reid's Texas *and* The Bullet Meant for Me. *He wrote this after returning from a trip to Mexico that went awry.*

POSTED Monday, July 6, 1998, at 4:30 P.M. PT

My friends say the gunman initially fired a shot at the pavement that night, trying to quell the rebellion. I have no memory of that. I just remember his glare as he came after me. I guess I thought that if I could land one punch I could back up the pistolero, and then I'd take my chances as I turned and ran. I threw the left well but the punch fell short. The Mexican robber looked me in the eye, pointed his gun at my midsection, and shot to kill me. The muzzle flash resembled a distant spark of lightning angling from sky to ground. The pain was immediate, enormous, and precise; I swear I could feel the bullet's spin. I fell and cried out: "I'm killed." Such a bad Hollywood line.

Four of us had gone to Mexico City to watch a prizefight. In April, *Texas Monthly* had published my article about Jesus Chavez, an engaging young boxer who had the uncommon distinction of gaining a No. 1 world ranking at the same time he was being deported. One of my travel companions edited the piece, another was the fact-checker. Jesus won his fight with a third-round technical knockout. The next night my friends and I drank and sang in Garibaldi Plaza, a mecca for mariachis and tourists. Then we got in the cab of a driver who delivered us to the two gunmen, who robbed us as the ride rolled on. Then as the cabbie pulled off a freeway, the robber who would shoot me said they were going to separate us. To me that sounded like a bad situation getting much worse. The fracas ensued—and my life can never be quite the same again.

Surgeons in Mexico City saved my life. The bullet broke both bones in my left forearm, narrowly missed vital organs in my abdomen, and came to rest at the base of my spinal column. The initial prognosis was paralysis from the waist down. Days later, in Houston, I came out of the netherworld of morphine and found I could move my toes and feet. Rays of hope. Today, after two months of recovery and therapy in Houston, I'm home in Austin, adjusting to life in a wheelchair and trying to believe the assurances that I may walk away from it someday. I'll always know the face of the man who tried to kill me. But could I pick him out of a lineup? I don't know. Not that there's much chance of that. To this day, no law enforcement official in Mexico has spoken to me. I don't dwell on the pistolero. He has no presence in my dreams. I escaped him in the outpouring of friendship and rescue that began with a spill of letters across my bed that first morning I regained my senses. From an old girlfriend came the best first line: "Dear Jan—Don't get in gunfights when you don't have a gun."

POSTED Tuesday, July 7, 1998, at 4:30 P.M. PT

"You'll have good days and bad days," doctors and therapists cautioned me. But they failed to tell me how often the good and bad would be rolled into one. The bullet that a Mexico City thug fired into me during an April 20 robbery churned to a halt in a mass of spinal nerves called the cauda equina—"horse's tail" in Latin. Two weeks after the shooting, my neurosurgeon in Houston let out a whoop when he saw the results of an MRI. Though he likened the bullet's effect on those nerves to a blast furnace, at least some of the nerves were capable of regeneration.

I had what's known as an "incomplete" spinal injury. That was good news. But not so cheery was the condition of my left leg. While the right grew stronger each day in the rehab hospital and soon would support my standing weight, muscles in the left twitched and fired, trying to remember what to do. The knee buckled and the leg was numb. In a way I was grateful. After I was shot, "referred" pain from the spinal injury had burned in my shins and feet like blazes of hell. The doctors brought this odd pain under control with drugs normally prescribed for epileptic seizures and depression. But more weirdness followed. First the symptoms felt like a fluttering surge of electricity moving slowly down my left leg. Then the phantom pains turned nasty. Doctors mumbled vague clinical explanations; the head physical therapist hiked her shoulders and said, "Aw, it's those funky gunshot wounds."

Now I'm back in Austin, Texas, doing outpatient rehab three days a week. Last night at dinner the outbreak began with a buzzing tightness in my left knee. By midnight these spasms came every eight seconds — I clocked them — and the periodic climax felt like a combination of a foot gone to sleep, a toe stuck in an electrical outlet, and a twisting, total, lockdown cramp that reached the thigh before the muscles relaxed. My groaning and hissing drove my wife to the guest bedroom. It was a miserable night.

As other people drove to work, I wheeled into the exercise room groggy and ill-tempered. My regular therapist said she had to do an evaluation of a stroke victim and introduced me to a young blond woman who would fill in for her today. Sarah was a contract therapist, working here and there as needed, and at one point she apologized for being so green about spinal injuries. "Green?" I said, surprised, because she was very good. On the exercise mat skilled physical therapists kneel and roll and pivot around their patients with the grace of dancers. The leg lifts and stretching moved me into that zone of relaxed airiness I once knew as an athlete. For 20 minutes I moved around the room on a walker. I lurched and wobbled, but in my mind I cruised. Outside the day looked glorious. "Slow down, take shorter steps," said Sarah. "But you're doing great."

POSTED Wednesday, July 8, 1998, at 4:30 P.M. PT

My first wheelchair was a one-armed bandit. Standard wheelchairs are designed to be propelled by both hands, but my left forearm had been broken by a bullet smashing through it. All I could do with a standard model was to send it in an endless left turn. Therapists at the rehab hospital in Houston mentioned the existence of a chair that could be driven with one hand. I told them to find me one of those — I wanted the exercise. But the only one available must have been of World War II vintage, for it handled like it had the tonnage of a tank. People in the corridors raised their gazes from mine because I crept so painfully and pathetically along.

The therapists took pity on me and delivered an electric-powered model. Soon I was zipping all over the place, never late for my appointments, steering with my index finger and thumb. Then a patient who had more legitimate need of my hot rod entered the hospital, and abruptly one night it disappeared. Left outside my door instead was a standard wheelchair. My arm was still in a splint. A nurse told me I could help in the steerage by throwing out my heels, digging them in the tile, and pulling the vehicle along. But the seat was set too tall for me. I flailed, kicked, and cursed, and when I finally came upon the responsible party, it's a good thing I didn't have a cane.

Now I'm home with a rented, standard, rather sleek model. My arm is tender but healed, and I've made a sort of peace with the mode of transportation. I sport a pair of mountain bike gloves, made in Sri Lanka, that look stylish and give me needed grip for

the ramps in my yard and house. I'm mobile. Thanks to the wheelchair, my working life goes on. But the dogs and cat recognize the
vehicle for what it is—a small car in the house that can veer out of
control. Our Austin home sits on a geological fault, and if you drop
a ball in the dining room it will roll through the kitchen to the living room wall. Now I don't find that eccentricity quite so funny. In
the kitchen I'm always spinning around, hitting a brake, as I try to
move a chicken breast from chopping board to skillet. To clean the
sink or load the dishwasher, I have to parallel park. Tonight I fed
the dogs and made a simple cold avocado soup for dinner. Nothing
to it on the cookbook page, yet the two light chores consumed
more than an hour. Afterward I looked at the water faucet and
glasses in one cabinet behind me and the whiskey bottle and refrigerator full of ice at the higher end of the kitchen. How much
trick driving do I have to do to make myself a drink?

POSTED Thursday, July 9, 1998, at 4:30 P.M. PT

Sometimes I think this episode has been hardest on my wife. After
I was shot that night in Mexico City, my friend Mike Hall, an editor and writer at *Texas Monthly*, kept a strong grip on my hand
and stayed with me during the ambulance ride. I told him I'd
rather die than endure such pain, except I wanted to see Dorothy
again. The remark found its way into an Austin newspaper story;
suddenly friends and strangers back home were making us into
Scotty and Zelda, Tracy and Hepburn. But life and love consume a
lot more soap than opera.

When Mike called Dorothy at 2:30 A.M. she didn't pick up the
receiver before the call rolled to the voice mail. I heard that message before it was erased, and I'm sure it was much like their conversation when he called again moments later: His shaken voice
strained for calm while my screams could be heard distinctly in the
background. Dorothy and my stepdaughter, Lila, were on a plane

to the Mexican capital early that morning. Neurosurgeons there told them I would be totally paralyzed from the waist down. On the emergency jet flight to Houston, Dorothy and Lila gaped as I snored loudly with my eyes wide open—not a good sign, a doctor told me later. On the ground I had to be resuscitated with breathing tubes as Dorothy screamed at the medical crew to get a helicopter. For her the pace never let up.

She took a leave from her job and assumed a manic gypsy life. Some days she lived in a borrowed apartment near the Houston Medical Center, learning from the therapists what my condition required of her. Then she was on the highway back to Austin, where she enlisted an architect and builder to modify the house. She admits to obsessive behavior; one day she was racing around wondering how she could possibly leave our housesitter with a spice rack devoid of peppercorns.

The strain took its toll, of course. At the rehab hospital, therapists agreed with her that while I worked hard at my exercises, other times I demonstrated a strange, spacey passivity. Was it the pain medication? Depression? Or was it having nurses attend to my every need? A few days before my discharge, the doctors wisely insisted that we spend a weekend away from the hospital. We checked into a nice hotel, drank and ate with friends, and once more enjoyed being in the same bed. But I forgot essential things related to my medical condition; she had to drive back and get them. On the hottest day of the year I insisted on keeping a social engagement; she had to haul the heavy chair in and out of the trunk.

"Are you depressed?" she said when we fought.

"I'm starting to be."

"I knew you were going to say that!"

Afforded a valuable glimpse of how hard it was going to be, we've tried to ease back into our life at home. None of the rowdy dinner parties yet. We've only gone out to restaurants twice. Our marriage always relied on equal division of labor. Dorothy cooked dinner one week, I cooked the next. Now I'm frustrated that I can't carry out the trash and take my turn going to the grocery store. She watches me struggling to put on my socks and wonders if she helps me too much or not enough. But we're getting there. Someday we'll drive those European back roads again and even go back to Mexico. In the meantime just lying here with happy dogs at our feet's enough.

Here's looking at you, kid.

POSTED Friday, July 10, 1998, at 4:30 P.M. PT

"You may walk again, and you may not," said the Houston neurosurgeon who had supervised my care. "It may take a year, 18 months, for this to play out. But you're going to have at least some movement of your legs. If you have to get around in a wheelchair, you can still work. You can drive a car. You can get on an airplane."

"A productive life," I said, trying to match his enthusiasm.

"Yeah. Now we're going to get you sitting up."

I laughed and said, "Sure." Confined to bed, I had come to feel like a brick slowly sinking in a lake of mud. All the strength I ever had was gone. But soon after the doctor left, nurses wheeled in a contraption that looked like a stretcher. When they lifted me over to it, one hit a switch, and this stretcher turned into a chair that vaulted me upright. I happened to look down, and something flopped like a salmon thrown out on a bin of ice. It was my right foot. Talk about a sobering bottom line.

The improvement came with time and with dogged, tedious effort in the rehab hospital. I couldn't feel sorry for myself. On the next machine or exercise mat someone huffed and puffed with injuries far worse than mine. Friendships formed. Jim was a linguistics professor who had made his life's work penetrating the mystery of the Tarahumara Indians in northern Mexico. He was also a competitive cyclist who had got bashed almost to extinction doing his daily miles in the Houston traffic. "I've got to walk again," he told me. "There's no other way to get to them." One day

I watched in awe as his legs gave out climbing a flight of stairs. He got to the top by turning around and lifting his hands and hips; then the therapist urged him to crawl.

Jesus was a Mexican immigrant. He had six kids at about age 40 and had bought a house and made his way as a landscaper. Now his back problems had put him out of that line of work for good, the neighborhood where he lived rang with the gunfire of gangs at night, and he had no medical insurance. One day he told me with an air of wonder: "I just got a bill for $145,000. That's a lot of money." Another night my leg pains were making me thrash and cry out. Jesus rose from his bed, restored the pillows I had kicked away, and stood for a moment with a comforting hand on my foot. It was one of the kindest gestures I've ever known.

Tom was a busy contractor called to look at a leaking roof. The shingles shot out from under him, and it was a long way to the ground. "This wheelchair business sucks," he e-mailed me the other day. "Thank goodness for hardwood and tile floors. Our bedroom carpet is like 6-inch bubble gum, but that's good exercise, they tell me. Whoopee."

Walking or rolling, we've all gone on with our lives. As I make my rounds of outpatient rehabilitation in Austin, I'm concerned with "gait," a noun I once associated with horses. With admiration and a nag of envy, I watch people saunter past me. How tall and confident they are! On my rear deck now is a protective rail that's just the right height. I lean forward and with a heave of exertion I stand up. Resting my hands on the rail, I pull my shoulders back, tighten my buttocks, and shift my weight from one hip to the other. I breathe the air that never penetrates a hospital and think of those friends and the bond we share. But so far I'm afraid to let go of the rail. My left knee starts wobbling, and with a sigh I lower myself to the safety of the chair.

Lucinda Rosenfeld

Lucinda Rosenfeld wrote a column about night life for the New York Post *from 1996 to 1998. She recently published her first novel,* What She Saw in Roger Mancuso, Günter Hopstock, Jason Barry Gold ...

POSTED Wednesday, April 30, 1997, at 4:30 P.M. PT

"I'm sorry—you're going to have to give me space," bitches the maitre d'. For a split second I think I'm hearing myself lecturing boyfriend G. Then I remember where I am. I'm at a restaurant called Balthazar in downtown Manhattan. It's a sumptuous art nouveau imitation of a famous Parisian brasserie. Silver egg trees line a polished zinc bar. The walls are painted a warm yellow-white. The mirrors are aged, and therefore kind. Balthazar has already been declared the restaurant of the moment. This means that by tomorrow it will be the restaurant of yesterday. It was my editor, S., who suggested I stop by. (At this late hour, I'm still looking for column material.) But the place is unbearably crowded. Wherever I stand, I'm in someone's way. Also in the way is the enormous glass vase of tulips that appeared at my office at six this evening—a conciliatory offering by G.

I earn money on the side doing administrative work for an Italian arts colony. I work out of a law firm, but I rarely talk to the lawyers, who walk right by me without acknowledging my presence. My friends are the secretaries. My closest secretary friend, L., was recently diagnosed with a stress disorder. She had been misdiagnosed the month before with Lyme disease. She resigned last Friday. She's already lined up a new job closer to her home, which is on Long Island. I'll be sorry to see L. go. I've grown accustomed to telling her my guy troubles. And I like her stories about high school in the late '70s. She was one of the so-called "burnouts." She used to get high in the forest behind the A&P.

Repositioning myself between the seafood bar and the drinks bar, I strain to overhear the conversation of a pair of 23-ish girls chain-smoking Marlboro Lights. I catch this much over the din. Says the brunette: "I think there are inherent characteristics about him that won't change." Says the blonde: "Don't think you can teach him something. But don't think you haven't taught him something already!" Squeals the brunette: "Tom and I are done!" Sighs the blonde: "I only wish I'd said that in my letter to Jack."

G. shows up early. We've made a date to dine together, but decide not to do it here. We take a cab down to a favorite place of his in Tribeca. For whatever reason, the flowers have ended up in his lap. He asks me if I like them. I tell him they're beautiful. It's an inadequate response. I know this. I don't know how else to characterize tulips.

My pasta isn't greasy, like last night. And G. and I are getting along again. But I'm anxious to get home. I'm tired. And it bothers me that my apartment is such a mess. Dirty clothes litter every horizontal surface in my apartment. The garbage needs bagging. By tomorrow, I will have run out of clean glasses. And I must buy a better shade for the bathroom window: The one I have is made of bamboo and isn't long enough and I am quite sure that all of my neighbors see me naked on a regular basis.

The couple downstairs who have probably seen me naked consist of a guy and his girlfriend, who lives in L.A. and comes to visit every few months. I know it the second she's back. I can hear her having sex. I know it when she's left, too, because that's when he starts playing the Police again. He plays this one song, "Message in a Bottle," over and over again.

POSTED Friday, May 2, 1997, at 4:30 P.M. PT

Feeling underslept and overextended, I cancel my lunch date with M., an editor at *Harper's Bazaar*, and go back to sleep. I wake up after 1 P.M. I sit at my desk eating oat-bran cereal and staring out the window at my neighbor's sheets and towels flapping in the wind. I glance at the papers. I shower. I don't have anything to wear. I hate my clothes. I resolve to shop this weekend.

There is a man on the subway platform wearing a shirt that says, "I don't date girls who use four-letter words . . . Don't. Quit. Stop."

After work, my friend A. and I meet in the lobby of the Waldorf-Astoria Hotel, which is exactly halfway between our offices. It is a beautiful hotel, though with its floral-pattern carpets, stuffed chairs, fresco ceilings, marble façades, and cocktail-hour pianist banging away on the mezzanine level, it cuts a slightly campy figure. So grand. So presidential. One half-expects the Reagans to step out from behind a potted fern. There is clearly some kind of black-tie function taking place. Middle-aged women with gold clutches and décolleté walk by with an air of purpose. A. and I briefly consider crashing, then realize we're dressed too shabbily.

On the F train home, I sit next to an Indian gentleman reading a printout titled "Reasons Why Delaware Is the Choice of Corporate America." I realize there may not be time in my life to learn such things.

I have barely removed my dinner from its brown bag when the phone rings. It's my editor, S., calling to inform me that Keith McNally, the owner of Balthazar, the hot spot I reviewed in my column this morning, is livid. McNally says Balthazar is nothing like the famous Parisian brasserie La Coupole, to which I compared it. McNally would like to talk to me. I take his number. I doubt I'll call.

Waiting for my shower water to warm up, I check in with my complexion. I started breaking out at 23, as opposed to 13, the age you're supposed to break out. As I grow older, the pimple problem grows worse. I hate myself for caring. Just as I hate myself for saying "thank you" to the wasted 1970s night-life degenerate who, standing two inches from my nose and slurring his words only slightly, declared me a "beeeaauuuttiiffuull wooomaaan" at the 21 Club Monday night. "She is beautiful," concurred the gossip columnist to his left, before smearing his hand down the side of my face. I remember thinking these were not my friends. And that, while it was true that I had failed to get into graduate school, it was still hard to accept the idea that at that moment, in that room, with these people, I was in possession of the life I deserved.

Chris Seay

Chris Seay is founding pastor of University Baptist Church in Waco, Texas, and is currently pastor of Ecclesia, Houston's Holistic Missional Christian Community.

POSTED Monday, Jan. 31, 2000, at 10:30 A.M. PT

I am a pastor, and that means I care for people. I am a teacher/storyteller, spiritual director, friend, mentor, and a giver of hope. I love it and am made for it.

My wife, Lisa, and 21-month-old daughter, Hanna, and I went to dinner Saturday night with a friend from Philadelphia who is traveling the United States and parts of Europe for the next year. He is a social worker and saved most of his salary last year for his adventure. After introducing him to Ninfa's (some of the best Tex-Mex you will ever taste), I drop them off while I go to rent a movie and close out Saturday night on a relaxing note.

As I pull into Hollywood Video, my Nextel phone screams, "YOUR APARTMENT IS ON FIRE! COME HOME!" I think it's a joke, but it's not. I race home. My wife and baby are safe outside, but there is smoke everywhere and the smell of burnt plastic is putrid and pouring out the door. I find a fire extinguisher encased in glass that will not break. It must be freakin' Plexiglas or something, because it takes 20 blows to shatter it. I run into our smoke-filled apartment to find a kitchen that is one big flame. I empty four extinguishers. Neighbors keep bringing another over just as I empty one. I can't see anything, so I just take a deep breath, run in, and hope for the best. Breathe...Run...Spray...Run and repeat until all the extinguishers are empty. I get most of the blaze out before the fire department arrives. But I suck in enough smoke to make me eligible for clinical trials for people with high risk of lung cancer. The firefighters convinced me to get some oxygen in the ambulance while they finish fighting the flames.

In the ambulance, the paramedic checks me out while I peek through the window to see how bad the damage is. "You must work out," he says. "Your pulse is incredibly low." I realize I am not in despair or distraught, and my pulse is not even racing. Perhaps it's because my family is safe. Perhaps I don't love my possessions and material comforts like I love God, friends, and family. Perhaps I do, but the shock of the loss of material things has not sunk in yet. Or I figure insurance is the great equalizer. Time will tell.

Fire destroys and smoke permeates everything. It leaves nothing untouched. My family spends the night in an empty apartment 20 blocks away and try to sleep as we sort out the ramifications of cleaning or replacing everything we owned and where we would live. Sleep mostly escapes me. My mind is focused on the joy of my "night-night" ritual with Hanna at home. We all play in our bed, sing in the mirror, read books, tickle each other, and fade off to sleep as a family. That routine seems weeks or months away from being reality again. So, my wife washes smoky clothes all night and we get ready for our church service on Sunday evening (I know most churches meet in the A.M., but we are not most churches. These young postmodern urban dwellers are happy to sleep to noon and worship late). My wife sends me to the store with a grocery list. It says: lemons (for a lemonade fast so I can detox all the carcinogens that I swallowed last night), paper plates, cups, a knife, papaya, distilled water, soy milk, and a pregnancy test. I think she's most likely paranoid that inhaling smoke and cleaning soot could endanger a potential fetus. If a $12 pregnancy test puts her mind at ease then it is a worthwhile investment.

So we cut the papaya, drink some water, and take the test. Holy Hellfire! There are two lines! Parents, you know what I'm talking about. There is a control line and a "You are great with child" line. Lisa is pregnant. We have our second child and I am now a father of a homeless family of four.

At 5:30, Ecclesia, our spiritual community, meets for our quarterly love feast. It is a celebration of Christian community. A time to share our stories of joy and sorrow. A great crowd is there for music, cuisine, and real-life stories. I share ours and the community finds ways to lighten our load. By the end of the night we find out we have countless people coming over to clean, $90 has been collected to buy supplies, and friends are making us dinner each night of the week.

POSTED Tuesday, Feb. 1, 2000, at 8:21 A.M. PT

I slept a few hours on my brother's cold floor last night. The vacant apartment that has become our temporary home, after the fire, has no phone line, and it seems that a cell phone alone cannot facilitate the work I do. So I chose to snooze on the floor near an Internet connection instead of in bed with my family and no connection.

Monday is my day off. Pastors work weird hours and Sundays can be exhausting. Monday is typically a day to recuperate. I return e-mails in the morning, have some kind of appointment for lunch, and the afternoon belongs to Lisa and Hanna. We go to the park, a museum, shopping, or relax and watch a video. It is the time each week that my cell phone is turned off, and my attention is focused solely on them. This will not be a typical Monday. We are homeless and I want to talk to the insurance adjuster!

9:00 — Cell rings. It's Todd, a church member who works with students at Rice University. He's the kind of guy everyone wants to be friends with. I enjoy our conversations and would like to meet around lunchtime, but I defer to the adjuster, in case he should call. Todd and I will meet tomorrow.

9:20 — You've Got Mail! — I could spend my whole life returning e-mails and never do another thing. I love technology. My laptop is a thin, lightweight Compaq with a DVD player that can turn a "We are sorry, we are going to circle the airport for the next few hours" into a personal film festival. Nextel is my flavor in cell phones: The combination of two-way radio and free incoming calls maximizes its usefulness. I carry a Compaq Aero 1530 as my PDA. I love never thinking about what I will do today or trying to remember a phone number or flight time. However, I often loathe e-mail. The sheer amount I receive daily is often paralyzing. I can mention a word or a topic in a sermon or a speaking engagement, and before I get home my box is loaded with questions, comments, and thanks. But I also love it. People share their hearts on e-mail. They feel safe and they pour themselves out and share who they really are. I was flooded today with messages of love and offers to help. I cherish them. Rudy, a friend in California who runs a community center for kids in East Los Angeles, read the article in *Slate* and knew of our joy and sorrow. He sent us his prayers electronically. But he knew that had its limitations, so he called and blessed me again, saying, "I just wanted you to hear my voice." He was right. The same force that creates a feeling of privacy also isolates. I love hearing people tell me in times like this that I am not alone. It is what I do with my life. I introduce people to a communal faith in Christ that says we are not alone in this world, there is a God, and we go on our faith journey not as individuals but together.

The cell rings all day with calls about one thing or another: an ad for the church in the *Houston Press*, an offer to wash some of our clothes from a single mom who has her hands full, a real-estate agent trying to find us a home, my parents wanting to take us to dinner and survey the fire damage, the pastor of my former church with more laughter than talking. Some people would say technology creates too much noise and distraction. I would agree. But the world is a better place when we really connect. I made connections with almost everyone today. Except the insurance adjuster.

POSTED Wednesday, Feb. 2, 2000, at 10:00 A.M. PT

I love being alone in a big crowd. I'm writing from one of my favorite spots in the city of Houston, the Compaq Center, watching my former world champion Houston Rockets. There are seven minutes to go in the fourth period. I just sat down for the game. I can't afford to buy tickets, so I just come for the last quarter. Tonight it helps me block out the reality that everything we own is smoke-damaged and our lives are in complete chaos. The help from our community has been touching. We have 100 offers for a place to stay and meals for the near future. It's great to be cared for, but for the last part of the fourth period I'm just going to ponder Kelvin Cato's shot-blocking ability, which is substantial, and Olajuwon's propensity to make a complete comeback, which is unlikely even in Clutch City. I live only a few minutes from the stadium and I love to do anything that is free. Wow! Steve Francis just set up Cutino Mobley for an alleyoop dunk that stirred my soul (by the way, the Rockets are up on the Hornets by 10). Basketball is a spiritual experience surpassed only by God's greatest gift... baseball.

Today has been a day full of meetings and conversations with all kinds of people including the insurance adjuster. My job is about people, helping them move closer to the "One True God." That means it is not about institutions, bureaucracy, or maintaining programs. Just people. I say all that to tell you it can be exhausting to be with people each minute of this day. Whether by e-mail, phone, counseling appointment, or everyday event I follow my calling as a pastor. When I get my hair cut, my oil changed, or go to the movies, people either recognize me or my vocation comes up in conversation and all normal interactions are suspended. Most reactions to clergy fall in three categories: Counsel ("I have a question I've been wanting to ask someone... "), Confession ("Pastor, we need to talk..."), or Evasion ("Sorry, Rev., I shouldn't say 'shit' in front of you"). The Evasive response is the one that is most troubling to me. It assumes that I am sitting in a place capable of judging. Christianity is about forgiveness and not accusation. I am the last person to be shocked when you say "shit" or "damn." I deal with people on a daily basis whose lives are often falling apart, including my own. Of course, we did a lot of stupid things to get to the place where we are. But these are the kinds of people and events that fill the pages of scripture. From Abraham, who pimps out his wife to the king of Egypt for a lot of cash, to Peter, the bigot who excluded non-Jews. The Bible says to us, "Judge not, or you will be judged." The Christian Coalition may be lobbying the Gideons to take that verse out of the latest edition, but for now it is still there. Blaise Pascal puts it this way, "There are two kinds of people: the righteous who think they are sinners and the sinners who think they are righteous."

The Rockets win, and the post-game interview with our rookie phenom wraps up. The event staff is telling me nicely to get another place to work on my computer. I'm inspired here, but I do as I'm told. As I walk out of the stadium, I pass a guy I went to college with. His name is David Wesley, a guard for the Hornets. He played well tonight, but he was not the enthusiastic player I watched play at Baylor. You see, David lost his best friend and teammate Bobby Phills in a car wreck recently. He was racing Bobby at the time of the accident. Both were in Porsches that were modified to exceed speeds of 170 mph. There is even speculation about holding David legally responsible for Bobby's death. It seems a dark cloud is hanging over him. I doubt he recognized me, but I wanted to let him know we are praying for him and hurting with him. I uttered, "Hang in there, Dave, we are praying for you and mourning with you," and he replied with a softspoken, "Thank you, thanks a lot."

I'm a believer in Justice. I just wonder how we are going to define it. David Wesley looks like a model citizen compared with Abraham. I for one am not prepared to sit in judgment.

David Sedaris

David Sedaris is a commentator for National Public Radio and the author of Barrel Fever, Naked, *and* Me Talk Pretty One Day.

POSTED Monday, Nov. 25, 1996, at 4:30 P.M. PT

It was 20 years ago, almost to the day, that I began keeping a diary. A friend and I had been hitchhiking from Oregon to Vancouver when, for no reason whatsoever, I scribbled the day's events onto the back of a restaurant place mat, not knowing that the activity would become obsessive. My earliest diaries are stored away in my father's basement, and I can't bear to read them. Entries are introduced with Joni Mitchell quotes and melodramatic sob stories that end with lines such as, "I know now that I must walk alone!!!" What makes these diaries extra embarrassing is the fact that I hadn't even started drinking yet. I can't blame the writing on drugs or alcohol — that was me talking. I'd like to know what I ate when I was 19 years old. How much did it cost for a pound of chicken or a pack of cigarettes? What did I carry in my wallet, and who did I talk to on the telephone? My earliest diaries tell me none of these things. They tell me not who I was, but who I wanted to be. That person wore a beret and longed to ride a tandem bicycle with Laura Nyro. He wanted to arrive at parties on the back of a camel and sketch the guests, capturing the look of wonder on their faces as they admired his quiet, unassuming celebrity. I've been tempted to destroy those early diaries, but the very urge reminds me that I really haven't changed all that much.

Hugh (my boyfriend) and I went to the 26th Street flea market, and then I went alone to see *Set It Off*, the fifth movie I've seen this week. The Sony Theater on 19th Street pumps the volume so high that it makes my fillings hurt. I sat through the movie with my fingers in my ears, but Queen Latifah made it all worthwhile. She plays a tough lesbian bank robber with such charming conviction that you lower your head in mourning when she finally goes down in a blaze of gunfire. She's bad, sure, but you can't help but love her, especially after she uses her heist money to buy her girlfriend a naughty outfit. After seeing the movie, I found myself wishing that Queen Latifah had been given both the Barbra Streisand role in *The Mirror Has Two Faces* and the Kristin Scott Thomas part in *The English Patient*. She's got this presence, an exuberance you don't see very often. The theater was rowdy, with beer bottles rolling down the aisles and teen-agers smoking joints. The woman behind me had brought her two young daughters. There were several children's movies playing at the theater, but this day was clearly about her, the mother, doing what she wanted to do. I wondered what the children thought of the violence and harsh language, until I saw them later on the escalator, where the mother cuffed her daughter's head, saying, "You'd better get your mother-fucking asses over here before I beat the shit out of both y'all bitches." She was a white woman, my age, with several missing teeth. She lit a cigarette in the lobby, and when the retarded usher asked her to put it out, the woman said, loudly, "Fuck you, Fuckface."

My sister Amy and I are working on a new play. It opens in two months and so far all we've got is the title, *The Little Frieda Mys-*

teries. We'll get together, throw out some ideas, and then, by the time I've started writing something, Amy will have decided that the character is blind, or paralyzed from the waist down. We're still in that phase where the story changes by the hour. I'll call her with a bit of dialogue and find that her phone has been disconnected by her rabbit, Tattle Tail, who regularly chews through the phone cord. Amy got this rabbit nine months ago, and now her entire apartment has been rearranged to accommodate its needs. Tattle Tail roams freely from one room to the next. She'll use a litter box, but only if it is placed upon the sofa. Great piles of alfalfa, dandelion greens, and parsley are heaped upon the living-room carpet. She's got all the carrots and dried food she can eat, but still she can't resist chewing the furniture and electrical cords. Amy will wake in the middle of the night to find Tattle Tail chewing her hair and fingernails. I left the outline of the first act on Amy's sofa and Tattle Tail was kind enough to edit it, chewing away the opening monologue and peeing on whatever was left.

POSTED Wednesday, Nov. 27, 1996, at 4:30 P.M. PT

J. called late last night to tell me she's got a new boyfriend. "OK, he's not a boyfriend, he's a crush," she said. She met the guy at a party, and two days later he moved into her spare bedroom. The problem is that the bedroom is right next to the bathroom, and J. doesn't want to be heard making any potty noises. As a result, she has taken to shitting in a paint can in the basement. There are other tenants in the building, and she worries one of them might come down to do a load of laundry and find her crouching there beside the furnace. She's already filled one bucket and is now wondering how to dispose of it.

I went early this afternoon to the NPR studio and recorded a Thanksgiving story for *Morning Edition*. It's always interesting to discover what can and cannot be said on the radio. A few years ago I spent time in Raleigh, N.C., where, on two separate occasions, I heard people say, "This show's boring. Hand me the nigger." The nigger is what they call the remote control, "because it's black and it does the work for you." I find this to be a curious bit of cultural information, but, no matter how hard I try, they won't put it on the radio. Next month I'm supposed to begin a series of recordings for the BBC. Whenever they call, I pick up the phone to hear an urgent voice whispering, "London calling, please hold the line." The producer uses words such as "Jolly" and "Cheerio!" and explains that I'll have to rework a few of the stories to fit what he calls "the British sensibility." I'm hoping that maybe they'll take all the stories I can't get on NPR. Maybe the English will listen, thinking, "Well, that's America for you."

My friend Paul sent me an issue of *Renaissance*, a magazine for people who wish they'd lived during the late Middle Ages. There are articles on medieval Christmas traditions, the brewing of mead, and filling in the gaps of your personal armor collection: "The process of making a chain-mail hauberk is really quite simple." The authors of the various articles are identified as "Contributing Scribes," and letters to the editor are signed "Lady Kimberly," and "Ayin." Available back issues offer cover stories on full-combat jousting and life as a town crier. These are people who frequently eat mutton with their bare hands and travel to fairs in Florida and Texas, where they stand in the hot sun wearing 80 pounds of clothing. What, I wonder, do their houses look like? Do they sleep on those dinky little sit-up beds, or curl up on a nest of straw? Do they own silverware? I love specialty magazines, my current favorite being *Bulk Male*, which is devoted to overweight men with lots of body hair. *Big Butt* was another good one. I can't look at these magazines without wondering what certain parents are forced to say when asked what their son or daughter does for a living. "Well right now he's a fact checker for *Bust and Booty*, but hopefully Brian will soon be moving over to an editorial position at *Juggs*."

POSTED Thursday, Dec. 5, 1996, at 4:30 P.M. PT

Amy came over late last night and we talked about the upcoming play. She'd recently gone to someone's apartment and borrowed three paperbacks from their bizarre personal library. These are books Amy thinks might help us with the play: *Llewellyn's Sun Sign Guide*, *Sexual Astrology*, and something called *How To Get Your Lover Back*, by Blase Harris, M.D. Dr. Harris' book contains chapters titled "Okay, So You Lost Your Lover" and "Loving 100 Percent to Get Your Lover Back." Amy's not sure how this book fits in, but we like the idea of someone using a manual in an effort to reconcile a failed relationship. ("It says here on Page 147 that in order to create a proper romantic trance state, I might want to somehow get Jerry beneath a canopy of leaves.")

The astrology books will definitely come in handy. Neither one of us knows anything about the zodiac, but we both get a kick out of hearing people say things like, "Whatever you do, never hire a Libra to clean your drapes," or, "That's a Virgo for you."

I never used to evaluate people on the basis of their birthdays. Before she died, my mother used to phone and read my daily horoscope from the *Raleigh News and Observer*. "Look for a big career breakthrough on the 15th," she'd say, and I would count the days, waiting for my big break. Nothing would happen, but that never dissuaded her from calling the next morning with news about my impending change of residence or surprise vacation. "This is a good day to tie up loose ends and just be yourself in the company of an understanding Leo." She wasn't raised to think this way. It just came upon her suddenly in the mid-80s.

The *Sun Sign* book begins each zodiac chapter with a list of tell-tale characteristics and key phrases. As a Capricorn, my phrase is,

"I use." My color is black, my flower the carnation, and my opposite sign is Cancer. Characteristics are as follows:

Positive Expression

Ambitious
Frugal
Conscientious
Cautious
Disciplined
Sensible
Patient
Prudent

Misuse of Energy

Controlling
Miserly
Rigid
Fearful
Repressed
Melancholy
Machiavellian
Inhibited

Whatever. The sensible thing certainly doesn't fit, and I'm not willing to lift the dictionary for "Machiavellian." I think that means I have a bad haircut. We're thinking that it might be nice to write characters for the play according to their zodiac descriptions. No one needs to know that so-and-so is a Cancer, we'll just follow the list and fashion an individual who is tenacious, protective, nurturing, patriotic, sympathetic, maternal, crabby, smothering, defensive, suspicious, anxious, and moody. Then we'll throw him into a room with his opposite sign and see what happens. Because I am a Capricorn, I think this is an excellent idea.

The third book, *Sexual Astrology*, is way out there. I looked up my sign and read, "Here's another erotic tip that delights a Capricorn male: The woman inserts the nipple of her breast into the opening of his penis. He'll love it and love you for doing it." What? I've never been with a woman, but if Hugh tried doing something like that I'd reach up and slap the shit out of him, hoping the force of my blow might bring him to his senses. Since reading the book, I've asked several straight couples if they've ever done such a thing, and they all thought I was making it up. The book warns men against touching the hair of Leo women during oral sex, and encourages women to pay extra close attention to the calves and ankles of Aquarian men.

Amy said that her friend has a lot of other great books, but I think these are more than enough to get us started.

Russ Siegelman

Russ Siegelman is a partner at the venture capital firm Kleiner Perkins Caulfield & Byers.

POSTED Tuesday, Nov. 17, 1998, at 4:30 P.M. PT

Most folks, if they have any idea about what venture capitalists do, probably hold at least two incorrect assumptions: that VCs spend most of their time chasing new investments, and the rest of the time they do financial engineering. The truth is that as a Kleiner Perkins partner I spend more than 70 percent of my time with companies that we have already invested in, and I spend no time doing financial engineering. The logic of these outcomes is clear when you think about the nature of the VC business. We stand to lose, and make, money only where we have already invested, so we have a natural incentive to make sure those companies succeed. As an early stage venture investor there are typically no revenues or assets when we first get involved—not much raw material for financial engineering. So we go about doing the only thing we can at this phase of a startup's life—help build companies.

This entails a lot of recruiting, advising senior management, helping raise money, and networking—introducing senior management to potential investors, employees, customers, partners, press contacts, prospective board members, or anyone else who might help the company. As the saying goes, you can to a large degree measure the value of a VC by the quality and depth of her Rolodex.

Today revolved around a series of intertwined calls and e-mails regarding five of my companies, each involving a separate set of recruiting, fund raising, or strategic issues. The calls and e-mails came in—sometimes more than one at the same time—and out throughout the day. First thing, I received a voice mail from a prospective investor for AdKnowledge. The message indicated that the investor was quite interested in participating in the upcoming financing but, because his parent company's operating unit had some hesitation, he was passing. I immediately called the CEO of AdKnowledge, and we devised a "diving catch" plan. I was going to call back the investor and get him to schedule a meeting between AdKnowledge and the head of the operating unit to see if we could turn him around.

While I was still on the phone, I read an e-mail from the CEO of one of my other companies, Resonate. I had been helping him recruit a new vice president of marketing, and the leading candidate, whom I had interviewed last week, was on the fence. I immediately picked up the phone and tried to reach him. In the meantime I realized that I had a call scheduled to talk to a senior executive of a publishing company that is in talks with a third company of mine, Academic Systems. After that call I realized that I had not got back to the prospective AdKnowledge investor, which I then did. After getting a commitment to meet, I called the AdKnowledge CEO back to discuss our tactics for the pending meeting.

The day continued in this fashion: several calls between me and various possible recruits for Resonate, including a cold call on a person I had talked to several months before as part of a due diligence process for a different company; a voice mail exchange with the CEO of Vertical Networks on recruiting; e-mail to update the CEO of Academic Systems regarding my call with the senior exec of the publishing company; a call with the CEO of Impresse regarding that company's impending financing and the agenda for Thursday's board meeting; a phone call with another of my companies about possible strategic alternatives for the company; a meeting with another prospective investor for AdKnowledge. And so on.

At the end of the day I stopped and pondered: What did I accomplish today except for filling up the e-mail in-boxes of my CEOs and running up my bill on several long-distance and cellular phone carriers? But it is the nature of the beast. Building companies from scratch requires forging little chunks of progress, bit by bit.

POSTED Wednesday, Nov. 18, 1998, at 4:30 P.M. PT

When I worked at Microsoft I traveled out of town from time to time but never drove around town for work. As a Silicon Valley VC, I rarely travel out of town, but I put a lot of miles on my car, because all the companies whose boards I sit on are between San Francisco and San Jose. Since we prefer to have board meetings on-site (nothing like being close to the action to see what is really going on!), I am often out of my office.

As a result, the pace and feel of the work can sometimes feel like a field salesperson's. I constantly find myself on the cell phone in foreign conference rooms and while strolling through parking lots doing business. (How did they do venture capital before cell phones? Pay phones must have been a VC's best friend.) Sometimes I don't need to be somewhere for another hour or so, but it doesn't make sense to travel back to the office, so I just plop down wherever I am and go to work. That's what I did this morning after I was done with my workout. I sat down in a corner of the Pacific Athletic Club and reviewed the books for tomorrow's board meetings. Then I went through my file of unread business plans.

KP gets hundreds of plans every year. The folklore is that the firm has never invested in a plan that came in over the transom. It may well be true. Nearly all the opportunities we invest in are referred to us by our network of CEOs, limited partners, friends of the partnership, or other VCs. Yet we still have to read plans. You never know what you might find. In any case, it is an educational experience. Spotting a good opportunity is a pattern-matching exercise. The more data you see—that is, the more plans you read—the more certain you are when you have found a match. This is one reason I often know after seeing the first 15 minutes of a company's presentation, and sometimes after reading the first page of a business plan, that I am not interested in investing. I have read the same plan, or heard the same pitch, five times before, and I know the tough questions (and possibly the answers). If they aren't being addressed, I am not interested.

I took two plans off my stack at random and, believe it or not, they were nearly identical business propositions! Both companies plan to become the leader in the "next great Internet play"—being an e-commerce portal. A sure reason not to invest in a company is that you have seen dozens of the same plan. I won't be investing in a new e-commerce portal. I rejected both plans.

The variations in the quality of the plans I read are amazing. Sometimes they look like the entrepreneur's dog has chewed them, and they are photocopied sloppily onto standard copy paper, with typos and coffee stains. Sometimes they arc glossy, well written, with plenty of Excel-generated charts and pages of financial projections. One might think that a good VC will get beyond the stains and the chewed pages and get to the business idea to make a judgment. But that isn't my view. If entrepreneurs don't present their ideas in a quality way, they probably aren't organized or professional enough for me to want to invest. I am not typically a form over substance kind of guy, but when it comes to business plans, I can't get to the substance if the form doesn't make the quality bar.

By 6:30 I'm home for dinner. Max and Jake eat slices of Max's birthday cake while I eat lasagna. After dinner Max and Jake help me build a fire, and we sit on the couch with Beth, roughhousing and listening to Max playacting as a helicopter pilot. By 8 they are in the shower, by 9 in bed. I tuck Max in, say happy birthday, and give him a good-night kiss. It is the most satisfying moment of the day.

Muriel Spark

Muriel Spark is the author of 20 novels, including The Prime of Miss Jean Brodie, Memento Mori, *and* Aiding and Abetting, *which will be published in 2001. She lives in Italy.*

POSTED Wednesday, Dec. 11, 1996, at 4:30 P.M. PT

A young woman reviewer of my latest novel, *Reality and Dreams,* complained that some of my characters are "nasty." I should have thought they were far worse than that; they are downright insufferable, even outrageous, and are supposed to be. I don't know why it is, but even in these feminist days, there exists a body of ladylike reviewers (and perhaps readers, although I put in a query here) who feel that women writers should write novels of boring virtue. I have always marveled when people have described to me, either in fiction or in real life, a creature who "hasn't a mean bone in her body" or who is "incapable of a mean thought." Who are these freaks of the human race, and where? I have never met them and hope I never will, arch-hypocrites as they most certainly are. One product of an immaculate conception in the history of religion is surely enough. And besides, to be "incapable of a mean thought" would surely cut us off from that imaginative empathy with the weaknesses of others that makes our imperfect world go round. Even that great English writer of the last century, Cardinal J.H.

Newman, declared he could not conceive a novel without sinful characters.

I had an editor at one of my English publishers who leaked information to the press—mostly the diarists—that I wanted to keep to myself. He always denied it was he who had done so. Therefore, I employed a technique we used during the war—when I was in the Foreign Office—to sniff out a leaker. I fed that editor disinformation, and fed it to him exclusively. Sure enough, it appeared in the papers as valid news, passed on by Bigmouth. Lesson: Don't confide in editors.

When I wrote my first novel, I had an editor in London who was deeply, distressingly, alcoholic. Eventually, he was fired. He gave an interview about me 35 years later, full of wild and chronologically impossible inventions. Was his memory impaired by alcohol, or had he been harboring some grudge for 35 years? Who cares?

I often think of the most charming editor of my life, the late Blanche Knopf of the Knopf publishing house. I was working in New York for a few years when I knew her. How she loved to meet me for lunch, and I, to meet her. She was always covered with diamonds, but somehow discreetly. Her clothes were Dior and Balençiaga. ("I don't care," she said, "if people don't know they are haute couture, so long as I know.") She had spotted and published 18 or 19 Nobel Prize–winners. She always wore her rosette of the *Légion d'Honneur*, which Gen. Charles de Gaulle had bestowed on her on the occasion of the liberation of France by the U.S. Army. (Blanche was there.) She put all her heart into the encouragement of my writing, for which I will always remember her with gratitude. I was the last author to talk to her, as she lay dying in her New York apartment. I was at East Hampton that weekend, right on the sea. I called to find out how she was. "Blanche," I said, "if I hold the receiver out of the window here, you could hear the sea." I held it out for a little while; then, when I got back to Blanche, she said, "Yes, I could hear the sea." She died that afternoon.

POSTED Thursday, Dec. 12, 1996, at 4:30 P.M. PT

Affectations: Someone has phoned to invite me to dinner, and I have accepted. They follow this up with a card with the date and time of the dinner, and "Pour memoire" written obliquely at the corner of the card. Do these people think I can't understand English? I feel happier, when in an English-speaking country, with "To remind," as sensible people usually put it. When I was very young, in the '30s, French phrases were scattered around everywhere for no apparent reason. Things were *de rigueur*, some people were *de trop*. Smart clothes were *chic*. People who dressed up in their best clothes for Sundays were *endimanche* (and rather common). You did not merely hurt someone's feelings, you offended their *amour propre*. And if you couldn't accept an invitation you were *désolé*. I should have thought we had said adieu to these phrases forever. But no, every wedding invitation still bids us *R[épondez] S['il] V[ous] P[laît]*; what is wrong with "Please reply"?

But even the English-using hosts and hostesses can be carried away by the rhetoric of the occasion. Not long ago I had an invitation to "refreshments" at 7:30 P.M. In the left-hand corner was written "Carriages at 9 P.M.," meaning the party was to be over at that hour. Carriages! Are these people for real? All they needed to put was "7:30–9:00 P.M." Sometimes I have known the word "Champagne" to specify on an invitation drinks before dinner, presumably an inducement.

Another recent affectation that assaulted my mind was contained in the following exchange I had with a man in a hotel lobby. We were discussing our dogs, which he insisted on calling "pets."

"Is your dog dressed?" he said.

"Is it what?"

"Is it dressed?"

"You don't mean castrated do you?"

"Well, yes," said the man, looking to right and left, terrified lest someone should have overheard.

Alessandra Stanley

Alessandra Stanley wrote this when she was a Moscow correspondent for the New York Times. *She is now the paper's bureau chief in Rome.*

POSTED Tuesday, Dec. 16, 1997, at 4:30 P.M. PT

How cold is it? It is so cold that when a small kiosk caught fire outside the Kievsky Railway Station a mile from my office, the fire hydrants were frozen, and the firemen had to douse the flames with buckets. The vodka, thank God, was spared.

The good news is that the firetrucks are working. The bad news is that the fire didn't spread to the train station, so the BBC crew that raced there to film kiosk disaster footage did so for nothing. But that setback had its own silver lining.

Today was our preschool's Christmas concert. I felt very virtuous for having recharged our video camera for the first time in two years. But I was outdone by my fellow working mom, Diana of the BBC, who arrived with the entire BBC film crew in tow to record the precious event.

I love Russian Christmas. The children's holiday pantomime consisted of acting out a folk tale in which a hunter (played with alarming verisimilitude by the *Philadelphia Inquirer's* driver Sasha, wearing a fur hat, long coat, and a huge rifle) viciously hunts down rabbits and deer with a rifle. My 4-year-old, Emma, wore a furry bunny tail and was killed instantly.

I went to a dinner party last night, and actually found myself sighing, "Caviar again?" The dinner was given by British journalists who have the best caviar supplier in town, a petite blond woman named Katya who smuggles about 30 kilos of contraband caviar into Moscow from the Caspian each month. She does her regular rounds — the Duma, the government building, a few favored restaurants, and Western news offices. Her caviar costs $120 a kilo and is always fresh.

How Katya manages her smuggling operation is no longer a mystery. My friend Richard once asked her, "Katya, aren't you afraid of the Mafia?" She gave him a long, hard look and replied, "Richard, I AM the Mafia."

Moscow dinner parties are a Washington hostess's dream. The most desirable Russian male guests never bring their wives, and are therefore free to flirt shamelessly with the Western single women (and us matrons).

But the guest of honor was Yelena Khanga, the hostess of Russia's first talk show entirely devoted to the subject of sex. Yelena is also Russia's first black TV talk-show host. Her grandfather was a black American communist who emigrated to the Soviet Union in the 1930s to build socialism. Basically, the show is *Oprah* without the diet tips.

Yelena, a former journalist, is funny, but well read and high-minded — more of a bluestocking than the fishnet kind, if you know what I mean. She now lives in New York and was very reluctant to do the sex show, but said she was talked into it by Leonid Parfyonov, a network executive. Her recruitment sheds some light on the art of business negotiation, Russian-style.

Leonid is young, good-looking, and knows how to charm. (He too came to the party wife-free.) When Yelena refused to come to Moscow, he flew to New York and took her to an expensive French restaurant. (Yelena was so worried by the extravagance she called a

friend in Moscow to ask her if Leonid could afford a 3-star restaurant. "Are you crazy?" was the answer.)

He didn't discuss salary, ratings, or perks. He asked her what
year she left Russia, then asked the waiter to bring a 1989 Bor-
deaux, handed her the cork, and said, "The next time we drink this
wine, you will be a star." Then he sang to her.

Yelena said she gave in then and there. "I'm a Russian woman.
We melt if a man just takes us for a tram ride."

POSTED Wednesday, Dec. 17, 1997, at 4:30 P.M. PT

I went to another party last night. I got there late, having filed a
story first, but got there just in time to see Alla Pugachova, Russia's equivalent of Liza Minelli/Barbra Streisand, leave, her full-
length black sable coat swinging angrily behind her.

It's not a party until a Russian Diva storms out. I have no idea
why she left early, but assume she felt slighted: The real Liza
Minelli was performing in town last week, and that has put all us
Divas in a bad mood.

The occasion was a birthday party for Vladimir Grigoriev, a
book publisher turned media tycoon, and one of my favorite people in Moscow. But this was not a typical Russian birthday party.

For one thing, it was held at Fellini's, a members-only restau-
rant-casino owned by one of Vladimir's media partners, Sergei,
who is one of the coolest—and scariest—New Russian businessmen. A one-time Komsomol leader and rock promoter, he now
owns an advertising company, TV stations, nightclubs, and lots
more. He travels in a convoy of jeeps with rifle-toting bodyguards.
He is a considerate host. Instead of the usual bootleg vodka, pickles,
and sausages, we feasted on champagne, roast beef, sturgeon,
caviar, and mountains of canapés as a live blues band played music
nobody danced to. There were lots of guys in black suits and black

turtlenecks and cell phones. New Russians often look like bit players in *The Avengers*, but it is a look that works for them.

To Vladimir's credit, there were also guests from his early publishing days, aging, tattered-looking writers and intellectuals who
looked almost as out of place as I did. (What do you wear to a New
Russian party when the temperature outside is 18 degrees below
zero Fahrenheit? Basic black long underwear.)

The one writer who fit in seamlessly was Viktor Pelevin, whose
novels have been translated into English and French. He choked on
his Cuban cigar when I asked whether writers are still as revered in
today's society as they were in Soviet times. "When I tell people
here I'm a writer," he said sourly, "it's like saying, 'I'm a loser.' "

I quickly moved on to a winner, Misha, who is in construction.
Misha is a big shot. As one guest put it, "He's the only man in
Moscow who can say 'fuck you' to the mayor." I savored the spectacle of Pyotr Aven, a pompous former government official turned
Russian megabanker (i.e., he doesn't return my calls), trotting behind Misha like an anxious terrier, a cell phone wedged in his ear,
trying to do a deal.

I had not seen Misha in a long time. He explained he had a bit of
trouble with the FBI this year, a "misunderstanding" that led the
feds to list him as one of Russia's top mobsters. I don't believe a
word of it. He did tell me his son was kidnapped (he got him back)
and that he himself was shot six times but survived. He pulled up
his cashmere sweater, Lyndon Johnson-style, to show me the entry
wounds, but I mainly saw chest hair.

When the men settled down to blackjack and roulette, I left. (I
love gambling, but the stakes were out of my league. Or Bill
Gates's, for that matter.)

I felt a bit misty. In the old days, departing foreign correspondents grew maudlin over memories of discussing art and literature
with dissidents over bad vodka until dawn.

I mainly feel nostalgia for the few, heady glimpses I got of the
new, raw Russian capitalists at play. They are a lot more fun than

New York investment bankers. Western reporters rarely get a chance to mingle with the real movers and shakers in this town, and when we do, we are a little like '30s debutantes tripping up to Harlem jazz clubs with boxers and mobsters for a "lark." We are indulged and tolerated, as long as we don't ask too many stupid questions. Like, "What's your name?"

A little goes a long way, but I would happily recommend Misha for a witness-relocation program if he should ever need it. And I know he would do the same for me.

POSTED Thursday, Dec. 18, 1997, at 4:30 P.M. PT

I am exhausted from all this party reporting, so don't expect too much. Actually, the real reason I cannot diarize today in depth is that I am co-hosting a party tonight for colleagues who are leaving and I have to file a story tonight off an afternoon press conference. (Presciently, I made the lasagna and salmon mousse last night. Recipes off the Web.)

I actually have a lot of work piling up, but I cannot resist this press conference, because it is to be given by Rufina, the fourth and final wife of British master spy "Kim" Philby (she's the much younger Russian woman he married after defecting to Moscow in 1963). She has just written her own memoir of the man, the latest in perhaps 10,000 books about the most famous mole of MI6.

Like a lot of foreign correspondents in Moscow, I am fascinated by the Cambridge spies and cannot hear enough about how they elaborately—and elegantly—betrayed their country. I just reread all John Le Carré's Smiley books. (Bill Haydon, as we all know, was modeled on Philby.)

I am particularly intrigued by Philby for perhaps a myopic reason—for years, he worked as a foreign correspondent as his "cover" and managed to file copiously and brilliantly, in addition to all his spying duties. And he drank like a fish.

I doubt Rufina has much of anything new to say about Philby (we took a quick peek at her book last night to check—the journalistic equivalent of making lasagna the day ahead). Personally, I have only one question for her: Whatever happened to Philby's silver cocktail shaker?

Rufina, like many Russian widows of famous men, put up a bunch of Philby memorabilia for auction at Sotheby's in London in 1994. A homburg hat; the shaker; and piles of books, photographs, and letters. I recently read that the sourpuss Tory government of John Major intervened and forbade Sotheby's from selling off the frivolous personal effects but let the manuscripts be sold. (I just called Sotheby's in London, and they said that, actually, the government didn't intervene, but "public disquiet" over auctioning off the belongings of a traitor caused them to hold back on a few items. Basically, Sotheby's doesn't remember what was sold and what wasn't.)

So where *is* the cocktail shaker?

I was never tempted by the auctions of celebrity memorabilia, Diana's dresses, Jacqueline Onassis' pincushions, or Judy Garland's pillboxes, but I have to say I would deeply love to own Philby's cocktail shaker. Imagine inviting the CIA station chief to dinner. "Care for a martini? Shaken, not stirred. And speaking of spies . . . "

Ben Stein

Ben Stein is a lawyer and actor in Los Angeles. He is the Emmy-winning host of the Comedy Central game show Win Ben Stein's Money.

POSTED Monday, April 3, 2000, at 10:00 A.M. PT

I'm trying to maintain my sanity. It's not easy. About 35 years ago, I had a teacher of economic history named Robert Lekachman. He smoked and he was a leftist and maybe depressed, but he was an amazingly smart man and incredibly effective at teaching. One of the many things he taught me in a little sunny room at Barnard (I was at Columbia but took a few classes at Barnard to meet girls, little dreaming I would someday be a major-league sex symbol, with girls chasing me all around Beverly Hills, but that's another story) was about the British Empire.

It never made economic sense for the Brits to have Kenya and India and Singapore. It would have been more efficient for the little country to just concentrate its efforts on making itself richer and more pleasant. But something deep in the human soul craves expansion, largeness, a global reach. Look at King Leopold and the Belgians.

Or look at me. Today, Friday, I went off to the doctor to try to find out why my heart is beating so fast and with so damned many beats per minute, a few too many it seems to me.

I think it has to do with lingering frantic screaming grief inside me about my father's death. With me holding his hand on one side and my sister on the other, reading him the Psalms and telling him he was about to go see my mom. Or maybe it has to do with my obsessive interest in the stock market, which has been volatile lately, to put it mildly—although I am bound to say I love it.

Or, maybe it has to do with the fact that I own six dwellings and am planning to buy more. It's not easy to be a man of property. Ask the Forsytes. Or maybe just one of the Forsytes.

Or maybe with the observed truth that the single hardest part of my day is making my son do his homework, which he generally absolutely refuses to do unless bribed.

Well, I went off to my doctor, celebrity doctor to the stars or else why would I be there? His echocardiogram woman, a lovely middle-aged blonde named Sue, attached the equipment and started to read the machine. She then told me she had a house in Brentwood Park (to be fair, I asked her where she lived), one of the most expensive neighborhoods in the world. She told me she got it because she had made so many smart buys in stock and real estate. She even had Qualcomm at a big profit. What a great thing to tell me. The Nasdaq's down about 400 points this week, and she's bragging about gains in tech? What a way to give an exam.

Of the *heart*!

Anyway, she said I was in wonderful shape, so all is forgiven. I guess it really is my son's refusal to even read his homework assignments that's the problem. I probably shouldn't have given him that million dollars for his 12th birthday.

JUST KIDDING!

Then, off across town to a meeting of my loyal producers to discuss my talk show and who the guests will be. The meeting was great. I sat on a huge couch, signing hundreds of photos of me taken when I was a lot thinner, reviewed possible guests for my talk show, decided which ones were big enough and which were not, and had everyone laughing at my jokes.

This is one of the great parts of being the star. Everyone laughs at your jokes as if you were a customer at a geisha house.

Then to a stereo store to look at receivers. I personally love everything Denon makes, but I also like KEF speakers and anything in the ES line that Sony makes. Stereo equipment is my obsession, and I need some good works so I can play *Austin Powers: The Spy Who Shagged Me*, over and over again. I want the room to rock when Dr. Evil's spaceship takes off—just like in my pal Phil DeMuth's house.

Then off to the set of *The Man Show*, starring my friend Jimmy Kimmel. I did a tiny guest spot, seated next to a young woman with blue toenails. Jimmy did a hilarious spot about being in a men's room talking to people at the urinals. He is the most naturally funny man in the world.

Then, back home to have a lovely dinner with wife and son. The son kept telling me how fat I was in Spanish. I'm not really that fat, but he's very thin. "How does it feel to be the best-looking boy in your school?" I asked him.

"That is something you'll never know," he said grimly.

Then, to bed to read my mother's diaries and wish she were here to talk to her about them, and to wonder if that stock-market whiz read my exam right or if I'm dying. There's too much happening. The Empire of Ben Stein is just too big and you haven't even seen a small part of it yet.

POSTED Tuesday, April 4, 2000, at 10:00 A.M. PT

My son is having friends over tonight to play some kind of role-playing game that is similar to Dungeons & Dragons. He's such a social kid; I really have to be happy about it.

Anyway, I went over to one of my many pieces of property—a condo I use as an office—and worked on my income tax. As I did, I had the immense windows open and a lovely summer breeze wafted in, along with the sound of men at the swimming pool nine floors below.

I listened to Bob Dylan softly on the stereo—maybe I should say "the surround"—and heard him tell about "The Lonesome Death of Hattie Carroll." She was a black woman caned to death by a crazed white man in Maryland long ago. It's a horrible story of racism in action. But in a way, thinking about it uplifts me. That caning—for which the perpetrator got a six months' suspended sentence, possibly because he was a relative of the governor of Maryland—would be pretty much unthinkable now in Baltimore, Maryland. I grew up in Maryland when it was largely a Southern state. The schools were segregated. Teachers called black people "coons" right in front of the class, and expected us to laugh about it. The only blacks you saw in good neighborhoods—meaning prosperous neighborhoods—were maids and gardeners. Blacks didn't even walk down the middle of the sidewalk in Silver Spring. They sort of slunk off to the side with their heads down. I can still remember when I saw a black couple walking cheerily, laughing and smiling on the sidewalk near a department store. I was simply dumbfounded. I guess I must have been about 13, and I was shocked at their self-confidence. I can still vividly recall the principal of our school making a black boy and his white dance partner leave a school dance.

Well, times have changed a lot. That's the good news. Human dignity is a huge issue and if we can have more of it, we're doing God's work.

However, I am still going crazy. I had the best year I ever had last year financially, and money poured down on me like rain in August in Washington, D.C. (Now, this is by my little standards. What I earn in a lifetime is what a successful venture capitalist or a partner at Goldman Sachs makes in a day. I am still operating on the expectations of a GS-11 who started after law school at $195 per week.) But despite that great year of money, I cannot find a dime to pay my taxes. I'll have to use my line of credit against my house. To be fair, I could find it fairly easily if I sold stock out of my account at E*Trade. But who wants to do that? I can't time the market and I don't want to even try. I feel as if I shouldn't have to pay half of what I earn in taxes anyway. It's peacetime. It's government-surplus time. Why do I have to pay so much?

Anyway, in my little mind, resting after my tax work, listening to Mozart's *Requiem* (written partly by others, I hear), I started to make a list of all the things on my mind:

- Doing my taxes;
- Finding the right guests for my talk show (we really want Bob Dylan and Mike Myers, but we can't get them);
- Making Tommy do his homework;
- Thinking how lonely I'll be when Tommy goes off to college if he ever does and how much I wish I had more children;
- How to take care of my three houses, two condos, and one co-operative apartment (I inherited it at the Watergate when my Pop died—I actually own half of it and my nephew and niece own the rest);
- Whether I should lighten up on tech stocks, of which I now own a lot;
- Whether I should go entirely to cash;
- How on earth I am ever going to get exactly the right sound on my stereo without electrocuting myself setting it up.

I started to make a list of what I own in the way of appliances: six refrigerators; innumerable air conditioners central and room; at least 10 computers, almost all Compaqs but a few Dells; so many stereo pieces I can't keep track of them; a lot of microwaves.

Then I gave up on that because all Americans have those things and they don't really mean that much. I have them because I'm too lazy to simplify my life, not because I'm smart. I started to think about why if I'm so smart and am a cable-TV star, I start to cry and hyperventilate when I see how much Regis gets paid.

> *The world is too much with us; late and soon,*
> *Getting and spending, we lay waste our powers....*

I wrote that. No, just kidding, Wordsworth wrote that.

Never mind, I have to go and supervise my son and his pals playing their nerd games.

I did that and occasionally watched a DVD of *Gone With the Wind*. Isn't it amazing that the defining movie of the 20th century in America is so clearly racist — and yet such a spectacular movie?

Then out to my house in Malibu to fight the army of ants who have moved in and taken possession of my bedroom. And to go through the endless boxes of papers and mementoes that the American Enterprise Institute has sent over from my Pop's office. I really am going to lose my mind if I have to keep reading my parents' words for the rest of my life and not have them to talk to.

Seth Stevenson

Seth Stevenson is a freelance writer and former Slate *staff writer.*

POSTED Tuesday, Feb. 24, 1998, at 4:30 P.M. PT

On the way to the GM Goodwrench Service Plus 400 Winston Cup Race at the North Carolina Speedway, we listen to "John-Boy and Billy's Rock 'n' Roll Racing" radio show. This is like any other classic-rock radio show, except that in the middle of each song, the deejays cue loud car-engine-revving sounds that drown out the music.

The North Carolina Speedway, in Rockingham, North Carolina, is known as "The Rock." Its track is 1.017 miles around, and high grandstands surround the entire loop. In the infield (the many acres inside the loop) people park their RVs and fire up barbecue pits. Most RVs fly Confederate flags from their antennas. The New South moneyed folks fly in by helicopter and sit in enclosed luxury boxes, far above the engine noise and gasoline fumes. The cheapest grandstand tickets are $35. This seems odd, since the average attendee does not look wealthy. *At all.* Yet this is far more expensive than a Major League Baseball game.

Outside the stadium is a National Association for Stock Car Auto Racing bazaar, where every product features the NASCAR logo: cup holders, T-shirts, posters, jackets, pins. I purchase 1) ear plugs, which the cashier says are the best investment I'll ever make (he is correct) and 2) an official NASCAR commemorative program (which is later stolen when I get up to get a beer). I do not purchase 1) a Jeff Gordon replica racing jacket, just like the one that champion NASCAR driver Jeff Gordon wears (not buying the jacket turns out to be a great move, for reasons that will become clear) or 2) a list of CB frequencies for the race that would let me listen in on the pit crews' radio instructions to their drivers (if I owned a CB radio, I definitely would have bought that list).

Right outside the grandstand entrance is the Skoal booth, and a replica of the green Skoal Bandit race car, which has "U.S. Tobacco" branded on its hood and rear bumper. A Skoal employee revs the car engine while onlookers cover their ears. Other booth attendants hand out free tins of Skoal chewing tobacco.

I take two tins of wintergreen-flavored Skoal. "Dipping," the use of chewing tobacco, is ubiquitous at The Rock—everyone's spitting brown. I end up dipping from lap 23 of the race through lap 48, spitting into an empty beer can. Net effect: slight headache, slighter nicotine buzz, annoying flecks of Skoal on my tongue, and a canker sore on the inside of my lip.

Free tobacco is everywhere. Winston smokers can hand in an empty pack of Winstons for a new pack, plus a free Winston Cup T-shirt. NASCAR is the last great refuge of tobacco sponsorship. Winston, Skoal, and Kodiak (another chewing tobacco) all sponsor cars. A huge percentage of fans smoke cigarettes throughout the race.

A huge number of fans smoke cigarettes throughout the race! This seems insane, since 1) the gasoline fumes, even up in the grandstand, are strong enough to make me slightly nauseated for the whole afternoon and 2) each of the more than 40 pit crews has vats filled with enough gasoline to run an extremely non-fuel-efficient car for more than 400 miles. One safety concession: About 30 seconds before the race starts, infield barbecuers are asked to extinguish open flames.

There is a 20-foot-high fence between the track and the grandstand. During the race, fans throw their empty beer cans at the fence. The cans hit, tumble down, and form a beer-can moat at the fence's base. Some fans flick their cigarettes toward the moat (and thus, the racetrack), often before the cigarette has been extinguished. (See above for the safety concerns this raises.) This chainlink fence is the only thing between the fans and the track. Upon first taking my seat, I become disturbingly enchanted with the fact that I might witness high-speed, flaming car crashes from a distance of 50 feet. Seconds later, I realize that tires and hoods could easily fly over the fence and into the grandstand at speeds in excess of 100 mph. Car racing is one of the few sports where spectators routinely die.

Throughout the race, nothing comes close to the fan excitement generated by a collision (of which there are many). When a car spins out and other drivers swerve to avoid it, the entire grandstand rises as one, gasping and pointing, eyes wide, hoping for a violent accident. I'm hoping too.

NASCAR gives us the sport of the future. It's already the fastest-growing sport in America. NASCAR is the latest benchmark in American sports' steady march toward speed and violence. Football and hockey, while both brutal and quick, cannot compete with 160-mph impacts, flying sheet metal, and the serious possibility of a fiery death.

NASCAR's biggest stars are Dale Earnhardt and Jeff Gordon. Real men root for Earnhardt. He drives a black Chevy Monte Carlo. (In the parking lot after the race, I suddenly noticed how many black Monte Carlos there were.) Earnhardt is nicknamed "The Intimidator," and he has a thick mustache, just like every guy in the stands. Little kids and some women root for Jeff Gordon. He drives a rainbow-striped car, and he is matinee handsome—young and clean-shaven. Most fans at The Rock hate Gordon with a passion I've never seen equaled at a sporting event. A man next to me flips Gordon the bird every single time his car comes by—all 400 laps, all afternoon, even though Gordon can't possibly see him.

Personally, I decide I kind of like Jeff Gordon, who eventually wins the race, but I keep very quiet about it.

Beneath Earnhardt and Gordon are the lesser gods, a pantheon of drivers who each have their own fan club. Everyone at The Rock wears a shirt or hat identifying their allegiance to say, No. 6 Mark Martin and the Valvoline racing team, or No. 9 Lake Speed (yes, that's his real name) and the Cartoon Network racing team (yes, that's his real sponsor). Sometimes the corporate allegiances seem a little funny (e.g., the bad-ass, mustachioed No. 36 Ernie Irvan fan who must wear a shirt that says "Skittles" in pastel letters). The crass sponsorship in NASCAR once again seems to make it the sport of the future, the endpoint toward which all sports are headed.

The pit crews are my favorite part of NASCAR. They gas up the car, change all four tires, and slip the driver a pinch of Skoal, all in less than seven seconds. Matching jumpsuits and choreographed, mercurial flitting make them seem weird and futuristic. The changing of a tire in three seconds is one of the most impressive feats I've seen in sports.

My favorite driver today is No. 17, Darell Waltrip, and his Speedblock/Builder's Square racing team. From the start, Waltrip putt-putts behind the other cars like he's driving an underpowered go-cart. Less than halfway through the 400 laps, Waltrip's Chevy hits the outside wall. He turns slowly into the infield, front end crumpled. It's just not his day. Later, I find out that Waltrip received the Goody's Headache Award, worth $2,500, given to the driver who runs the unluckiest race.

Daniel Sullivan

Daniel Sullivan is a New York–based stage director who recently staged A Moon for the Misbegotten, *starring Cherry Jones and Gabriel Byrne.*

POSTED Wednesday, March 15, 2000, at 10:00 A.M. PT

Back to the grind after a day off. If you can call that a day off. Woke to what felt like a hangover. Haven't had a drink for a few years, but the feeling is a familiar one from days of yore. I've been working on this play too long.

The stage door of the Walter Kerr Theatre is an awkward affair. The door opens off the street into an incredibly cramped cubicle, about 4 feet square, where a stage-door guard sits on a swivel chair occupying the entire space. He watches a small television to take his mind off his hellish employment and, with eyes still glued to the television, swivels the few available inches to accommodate your squeezing by him and into the stage area proper. It's an absurd but somehow fitting entryway into the damned-up world of Eugene O'Neill.

This is the final preview week. You can hardly even call it a preview week since the critics start coming halfway through it. Opening night is Sunday, but the critics come midweek so that they can write their ever-so-thoughtful reviews over a space of time. So I really sort of have to keep my hands off the production now. The actors need to play it freely, minds uncluttered with last-minute notes. And I have to be careful not to have any more ideas. I've learned that the hard way. Years ago, I was doing a hostage drama and I decided at the last minute that the man playing the hostage didn't look enough like a low-level bureaucrat, so I insisted he wear a moustache. A moustache was hastily constructed. Opening night, a few minutes into the first act, the right side of his moustache became unglued. Now, if you're quick, and the glue is still wet, you can press your hand against it and it will reseal itself. The problem was, the man was playing a hostage and he was handcuffed with both arms behind a chair. Excruciating minutes went by. The moustache began to flap a little whenever he talked. The actor playing the terrorist saw the problem and thought, "Sorry, I'm a terrorist, why would I fix his moustache?" An understandable demurral for a man about to blow up Washington, D.C., but ruinous to this particular opening night. Late in the act, the terrorist undoes the man's handcuffs so that he can eat. The actor immediately reached up and ripped off his own moustache to a chorus of sniggering from the audience.

So I don't have ideas close to openings anymore. Then what am I doing there, sitting like a useless lump in the audience, too worn out to act the cheerleader as I probably should be doing now? Good question. Oh let's face it, I've never played the cheerleader in my life. An actress I recently worked with called me "Sunshine" with a devastatingly cruel inflection every time I appeared backstage. At this point, actors want what they usually refer to as "feedback." Feedback is not notes or suggestions or ideas. Feedback is, as I've come to understand the term, immoderate and unqualified praise. "Honey, that was inspired." "My God, it's perfect." And, you know, after all the struggle, they damn well deserve it and need it. And I do my best but I can see the little glint of suspicion as they listen to my half-baked performance. "Thanks, Sunshine." It's not that I don't need it. I just feel I'm auditioning for the role of enthusiast and I'm wrong for it.

Notes were getting harder to give on this play anyway. Hard to orchestrate the deterioration of an alcoholic. Emotionally wearing. Most of the subtextual work is done early in the rehearsal period, the play broken down beat by beat, the huge discoveries as we probe beneath the surface of the play. And the play is all subtext. Characters hiding from one another and themselves. As we move toward opening night, the detail work becomes more and more important. Exactly how much alcohol should the character of James Tyrone consume. "Don't take so much there. Drink a little more there." I began to get very depressed after these note sessions and I came to realize that it had something to do with my late father's alcoholism. Among the children, I was the designated caretaker, and I would watch his intake with a chemist's precision. Every night at the Walter Kerr, I seemed to be living it again, trying to control the flow.

In the end, the play itself offers some relief. O'Neill was obsessed with the masks people wear to hide from the world and themselves. In most of his plays, the masks hide a grim reality. *Long Day's Journey Into Night* begins with a family seemingly contented on its surface before it quickly and terrifyingly unravels to show the miserly, haunted, addicted people beneath. In *A Moon for the Misbegotten*, the face beneath the mask is love. The hardness these people affect is a protection for the fragile, needful affection they have for one another.

This is O'Neill's last play, his last word on the subject, and it's interesting that he came to hate it. I think maybe it's because he couldn't accept its goodness, its conclusion that we can ever "rest forever in forgiveness and peace."

POSTED Friday, March 17, 2000, at 12:00 P.M. PT

The *New York Times* critic was there tonight. Even though his review doesn't appear until Monday, it's pretty much all over, and the weekend's shows can be played with the knowledge that the horse has left the barn. Sad to say, the *Times* is the only review that really counts. If he likes it, the play will be a hit. If he doesn't, it will have to fight for its life. This isn't the case with the theme-park musicals that currently rule the landscape of Broadway. They survive no matter what the *New York Times* says. But a serious work needs to be anointed by the *Times* to succeed. There is no exception to the rule. So relax, everybody. Nothing we can do about it now. The deed is done. Sure. Just try to relax until Monday. The panic may be over, but the demon reputation will haunt us as Monday morning grinds slowly toward us. I liked the old days, when the critics came opening night and delivered the coup de grâce quickly the next morning. No waiting. Off with their heads. This new method is a product of producers' caving to pressure from powerful media interests. The fiction goes that, with the present system, we theater folk will have an opening night free from the tensions of the press. That's like throwing a nice party for the Christians in the basement of the Coliseum. We know what's coming.

An eventful night. A large off-stage crash during the first act. I'm not even going to ask. A man with a crazy laugh who laughed at inappropriate times. During the second act, this same man, clearly drunk, began to sob audibly. He struck the man sitting next to him who was trying to hush him. The head usher removed him, and he was arrested outside the theater. The man who was struck was brought outside to press charges. But he was so involved in the play that he kept running back into the theater to watch, banging the entrance door repeatedly. I wanted to have him arrested. The drunken man was taken away in handcuffs. An odd, rather chilling event. The stage action that seemed to have precipitated the man's breakdown was the drunken, dying figure of James Tyrone crying out in an agony of shame and guilt. And the poor man lurching up the aisle with the usher seemed suddenly to be the mad, restless ghost of James himself, haunting his beloved Broadway. You can never find peace, he seemed to be saying. Never find it.

So if you ask me how the play was tonight, I'll tell you what I told the actors: "Couldn't have been better." The truth is I have no idea.

And I haven't had an idea for a while now, truth to tell. There comes a time when you don't see the whole picture at all anymore. When it becomes one big blur of distracting details and you know that, whatever it's become, you just have to let it go. It's like letting go of the back of the bicycle when you're teaching your kid how to ride. It feels like she's balanced, but you'll never really know until you let go. Unfortunately, I remember the time I did this with my youngest daughter, Rachel. I let go and felt that heart-soaring moment as she took off on her own. The problem was, she was in a rage at me for the inadequacy of my teaching methods and realized, as she took off, that she could just keep going, running away from home in one clean burst of speed. And suddenly she was gone. My wife and I jumped into the car and went after her. We found her charging away down a truck route, huge semis whizzing by, determined but clearly afraid. We pulled alongside and asked her if she had enough money for lunch. She allowed as how she didn't and that maybe she'd have to stay until tomorrow.

There's always that unknown, when you let a show go. Will it stay upright? Will it take off in some direction that seems wrongheaded? If you've put it together right, probably not. The pieces will be too linked to twist apart. But I have done shows that have happily surprised me; I've come to see a show a month after letting go to find something very different. Moments transformed by some new inspiration that was not what I'd had in mind at all, but much, much better. You like to tell yourself that maybe you planted the seed that made that happen, but probably not.

I'll be happy to set this show free. To not come around for a few weeks. And then to visit, hoping to see something new, something surprising. It's a good, strong-willed group, and they're speeding away even as I write this.

Erik Tarloff

Erik Tarloff filed this from the 1996 Democratic Convention. He is a novelist, screenwriter, and the husband of Laura D'Andrea Tyson, former chair of the National Economic Council. His latest novel is The Man Who Wrote the Book.

POSTED Wednesday, Aug. 28, 1996, at 11:10 A.M. PT

A morning run along Lake Michigan is clearly the activity of choice at this convention. You can spot more luminaries on the jogging path than in the convention hall itself. And what's more, they're in their underwear!

Yesterday, as I was pounding the pavement and trying to convince myself that the view of the lake mitigated the ordeal, I found myself abreast of Federico Peña. We ran side by side for a mile or two, exchanging personal news and whatever tidbits of gossip we'd managed to scrounge. It was a pleasant encounter, but vaguely unsettling: You don't expect to see the secretary of transportation on foot.

And today, going through the same process, I was hailed by Heidi Schulman, Mickey Kantor's wife, power-walking in the company of a prominent California politico I've met three or four times. He clearly didn't have the vaguest memory of having met me. Perfectly understandable in an ordinary person, but a serious flaw in a politician. I know this to be the case because, although I found his forgetfulness perfectly understandable, it also annoyed the shit out of me.

And then, perhaps a mile on, was Paul Begala, working up a Texas-sized sweat. He was gracious enough to change direction and run with me awhile, and eventually even switched off his sports radio. But then it emerged that he had an agenda: He wanted my opinion of a joke he had written for the first lady. My opinion: Good joke. I even laughed while running, something Gerald Ford could never have managed.

Speaking of joke writing, I also stumbled across Mark Katz yesterday as he attempted to gain entry into my hotel (I'm obviously not the only one who's had credential problems). He's supposed to be helping out with the vice president's speech, leavening it with some humor, but found himself barred from the hotel by security personnel. Security at the Sheraton is awfully tight, since the first and second families are staying here (if I have to endure one more deep cavity search, I swear I'll start taking it personally). Anyway, Mark must have finally made it in—I don't want to think about what lengths he had to go to in order to convince the Secret Service of his essential innocuousness—because he phoned me a little later and invited me up to the vice president's floor to lend a hand.

All that was needed were two simple jokes, one for the vice president, one for Tipper. No problem, you'd think. At the top of his form, Mark is a virtual human joke machine, and working together, he and I have generated scores of lines in an afternoon, some of which were even usable. But maybe we've just ground out too many damned Al Gore-is-boring jokes over the last four years. Because a small group of us sat there in the speech-writing room for over an hour yesterday and produced virtually nothing, scratching our heads and staring disconsolately at the ceiling, waiting vainly for the divine afflatus to pay a visit. We eventually started to get giddy at the very fact of our own incompetence. "Al

Gore is so boring, he's ... REALLY BORING!" was one attempt that reduced us to helpless, teary-eyed, stomach-clutching hilarity.

Thank goodness my contributions are pro bono. If I actually got paid for this work, I'd feel terrible.

Elizabeth Drew made a characteristically shrewd observation the other night. We were standing in the middle of a party, chatting inconsequentially, when she suddenly narrowed her eyes and said, "I just noticed something. There are a lot fewer cell phones here than in San Diego." This was quintessential Elizabeth, who would have been a welcome guest at 21B Baker Street.

What one extrapolates from her observation may depend on personal bias, but I can't help feeling it suggests something important about the differences between Republicans and Democrats.

It puts me in mind of something our assigned driver told Laura and me during Inaugural Week almost four years ago. He was a man who had driven in the previous inauguration as well, and he said, "You know, it's different this time. Republicans just hand you their bags. With Democrats, you have to ask."

Speaking of security (yes I was, several paragraphs ago): Here's something unexpected I saw this morning while eating my buffet breakfast in a very public section of the lobby. Without any fuss or to-do, Chelsea Clinton arrived at the hotel. Sure, she had a few people in tow, but they were few, and no one was murmuring into a wristwatch as the group strolled across the lobby. She was even carrying her own backpack. What made this especially interesting is that I seemed to be the only one in the vicinity who noticed. She and her party just walked toward the elevators without attracting any attention at all. It's a sort of *Purloined Letter* approach to security, and it might be just as effective as brute intimidating force.

I finally got to the convention hall today, putting those new credentials of mine to the test. And they worked like a charm, I have to admit it. I wandered the corridors, hung out in the *Washington Post* headquarters with Richard Cohen, and grabbed all the freebies I could get my hands on. But good as these credentials may be, they don't do everything. As I was walking down one corridor, I saw a sign for the *NewsHour with Jim Lehrer* office. Thinking I'd drop in to say hello, I started to enter the room, but a guard stopped me. Did I have a *NewsHour with Jim Lehrer* pass? he demanded.

I admitted I didn't. "But I won't be long. I just want to say hello."

"Who to?"

"Jim Lehrer."

He grimaced, concentrating hard. Then he said, "Who's that?"

I swear he wasn't kidding. But I couldn't help laughing anyway. It seemed to me to be the equivalent of wondering what Lou Gehrig died of.

Shashi Tharoor

*Shashi Tharoor is an Indian writer of both fiction (*The Great Indian Novel, Show Business*) and nonfiction (most recently,* India: From Midnight to the Millennium*). He is also director of communications and special projects in the office of U.N. Secretary-General Kofi Annan.*

POSTED Sunday, Aug. 9, 1998, at 4:30 P.M. PT

This is going to be the "Diary" of an untypical week. Not that I have such things as typical weeks: Mine are usually characterized by what cricket writers love to call the "glorious uncertainties of the game." Last week I was helping U.N. Secretary-General Kofi Annan cope with the latest Iraq crisis; the week before I was in New Delhi in my other guise, doing readings to mark the launch of the paperback edition of my most recent book, *India: From Midnight to the Millennium.* This week I'm at the Aspen Institute in Aspen, Colorado, attending its flagship executive seminar. Unless, of course, a new crisis supervenes and I'm summoned back to U.N. HQ. It's been known to happen.

Aspen is, of course, the very expensive, very tony resort in the Colorado mountains where all visitors are rich or famous (or think they are). Not the most likely spot for impecunious writers or international civil servants (and I'm both). But the institute's campus at the pleasantly laid-out Aspen Meadows is a place where beautiful ideas take precedence over beautiful people. Last December, in England, I co-moderated, with David Gergen (who is always, of course, a moderating influence), an Aspen Institute seminar on "Persistent Poverty in Developing Countries." It went well enough that I was asked whether I'd be willing to moderate an executive seminar. I said I'd need to attend one first as a student. So they invited me.

I don't normally lead the kind of life that allows me to spend a week in sylvan surroundings musing on the Great Ideas of human civilization, which is what executive seminarians do. But it's precisely the frenetic pace of my daily existence—governed by the interminable tyranny of meetings and deadlines, the insistent clamor of the telephone, incessant streams of visitors and inescapable social obligations—that prompted me to accept the invitation. It's been 20 years since graduate school, and that portion of my mind that hasn't been totally numbed by reality could use some intellectual stimulation. It helps, of course, that this particular session is taking place this week. The hope that mid-August, with the secretary-general away, might be a relatively safe time to make my escape from U.N. chores had crossed my mind. But I'm hardly invulnerable. August has been a busy month for international crises: World War I began in August 1914, Pakistan went to war with India in August 1965, Iraq invaded Kuwait in August 1990. Perish the thought.

My fellow participants are an interesting group, overwhelmingly from the private sector—senior executives of Toyota and American Airlines among them—and even a woman from the CIA. (There are also, amazingly enough in a group of 19, two other Indians—the CEO in India of the British multinational ICI, and an academic based in Thailand. And we're the only non-North Americans.) They're all here because their corporations believe a renewed grounding in the major ideas of political economy and moral philosophy will help equip senior managers to make better decisions. I don't know to what extent that's true, but it seems to work, because the executive seminars have gone on for decades and executives keep paying to come to them.

Time to drag my unwilling carcass over to the health club before the first session. Most of the time, my only form of exercise is jumping to conclusions.

POSTED Tuesday, Aug. 11, 1998, at 4:30 P.M. PT

The executive seminar is going well. It's been salutary, and in some ways exhilarating, for business executives to discover how much pleasure and instruction they can in fact receive from parsing Aristotle or dissecting the Declaration of Independence. We've all been doing it with brio, and probably surprising ourselves a little in the process. I even found five lines in John Locke's *Second Treatise of Government* that could be read as a prescient, if probably unintended, attack on the basic premises of colonialism, which gratified my liberal Indian heart no end.

The initial sessions have focused on issues of rights, responsibilities, and liberty—including some fairly intense discussion of slavery, for which the ancient thinkers managed to find some tortuous rationalizations. Aristotle's views ("the lower sort are by nature slaves, and it is better for them as for all inferiors that they should be under the rule of a master") probably caused the most offense, but he had some pretty tough competition from himself on the subject of women ("the male is by nature superior, and the female inferior; and the one rules, and the other is ruled; this principle, of necessity, extends to all mankind"). There's much more along those lines from the most influential thinker of ancient Greece, but one lesson I learned immediately was to beware of philosophers who use the phrase "by nature" (or, for that matter, "by necessity"). The most untenable arguments can be ascribed to the way things just are, "by nature"; and if a proposition follows "by necessity," you can be pretty sure the necessity is the philosopher's, not nature's.

But then what can you expect from the man whose most successful pupil was that mass murderer Alexander the Great? You spend years teaching a kid philosophy and ethics and reason; then he goes out and sees one of the great conundrums of the age, the Gordian knot, which experts from all over the world have been trying for years to unravel; and all he can do is run his sword through it. Barbarous, but if that's all he took away from his Aristotelian education, I don't think we'd have welcomed young Alex to Aspen.

I've had a couple of U.N. phone calls, including one from the secretary-general (currently traveling in Portugal), and a flurry of e-mails, but so far no clamorous summons to abandon my ivory tower and return to HQ forthwith. The tragic bombings in Africa have nothing directly to do with the United Nations, of course, but Iraq remains an ongoing worry. As the secretary-general told the Security Council, the Iraqis seem to have convinced themselves that nothing they do will get the sanctions lifted, so they see little incentive to comply with the U.N. disarmament demands. Our job is to ensure they cooperate with our work and comply with the Security Council resolutions; it's for the council, in turn, to recognize any progress that's made. Everybody agrees that in the end the world needs an Iraq that's effectively disarmed and poses no threat to its neighbors, but also an Iraq whose people are given their place in the community of nations, free of sanctions. As always in international affairs, identifying the goals is easy enough; it's getting from here to there that's difficult.

Just the note on which to set off up the mountain to an outdoor cookout. At the cookout, we'll be rehearsing for an all-but-impromptu production of Sophocles' *Antigone*, a vital part of our course. And why not? After all, the seminar couldn't be all work—and no play!

Butch Traylor

Butch Traylor is a driver for United Parcel Service and a former shop steward for the Teamsters Local 728 in Valdosta, Georgia. He wrote this shortly after returning to work following a 15-day strike.

POSTED Thursday, Aug. 28, 1997, at 4:30 P.M. PT

I arrive at the center at about 8 A.M. Dennis Moore, my union business agent, calls to confirm arrangements for a contract presentation meeting this Saturday. I tell him that I have received a half-dozen pending grievances since coming back to work. He says that the Tifton, Georgia, center has filed over 200 grievances since last week. It appears that local management is violating the contract on a wholesale level since losing the strike. Most of the grievances involve seniority violations, where the company has brought back scabs before more senior employees who honored the strike.

The part-timers in my center are all back at work, and my load of packages is at about the normal level for this time of year. The only bad news is that the air packages are late arriving at the center and the drivers must wait for them.

At 9:30 A.M. I pull out of the center parking lot and head for downtown Valdosta. The dog days are back and I'm thinking that this is going to be a rough day, but at a red light I look at the car in front of me and see a bumper sticker that reads, "I fantasize about the UPS man." Man, I love this job!

A middle-aged woman named Claire stopped me in the afternoon. She had come out to the picket line during the strike, but I hadn't had a chance to meet her then. She said that she worked at a large craft store as a department manager. Even though her store and department had increased sales, she had been shifted from full-time to part-time and had lost her health benefits. Claire was also still responsible for the same work. She said that she was going to have to quit soon, because it was too expensive for her to commute for only part-time pay. She wanted me to know that she supported us and that the exploitation of part-time employees extended to the white-collar workforce as well.

I got a call from an old friend. She was in the area last week visiting her in-laws when she saw a news story on the strike. She joked that she wanted to get my autograph while it was still worthless. I assured her that my signature would be worthless for a long time to come, and that my 15 minutes of fame are about up, but I would treat her to lunch the next time we met. For a while it was exciting to have television cameras pointed at you with people interested in what you had to say, but I am looking forward to slipping back into the anonymity of just being known as the UPS guy.

POSTED Friday, Aug. 29, 1997, at 4:30 P.M. PT

Bart Johnston was my predecessor as the shop steward at UPS. We have worked beside each other for the past 20 years, and he has been both my mentor and my friend. During the strike Bart's dad passed away. Normally I am as involved in the personal lives of the drivers as I am in their professional lives. Being a shop steward is a lot like being a priest, without the celibacy. I have spent as much time in hospital rooms and funeral homes as I have in grievance hearings. But when Bart's dad was buried, I was unable to attend the funeral because of a crisis on the picket line. I have felt guilty for missing the funeral, and today I apologized for not having been there. Bart reassured me that he understood.

Today was filled with several ironic twists. At the prework meeting I received my 20-year service award from the managers. My 20th anniversary was actually on the first of the month. I was, however, on the picket line at the time, and I assume management thought it might be better to put off the ceremony until after the strike. Today is also the 90th anniversary of the founding of UPS. The company provided a cake and orange juice, and the atmosphere was lightened for a short time.

We are late getting started again today, and I have to run for the first hour in order to make service on the next-day-air packages. By midday things begin to go more smoothly. I stop and make a call to Ken Paff. Ken is an organizer with Teamsters for a Democratic Union. TDU, as it is better known, is an organization of rank-and-file Teamsters that was largely responsible for the democratic reforms that swept the union in the 1990s. They were also primarily responsible for Ron Carey's 1991 and 1996 election victories. They provided an army of member activists who phone-banked, leafleted, and campaigned on behalf of the Carey slate. Without TDU there would never have been any Ron Carey. I rely on Ken and TDU for accurate information on both the union and UPS. Ken says that the contract appears as good as we first thought. He tells me that UPS is trying to discipline drivers around the country because of incidents that took place on the picket line during the strike. TDU publishes a newspaper called *Convoy Dispatch*. It is due out soon, and Ken tells me to expect it before the contract vote.

I hope to have time tonight to catch a movie after work, but first I have to finish writing thank you letters to all the churches, businesses, labor unions, and individuals who supported us during the strike. The public support we received is why this strike was successful. I hope that what we saw happen at UPS will not become a unique event but a model for future trade unionism.

Untenured

Untenured is an assistant professor at a well-known private American university.

POSTED Monday, Feb. 15, 1999, at 10:30 A.M. PT

The first thing you need to know about the average assistant professor is that she or he spends the year before the Day of Judgment—in which it is decided whether or not she or he gets tenure—in a state of anxiety and paranoia. As a former professor once observed, "Never forget that every paranoid's discourse contains more than a small grain of truth." Whether justified or not (and you never know until it is too late to matter but you always know once it is too late to matter), this paranoia is a breeding ground for more paranoia. The assistant professor about to undergo a tenure hearing seems to attract horror stories from well-wishers and sadists alike eager to commiserate or to tell sordid tales of brethren who got the ax.

Just last weekend, as I was innocently trying to choose between Gruyère and cheddar at the local grocery store, I bumped into the shiny face of a tenured colleague from a related department who raced across the aisles to ask me "how I was holding up" and "whether I knew who would vote for or against me" on the Big Day. I replied that I was "holding up" quite well, thank you, and then ran home to lie down for several hours.

And in the past few weeks I have heard about: one tenure decision that ended in litigation; another one that seems likely to; an assistant professor whose tenure case was scuttled by his closest "friend" and "mentor"; and a healthy number of tenure-related narratives detailing the hilarious or catastrophic consequences of misdirected e-mail. (Misdirected e-mail has become its own sub-genre of academic nightmare; the nefarious possibilities are infinite. In particular, graduate students are carrier pigeons from hell. They are known to forward anything sent to them to the worst possible recipients. They are particularly adept in the art of making your "helpful advice" seem like an attack on a colleague.)

Let me assure you that I love my job. This is no mean feat given some of the drawbacks of academic life. Academic survival requires that you endure a Darwinian test that selects for a peculiar cocktail of masochism, sadism, perversity, and the ability to withstand large quantities of institutionalized torture over long periods of time with few measurable rewards. Masochism? You spend years and years and years writing a book that will be read by ten people and then remaindered. Sadism? You are on the board of a university press that publishes those sorts of books and have to decide whether to publish one that some other poor professor has spent years and years writing. Perversity? You have to give a glowing introduction to a guest speaker who, you just learned, single-handedly made sure you weren't hired at his institution. Torture? At some point during the tenure process, a damning letter suddenly appears in your file from a student you thought you treated well —and you don't find out until it is much too late.

For all this, the pay is lousy and academics get no respect. Being populists, Americans tend to treat higher learning with distrust, disdain, and/or uncomfortable awe. I have a philosopher friend who learned long ago that mentioning his profession was a sure-fire way to stop conversation at a social gathering. And within the university, while there is no foolproof standard of success, there are many forms of failure — some of which are so baroque that they take years to become, as a doctor might say, "emergent." At

the end of the day, when and if the tenure battle is won, one faces
the even more frightening prospect that one could join the ranks of
"deadwood," "dinosaurs," or any of the other species of Tenured
Undead who end their days pickled in the brine of their unwritten
books and unfulfilled aspirations.

POSTED Tuesday, Feb. 16, 1999, at 10:30 A.M. PT

Today I bumped into a former student, the incomparable young B.
I met B. last year, when he was just a nubile freshman. B. had liked
to let it be known that he had already read everything we were
going to read in class "for fun." He spoke in aphorisms, quoted
Pynchon and Nietzsche, and wrote me daily e-mails requesting
that I answer his arcane questions about the finer points of decon-
struction. I would awaken to find his daily missives addressed to
"yo, professor." He stalked my office hours on a regular basis to
seek my advice about philosophy, literature, life and, of course, his
glorious future. In short, for a good 15-week span of time, we developed a relationship of sorts.

But that was last year. Today, I catch my first glimpse of his sophomore self. When he sees me, he saunters over and says, "Hey, professor." I say, "Hey, B., what's new?" He says, "You know, I'm taking
this grad course with Professor N." (He lingers over the word grad).
I say, "Wow, that's great!" (Professor N. is, in fact, a friend of mine, so
I actually am quite pleased.) But does he stop there? No. He says,
"Professor N. is really cool." I'm still fine with that. Does he stop
there? No. "Professor N.," he says, looking at me intently, "is who I
want to be when I grow up." That's just fine, I think. Professor N. is
smart, hip, sexy, and gay. I wonder if B. has any idea. Then he narrows his eyes and delivers the zinger: "I took an undergrad class with
him, too. He really knows how to handle a class." Okay, okay. So now
I want to turn around and shriek, "So what am I, chopped liver?"

Teaching often leaves one feeling a little like chopped liver. It is like some intense romance which retroactively turns into a one-night stand. But weirder still—it is like a one-night stand you keep having over and over. Students come and go but always stay the same age. I sometimes have the feeling that I have had several similar relationships with generations of their slightly older prototypes over the years. I had met B. in his many previous incarnations. In my graduate student days, he might have been what we liked to call the Heidegger boy. The Heidegger boy would always find a way to fit a discussion of Heidegger into any and every conversation. The Heidegger boy is brilliant, aloof, and a bit cold around the edges. The Heidegger boy has some interpersonal limitations.

But emotional attachment to students takes many archetypical forms: These range from grand, unconsummated, courtly passion to raging, unconsummated, stuttering lust. There are more complex forms as well. There is the love one feels for the beautiful young woman who doesn't know she is brilliant and the love one feels for her twin—the brilliant young woman who doesn't know she is lovable. There is the earnest frat boy who learns to think. The boy one wanted to date in high school but didn't. I have always had a particular penchant for young men of 20 whose intellectual excitement translates into a steamy sort of vulnerability. Sometimes one falls in love with a class as a whole, like an adorable Borg whose every part is equally adorable. During these semesters, a random absence from any student feels like an amputation.

Sitting on my desk is a stack of this semester's students' first papers. I have promised to read them by tomorrow, but I don't dare to look at them. I have been teaching long enough to know that the minute I look at those papers, I will enter a new phase of relations with my students and that the current honeymoon will be over. Although I was initially quite enamored of them, I am starting to suspect that they're humoring me—they don't really want to be there—but they're too polite and well-groomed to let me know. I'll probably know by the end of the week whether we're headed toward civil cohabitation, guarded distance or, perhaps, some lighter passion.

Sarah Van Boven

While on a leave of absence from Newsweek *magazine, Sarah Van Boven returned to the summer camp she attended as a child and filed this. She is now an editor and writer in Hanoi, Vietnam.*

POSTED Monday, Aug. 9, 1999, at 10:30 A.M. PT

Much like the universe, summer camp is always teetering precariously on the knife's edge between order and chaos. Appropriately enough, this is nowhere more evident than in the dining room. There are two weeks left in this session, and I am struggling to maintain a veneer of etiquette at a table of eight girls who — despite elevated socioeconomic status and some of the best elementary educations money can buy — resemble desperate refugees awaiting an overdue aid shipment when turned loose on a platter of chicken drumsticks. During the 50 minutes of dinner on Sunday, I found myself saying each of the following phrases at least once:

1. "Baked potatoes with butter are not finger food."
2. "Please sit on the bench with both feet on the floor. Very funny — on the floor in front of you."
3. "There is really no need to stand up when passing bowls of food."
4. "No talking between tables, please."

5. "No exaggerated silent pantomime of talking between tables, please."

6. "I'm sorry you forgot that you are 'allergic' to chicken,
   but once it's in your mouth you do have to swallow it."

Because of commands like these, and despite my belief that
rules exist for reasons other than the suppression of all that is fun
in the world, I am often referred to as a Mean Counselor—though
certain allowances are made for my extremely advanced age of 26.
(I returned this year to the New Hampshire girls' camp where I
summered as a child and young adult to rest up before departing
for an editing job overseas. I utterly forgot how exhausting it can
be to be a camp counselor, but it's not a bad place to hang around
waiting for a Vietnamese work visa.) At my table this week, we
have already had several discussions of my decrepitude. A 10-year-
old named Casey guessed that I was 45, and all expressed unani-
mous amazement that Hannah, the other counselor sitting at our
table, was once a camper in my cabin way back in the early '90s.
Despite Hannah's testimony that I was indeed this "mean" in the
olden days, it has been decided that much of my strict demeanor
springs from many years of living in New York City. I can't help
but laugh when Brianna, a brassy little blonde in pigtails, responds
to my request that she please go get more French bread with, "You
can't just order me around. I'm not a *cab driver*."

If my friends back in Manhattan could see me now, I think they
could get over my regulation forest-green uniform, my unwashed
hair (yes, there's a drought up this far north, too), and the ball-
point-pen tattoo inked onto my ankle by a bored camper. The irrec-
oncilable cognitive dissonance would probably come when they
saw me joining in the songs in the dining hall.

Here at camp we start off each meal by singing grace. Loud. The
senior campers (ages 13, 14, and 15) then have the privilege of
starting a variety of raucous songs that are inevitably sung in various simultaneous pitches. The juniors, ages 7 to 12, join in and

spend what little downtime there is in between songs engaged in more exaggerated silent pantomime, hoping (usually in vain) that someone on the senior side of the dining room will take pity on them and start the tune of their choice. Should a counselor need to cut into the din, the entire room breaks into one of several vaguely insubordinate announcement songs, such as "Announcements, announcements / We sold our cow / Don't want your bull / Announcements, announcements."

Everyone sings—no exceptions, and the louder the better. For example, the camp has a sizable number of young kids shipped up from Venezuela by their parents to work on their language skills. It never fails to amaze me when I see a little girl who didn't know the English word for "lake" two weeks ago belting out rapid-fire nonsense songs. Just tonight, a timid, dark-eyed Venezuelan at my table named Ana was able to effortlessly belt out these lines:

> *The peppiest camp I ever did see*
> *It never goes a' pokin'*
> *If I could tell you the pep it has*
> *You'd think I was a' jokin'*
> *It's not the pep in the pepper pot*
> *Or the pop in the popcorn popper*
> *It's not the pep in the mustard jar*
> *Or the pep in the vinegar stopper*
> *It's good old fashioned P-E-P*
> *The kind you can't knock down*
> *We're the peppiest camp around.*

She was, of course, stuffing buttery baked potato into her mouth with her fingers the entire time, but not even I am mean enough to quash that one.

POSTED Wednesday, Aug. 11, 1999, at 9:30 A.M. PT

Can there be a more pastoral scene than that of 10 teen-age girls shaving their legs by bucket and flashlight in the middle of the woods? I wandered by this tableau tonight at 7:45 P.M., 15 minutes before the boys from a neighboring camp were due to arrive for a social. The two-minute shower limit is never popular, but once the senior girls stop howling on dance nights about the great injustice of water rationing, they do get resourceful.

We have dances just about every week of the summer, but you would never guess from the atmosphere in Senior Alley. All decked out in slip dresses from The Limited and liquid eyeliner from the drugstore, the oldest campers resemble the populace of the all-female planets often featured on *Star Trek*—the distant farming colonies where lady aliens hadn't seen men in many millennia and were all ready to rip off William Shatner's mustard yellow uniform. The other head counselors and I actually have to check each girl as she enters the Lodge for visible bra straps and violations of the Fingertip Test (skirt hems must extend at least a millimeter below hands hanging by a camper's sides).

Of course, for all their tartish comportment, the campers are essentially so innocent that you want to reach out and ruffle their moussed hair. For example, one Pixie with a black belt in tae kwon do informed me last session that I had better keep a close eye on her because she danced "like a 21-year-old on *The Grind* on MTV"; as a matter of fact, she bobbed around like a skinny 12-year-old at a camp dance. Last night, the girls clung anxiously to each other, belting out lyrics to Backstreet Boys songs without a trace of irony (and scowling at me when I pointed out that "Ain't nothing but a mistake/ Tell me why/ I never want to hear you say/ 'I want it that way'"is utterly nonsensical). The boys cruised the Lodge like sharks in a crowded aquarium: around and around and around— inexplicably, almost always in a counterclockwise direction. During the first hour of the dance, they stopped circling only long enough to shuffle back and forth next to girls during nonthreatening crowd-pleasers by Ricky Martin or Will Smith.

During the second hour, seemingly fortified by the red dye and sugar of 15 gallons of "bug juice," the campers actually mingled. I got to enjoy the spectacle of homophobic, oblivious teen-age boys gesticulating along with "Y.M.C.A.," the Village People song that always furthers mixing since teen-age girls seem equally fond of this paean to anonymous gay sex. By 9:45, campers were actually requesting slow songs. The girls who were highest-pitched in their squeals of pre-dance anticipation either loitered longingly or danced in stiff-armed lockstep with boys shorter than them by at least two inches. Other than a few obvious bombshells, it was the campers I least expected to be aggressive who actually snuggled up to young men during the interminable riffs of "Stairway to Heaven" (the traditional last song for going on three decades now). One peculiar, poetry-spouting 14-year-old who had announced, "I'm going to find another outcast," did just that, God bless her.

Cindy, the program director, and I spent the last few minutes of the dance practicing the hallowed Hand Check tradition: roaming the floor removing impudent male palms from our campers' behinds. The boys are mortified by this particular manifestation of my fabled Meanness, but I can't say I care. Only one girl looks anything less than relieved, and her scowl and rolled eyes produce the only episode of true cattiness I witnessed the entire evening. "She's such a slut," said one camper to another, just within my earshot. "I mean, she lost her cybervirginity at 13." Right now I'd do anything to have this be the worst thing they can think of forever and ever.

Good night, girls. Sleep tight.

POSTED Friday, Aug. 13, 1999, at 9:07 A.M. PT

Camp is just unchangeable enough that I have, on several occasions, woken up in the morning and had to think hard before remembering how old I am. The four-inch-high inscription "SARAH VAN BOVEN 1987 SILVER BIRCHES!" on the rafter directly above my head doesn't help one bit. Inking "SVB Summer of Regression '99" could be useful for space-time orientation, but I plumb forgot to bring thick, green Sharpie markers to camp this year.

For the most part, this constancy is lovely. Yesterday, for example, a Scotch Pine camper named Spring sat next to me in the white van while I drove a team of archers to a tournament at a boys' camp down by Lake Winnepesauke. One of the few girls old enough to remember me from the early '90s, she was eager to prove it. Spring told the entire van a long story about the night I orchestrated a prank for despondent Juniors to play on the lucky Seniors who had gone off to a dance: dozens of pounds of confetti secreted in their belongings — shoes, trunks, riding helmets, soap dishes, you name it. (The Seniors were coming across stray bits of confetti for years quite literally. It was well worth the reprimand I received from the camp's director.) I decided to risk publicly reminding a 15-year-old just how sweet she was when she was an Elf and pointed out that I still remember what she said while helping me sweep out the Arts and Crafts room just before the Seniors arrived back in camp: "Sarah, this was the best night of my life!" Unaware that I was steeling myself for eye-rolling and the one phrase all counselors hate most ("Whatever ... "), Spring just swiveled in the captain's chair of the GMC and thought for a few moments. "Well," she said, "it was really fun."

If there is anything better than knowing you were never forgotten, I'm having a hard time thinking of what it might be just now. Campers have shyly informed me that back when they were little they thought I was very strict, but still "nice," because I would play long, sweaty games of Kick the Can with the Juniors every night after dinner. A young counselor named Stephanie told me she read her girls S.E. Hinton's *The Outsiders* this summer because I read it to her many years ago. She is one of several Pixies from my cabin in 1993 who have apparently subscribed to

Newsweek ever since; their tales of running up and down the halls of school or home waving one of my articles yelling, "Sarah wrote this! I know the lady who wrote this!" astound me. They remembered me after I was gone.

I can say with confidence that the Manhattan neighbors I never met haven't noticed I left. My cat has bonded nicely with her new guardian; she stopped mewing plaintively weeks ago, probably a few weeks earlier than I would have liked. And my office surely has a new occupant by now, someone who never spills coffee on the computer keyboard and knows me only as a scratched name plate. Camp remembers. Camp remembers the summer I almost shot a local dirt-biker when he came roaring over the hill behind the riflery range and the ill-fated Dining Room Rules chart I made in 1991, even if my name isn't attached to either incident. I remember stories about silly, brave campers long since lost to the world of school and work and traffic and husbands, and I tell them to girls who know them only as names written on cabin walls. I hope that I taught a few campers a few things this summer, that my jokes were funny and that my games of Kick the Can helped a few lonely Gnomes forget to be homesick for an hour or two. Because I feel awfully lucky to be known by a whole new generation of witty, noisy little girls—girls who know so much more than I did at their age, when I was sleeping on the same bunks they are sleeping on now. Songs and socials and Color Wars may be silly, but collective memory is precious.

Rob Walker

In 1999, Rob Walker quit his job as a magazine editor in New York to move to New Orleans. He now writes Slate's *"Moneybox" column.*

POSTED Monday, Jan. 3, 2000, at 10:30 A.M. PT

Random bullets are a problem in New Orleans, especially on New Year's Eve. Apparently it's something of a tradition among certain locals to step outside and pop off a few rounds. I just moved here with E, my girlfriend, and we didn't know about this. Then she noticed a billboard showing a hand firing a gun into the air and the warning "Falling Bullets Kill." And I read in the paper that "police officials urge residents...to avoid firing weapons into the air."

Somehow "avoid" seems a little nonchalant to me. I think one avoids fatty foods; one simply does not fire weapons into the air in an urban setting, even on special occasions.

But maybe that just goes to show that I have a lot to learn about my new home.

The *Time Out Guide to New Orleans* notes: "Orleanians are proud of their culture.... Visitors are expected to be as enthusiastic about the city as the natives are. If you like the city, tell everyone; if you're not happy in New Orleans, keep it to yourself."

In addition to falling bullets, the reasons not to move to New Orleans include: a largely moribund economy (though it's perkier than it was), a high crime rate (though this, too, has improved), crushing summer heat, and the legitimate possibility of being wiped out by a hurricane or flood. These are good reasons. Incidentally, the population here has fallen from about 628,000 in 1960 to 466,000 in 1998.

So why are we here? We're here, actually, because we really are as enthusiastic about the city as the natives are. This is the second time I've moved across the country; the first was from Texas, which is where I'm from, to New York City, where I spent the last eight or so years. We liked New York. I had a good job as an editor (at the *New York Times Magazine*), and E had a good job as a graphic designer (at a big-deal design firm), and we have many wonderful friends there.

But to make a long story short, we just like it here more right now. We're in this great big duplex — or a "half double," as the local parlance has it — instead of our awful little Greenwich Village railroad apartment. We live in a quiet, pretty neighborhood. It's been about 75 degrees and sunny every day so far. We like the food, the music, the way people talk. And, maybe more to the point, it's been such a short time that it still feels like we're on vacation. What we have is a big, huge crush on New Orleans. We're walking around thinking, "Oh, falling bullets, that's not such a bad thing, I'm sure it's just a phase."

When you move a long way, to a place you don't know very well, life is a weird mix of quotidian tasks and we're-new-to-these-parts wandering. Yesterday, Sunday, we hunted down a *New York Times*, stopped at Ace Hardware for some paint, bought some coffee filters. Then we shifted to tourist mode and drove around to various points on the levee that keeps the Mississippi from flowing across

New Orleans' streets, some of which, I gather, are as many as 18 feet below sea level. Eighteen feet! I just finished John Barry's excellent book about the 1927 Mississippi flood, *Rising Tide*—which a New Orleans acquaintance insisted I read before crossing her threshold again—and I wanted to look at the river.

I can't say I feel quite at home yet, although I came close on New Year's Eve. First we went down to the French Quarter, but it was choked with foolish young drunkards from the four corners of the New South, so we scurried back to our new neighborhood—which is called Bayou St. John, or Faubourg St. John, or simply Over by the Whole Foods—and went to the local bar. Liuzza's, this place is called, and there were four people there at 11:20. We ordered drinks. E is kind of obsessed with Liuzza's, because it seems like a real neighborhood place, it's very unpretentious, the gumbo is good, there is Abita on tap, the clientele is friendly and so is the bartender. At 11:35 or so people started showing up. Regulars. Everyone in the bar knew everyone else, I think, except us. Some brought their own bottles of champagne; some brought their own champagne glasses; one woman literally danced in the door with both. With maybe 20 people, the place felt full by 11:45. A guy bought a round for the house. Janis Joplin sang "Bobby McGee" on the jukebox. We all looked at the TVs for the big countdown. It was a wonderful moment.

The next morning I walked over to the Circle K and bought the paper, which said that five people had been hit by random bullets, fallen from the sky.

Philip Weiss

Philip Weiss writes a column for the New York Observer *and is working on a novel called* My Wife, A Life.

POSTED Thursday, Aug. 6, 1998, at 4:30 P.M. PT

I crept out of a friend's house in Minnesota at 5 this morning, trying not to wake anybody, but the hinges squeaked. The foyer's inner door wouldn't stay where I left it but fell away with a long cry, then the outer door opened with a sharp meow. I thought I could keep the meow from getting into the house by closing the inner door after me, but I had my backpack on and couldn't fit through without both doors being open . . . well, you get the picture.

The cab was there to take me to the airport. I was pensive, trying to remember the first place that I and a friend I'd seen at a party last night made love. It was 21 years ago, and I'd never been so intoxicated. She was insouciant, dissolute, beautiful. Now I couldn't remember that first time. I wondered if it was my small apartment in the Indian neighborhood, or her room under the eaves of her parents' house overlooking the Mississippi. My apartment, probably. I thought of our first date, when at 4 in the morning we made out on the River Road and I asked her if I could touch her "here" and she said not if you have to ask.

The party was at her brother's house in Minneapolis. He was as dissolute as she was back then, but sweeter. He has always made me laugh. I loved her big, smart family. In one giant step I'd gone from my sheltered, scientific Jewish family to a politically prominent but ambitionless Nordic family, and the change felt dizzying. She kept me out too late and we did mescaline and she twisted the dial of the car radio impatiently to find James Brown. It was the surreal Minnesota winter. Her boyfriend was in prison on drug charges. That summer she dropped me for a musician, at a party on Nicolet Island where we drank rum from jars.

She and I have always kept in touch, and in the cab I thought of writing her a letter to ask: Where, Mo? I imagined she would write back in her good script to say that it isn't something she wants to think about now. When I saw her last night, a jeweled crucifix hung down on her pretty breastbone. She talked of partying and stubbed out cigarettes behind her on the porch rail, soon a bunch of cigarettes, burned right to the crunched filter. She has had a hard life. Always merry and bright, she used to say, ironically. But I'd never judge her. I still feel so grateful, she brought me out into the world.

PublicAffairs is a new nonfiction publishing house and a tribute to the standards, values, and flair of three persons who have served as mentors to countless reporters, writers, editors, and book people of all kinds, including me.

I.F. STONE, proprietor of *I. F. Stone's Weekly*, combined a commitment to the First Amendment with entrepreneurial zeal and reporting skill and became one of the great independent journalists in American history. At the age of eighty, Izzy published *The Trial of Socrates*, which was a national bestseller. He wrote the book after he taught himself ancient Greek.

BENJAMIN C. BRADLEE was for nearly thirty years the charismatic editorial leader of *The Washington Post*. It was Ben who gave the *Post* the range and courage to pursue such historic issues as Watergate. He supported his reporters with a tenacity that made them fearless and it is no accident that so many became authors of influential, best-selling books.

ROBERT L. BERNSTEIN, the chief executive of Random House for more than a quarter century, guided one of the nation's premier publishing houses. Bob was personally responsible for many books of political dissent and argument that challenged tyranny around the globe. He is also the founder and longtime chair of Human Rights Watch, one of the most respected human rights organizations in the world.

———

For fifty years, the banner of Public Affairs Press was carried by its owner Morris B. Schnapper, who published Gandhi, Nasser, Toynbee, Truman and about 1,500 other authors. In 1983, Schnapper was described by *The Washington Post* as "a redoubtable gadfly." His legacy will endure in the books to come.

Peter Osnos, *Publisher*